Einstein
A to Z

Karen C. Fox

Aries Keck

WILEY

John Wiley & Sons, Inc.

For Mykl and Noah

For general information about our other products and services, please contact our Customer Care Department within the United States at (800) 762-2974, outside the United States at (317) 572-3993 or fax (317) 572-4002.

Wiley also publishes its books in a variety of electronic formats. Some content that appears in print may not be available in electronic books. For more information about Wiley products, visit our web site at www.wiley.com.

Library of Congress Cataloging-in-Publication Data:

Fox, Karen C.
  Einstein : A to Z / Karen C. Fox, Aries Keck.
    p. cm.
  Includes bibliographical references and index.
  ISBN 0-471-46674-3 (pbk.)
1. Einstein, Albert, 1879–1955. 2. Physicists—Biography. I. Keck, Aries.
II. Title.
  QC16.E5F68 2003
  530'.092—dc22   2004003016

Printed in the United States of America

10 9 8 7 6 5 4 3 2 1

Contents

iv Contents

Timeline

1879 On March 14, Albert Einstein is born in Ulm, Germany, to Hermann Einstein (1847–1902) and Pauline Koch Einstein (1858–1920) at 11:30 A.M.

1880 The Einstein family moves to Munich.

1881 On November 18, Einstein's sister Maria (nicknamed Maja) is born in Munich.

1885 Six-year-old Einstein begins taking violin lessons, which he dislikes at first, but grows to love.

1885–1888 Einstein attends primary school. At home, a family relative gives him a Jewish education.

1888–1894 Einstein attends the Luitpold Gymnasium for secondary school. During this time, the family becomes friends with Max Talmey (né Talmud), a medical student who introduces Einstein to many scientific books and topics.

1890 Einstein experiences what he later will describe as his brief "religious paradise," in which he embraces Judaism whole-heartedly and keeps kosher.

1892 At the age of thirteen, Einstein rejected organized religion and chose not to have the traditional Jewish bar mitzvah.

1894 The Einstein family moves to Milan, Italy, but they leave Albert behind in Munich so he can finish school. Einstein is so miserable that he drops out of school and shows up unannounced in Milan.

1895 Einstein takes an application exam to enter the Swiss Polytechnic University, known as ETH, but he fails anything that doesn't have to do with science and math. He goes off to the Swiss town of Aarau to study before retaking the exam. Einstein writes what might be termed his "first paper," a study on how ether reacts to magnetism, which he mails to his uncle Caesar Koch. He also meets his first girlfriend, Marie Winteler.

1896   Einstein renounces his German citizenship. In the fall, he enters the ETH as a physics student and meets a fellow student, Mileva Maric (1875–1948). Einstein's parents dislike Mileva the moment they hear of her, but she would come to be his first wife.

1900   Einstein graduates from the ETH, but does not have a job. He submits his first paper (on capillarity) to the renowned German journal *Annalen der Physik*.

1901   Einstein officially becomes a Swiss citizen, and within a month is informed he doesn't have to serve in the army due to flat feet. Unable to find other work, he takes a job as a tutor in Schaffhausen. He and Mileva have a secret tryst in Italy where she becomes pregnant. Once visibly pregnant, Mileva moves in with her parents in Hungary.

1902   Einstein moves to Bern, hoping that a job at the patent office will come through. Mileva and Einstein's daughter, Lieserl, is born. Einstein never meets his daughter and it is unclear whether she died at a young age or was given up for adoption. Einstein gets a job at the Bern Patent Office, where he will stay for seven years. His father, Hermann Einstein, dies in Milan, but on his deathbed he finally gives permission to his son to marry Mileva. Einstein publishes two papers in *Annalen der Physik*.

1903   On January 6, Einstein and Mileva marry. Einstein, Conrad Habicht, and Maurice Solovine start the Olympia Academy, a group of friends that discuss scientific and philosophical thoughts of the day. Einstein publishes one paper in *Annalen der Physik*, describing the theory of the foundations of thermodynamics.

1904   Einstein's first son, Hans Albert, is born on May 14.

1905   Known as Einstein's "miracle year" or "Annus mirabilis," Einstein publishes five papers in the *Annalen der Physik* including his papers on the photoelectric effect, Brownian motion, special relativity, and $E = mc^2$.

1907   Einstein begins to incorporate gravity into his previous theories. This will eventually grow into the general theory of relativity.

1908   Einstein takes a part-time, nontenured teaching position at the University of Bern. He works with a co-author (J. J. Laub) for the first time, and together they publish two papers in *Annalen der Physik*.

1909   Einstein is finally offered a full-time professorship and he quits his job at the patent office to work at the University of Zurich.

1910   On July 28, Mileva and Einstein's second son, Eduard (known as Tete) is born.

1911   Einstein moves his family to Prague for a new job at the Karl Ferdinand University. In October, at the age of thirty-two, Einstein is the youngest scientist invited to the first ever Solvay Conference in Brussels, and he is honored with giving the closing presentation.

1912   The Einsteins move back to Zurich, where Einstein takes a job as a professor at the ETH, his alma mater. On a visit to Berlin, he re-meets his cousin Elsa Einstein and begins an affair with her.

1913   Einstein attends the Second Solvay Conference in Brussels.

1914   Einstein moves to Berlin to take a job at the Kaiser Wilhelm Institute. Within a few months, Mileva and their sons move back to Zurich and so begins the formal separation of Einstein's marriage. In August, World War I begins and, in response, Einstein signs the pacifist document the "Manifesto to Europeans." This was the first of many political documents that Einstein signed.

1916   After several years of constant revisions, Einstein publishes the complete version of the general theory of relativity. The paper, "The Foundation of the General Theory of Relativity" is published in *Annalen der Physik*.

1917   Einstein publishes his first paper on cosmology and introduces the cosmological constant. Possibly exhausted after the intense work of the previous years, Einstein collapses and becomes seriously ill. Elsa Einstein helps nurse him back to health, though he does not fully recover until 1920.

1919   In February, Einstein and Mileva finalize their divorce and, a few months later, Einstein marries Elsa. In May, Sir Arthur Eddington leads an expedition to view a solar eclipse and see whether starlight bends around the sun according to the laws of relativity. It does, and the general theory of relativity is therefore heralded as being "proven." Overnight, Einstein becomes a celebrity.

1920   Einstein's mother, Pauline, who has been living with him and Elsa, dies at his residence. Einstein feels the first obvious effects of anti-Semitism as the Anti-Relativity Society holds a conference rallying against his "Jewish" theories. Einstein uncharacteristically writes a heated defense of his work in a Berlin newspaper.

1921   That spring, Einstein visits the United States for the first time, not to give science lectures, but for political reasons: he travels with Zionist Chaim Weizmann to raise funds for the Hebrew University of

Jerusalem. President Warren Harding invites him to the White House. While he is in Chicago, Einstein meets the Nobel Prize–winning physicist Robert Millikan, who will eventually lure him to the United States with a job at Caltech.

1922   Einstein publishes his first paper on unified field theory, the still unfinished attempt to join the theories of relativity and quantum mechanics on which he would focus for the rest of his life. On June 24, foreign minister Walther Rathenau, a prominent and assimilated German Jew, is assassinated. After being told he may be next, Einstein leaves Berlin for awhile. He takes a lecture tour through Japan and in November it is announced that he has been awarded the 1921 Nobel Prize in physics for his work on the photoelectric effect.

1923   On the way back from Japan, Einstein stops in Israel, delivers the inaugural address at Hebrew University, and is made the first honorary citizen of Tel Aviv. In July, he travels to Gothenburg, Sweden and delivers his Nobel Prize lecture. Despite the fact that he won the prize for the photoelectric effect, he gives a talk on relativity.

1924   Satyendra Nath Bose of Dacca University sends a paper to Einstein entitled "Planck's Law and the Hypothesis of Light Quanta." The two men will collaborate to describe a new state of matter today called Bose-Einstein condensation. Einstein's stepdaughter, Ilse, marries writer Rudolph Kayser.

1927   In May, Einstein's oldest son, Hans Albert, marries Frida Knecht against his father's wishes. Einstein attends the fifth Solvay Conference along with Niels Bohr and other early crafters of quantum mechanics. While many of the scientists leave feeling comfortable that they have hammered out the proper interpretation of the new science known as the Copenhagen interpretation, Einstein disagreed with it vehemently.

1928   Helen Dukas, Einstein's secretary on whom he would grow more and more dependent, begins to work for the Einstein family.

1929   Einstein is invited to visit with the Belgian royal family. He meets Queen Elizabeth of Belgium and they write letters to each other for the rest of his life.

1930   Einstein travels to the United States for the second time, visiting the California Institute of Technology as a visiting scholar. Einstein's first grandson, Bernard Caesar, is born to Hans Albert

Einstein. Einstein's stepdaughter Margot marries Dimitri Marianoff, who, after their divorce, would write a tell-all biography of his ex-father-in-law.

1931   After Edwin Hubble shows that the universe is expanding, Einstein rejects his previous notion of a "cosmological constant," a term he'd included in his general relativity theories specifically to explain why the universe was *not* expanding. Einstein visits the United States for the third time, again to teach at Caltech.

1932   Einstein receives an offer for a professorship at the Institute for Advanced Study in Princeton, which he accepts. Originally planning to maintain a part-time job in Berlin, as well, he leaves Germany for the United States in December.

1933   On January 30, the Nazis are voted into power in Germany. In March, they raid Einstein's summer house. Einstein briefly returns to Europe, staying in Belgium, but he never sets foot in Germany again. He resigns from the Prussian Academy of Sciences and then the Bavarian Academy of Sciences. In October, Einstein moves to Princeton for good, along with his wife, Elsa, his secretary, Helen Dukas, and research assistant, Walther Mayer.

1934   Einstein publishes his first collection of popular articles, entitled *Mein Weltbild (The World As I See It)*. His stepdaughter Ilsa Kayser dies in Paris, at the age of 37. His other stepdaughter, the newly divorced Margot, moves to Princeton.

1935   Einstein applies for permanent residency in the United States. He publishes a paper with Boris Podolsky and Nathan Rosen, in which he presents an argument that quantum mechanics is not a complete theory and needs additional work.

1936   On December 20, Einstein's wife, Elsa, dies at the age of sixty.

1938   Einstein co-authors a book called *The Evolution of Physics* with Leopold Infeld.

1939   Einstein's sister Maja moves to Princeton. On August 2, Einstein sends a letter to President Franklin D. Roosevelt cautioning that the Europeans have discovered how to control nuclear reactions and that the United States must invest in similar research lest the Axis powers create atomic weapons.

1940   Einstein becomes a U.S. citizen in October. (He retains his Swiss citizenship.)

1944   Einstein handwrites a copy of his 1905 paper on special relativity and it is auctioned for six million dollars. The money is donated to the war effort.

1945   Einstein formally retires from the Institute for Advanced Study in Princeton, but he continues working on physics theories. His focus for much of the rest of his life is on perfecting a unified field theory that he believes will bring the theories of quantum mechanics and relativity together.

1946   Einstein becomes the president of the Emergency Committee of Atomic Scientists. He continues to speak out against war and writes a letter to the United Nations calling for a single world government.

1948   In August, Einstein's first wife, Mileva, dies in Zurich. Doctors discover that Einstein has an aneurysm on his abdominal aorta.

1949   Einstein publishes *Autobiographical Notes*, the closest he ever comes to an autobiography. He does not write about his personal life, but instead, discusses how he developed his scientific theories.

1950   Einstein signs his will. He publishes his second collection of popular works, *Out of My Later Years*.

1951   Einstein's sister Maja dies in June.

1952   Einstein is offered the presidency of Israel. He declines.

1954   Einstein writes in support of J. Robert Oppenheimer, who has been accused of anti-Americanism by Senator McCarthy.

1955   Einstein's last scientific paper, "A new form of the general relativistic field equations," co-authored with Bruria Kaufman, appears in *The Annals of Mathematics*. Einstein's last political statement, the Russell-Einstein manifesto, speaks out against the arms race. On March 15, Einstein dies of a ruptured aneurysm.

1965   Einstein's younger son, Eduard, dies in Zurich.

1973   Einstein's older son, Hans Albert, dies in Boston.

1982   Einstein's secretary, Helen Dukas, who guarded his correspondence ferociously after his death, dies.

1986   Einstein's stepdaughter, Margot, dies.

1987–today   Einstein's letters and papers are collated and published. Historical information about the scientist suddenly becomes plentiful and numerous pieces of information that had been held under wraps are made public.

Introduction

Tackling a human life in alphabetical order is a fascinating task. Instead of a continuous story that includes highs and lows, descriptions of a personality with both strengths and weaknesses, a tale of triumphs coupled with failures, an encyclopedia spotlights a single topic to the exclusion of others. Every aspect of the subject's life is presented starkly and without mitigating factors.

Consequently, as we wrote these entries about Albert Einstein, our impressions of him regularly changed as we were confronted with different—and sometimes contradictory—slices of the man's life. When writing about his theories, we were in awe that he had the genius and imagination to make such creative leaps. When writing about his family life, we were forced to accept that he was a poor husband and father, casting away his first wife and two sons and cheating on his second wife. He was obsessed to the point of eccentricity with the support of pacifist causes, yet he urged on the development of the first atomic weapon. He created modern relativity theory, and yet refused to accept the second great theory of the twentieth century: quantum mechanics. He was a statesman on par with the world's greatest political leaders, yet he was a homebody who demanded in the United States a re-creation of his German household, never comfortable in his adopted country. He was a devoted Jew who detested religion.

And yet, parsing out a biography in this way has its advantages. *Einstein: A to Z* is designed to be as casual or as specific as the reader wishes. You want to know if Marilyn Monroe ever met Einstein? Turn to "M." How did Einstein's theories open up the possibility of time travel? Go to "T." Flip to "Children" and learn of Einstein's illegitimate daughter and his messy, complicated, and all-to-human family life. Go to "Relativity" or "E = mc^2" and you'll get a detailed description of Einstein's science. Read the book straight through, from "Absentmindedness" to "Zionism," and you'll know it all. (If you're looking for a place to start, Aries's favorite entry is "Brain" and Karen's favorite entry is "Wormholes.")

Most important, you will learn that the contradictions of Einstein's life could not obscure his contributions. His theories, one more elegant than the last, nourished and created the very foundation for twentieth-century science. Ultimately, as we wrote this book, we realized that Einstein quite simply was all his contradictions simultaneously: stubborn, brilliant, modest, self-centered, generous, passionate. A biography presented in bite-size entries, as this book is, offers the chance to see the truth behind an icon in a way that is rarely possible.

So, flip to a random page, read the book in order, or put it on your shelf as a desk reference. We hope you enjoy it as much as we've enjoyed writing it.

Absentmindedness

Unkempt hair, wrinkled clothes, and disorderly class lectures. Einstein's famous persona embodied—indeed, created—the image of the "absentminded genius."

Whether a love of science automatically results in an inability to keep track of day-to-day details, anyone immersed in thought does learn to block distractions. And since Einstein's work was often on his mind, it's no surprise that anyone who wanted him to focus on practical matters sometimes found him mentally out to lunch.

Einstein could get so caught up in his ideas that he would overlook the basics of life; when he was coming up with his general theory of relativity he neglected to sleep or eat. And once when his friends in Switzerland bought him a full tin of caviar for his twenty-fourth birthday, he was so engrossed in discussing inertia that he wolfed down the entire treat without noticing. (They made up for it a few days later, presenting him with a new tin of the stuff; this time chanting "Now we are eating caviar" to make sure their friend was paying attention.)

Einstein could become so engrossed in thought he'd forget where he was—once coming to a dead stop in the middle of a busy Princeton street—arguing his point as cars drove around the unconcerned scientist.

But nothing quite epitomizes the absentminded professor more than poor choice in clothing. The lecturer who shows up to class having forgotten to put on his pants is a timeless image, and Einstein had his share of similar stories. A classic comes from James Blackwood, who lived next door to Einstein and his wife, Elsa, in Princeton. In the biography *Einstein: A Life* by Denis Brian, Blackwood remembers his mother was once sitting in the Einstein living room, "talking with Elsa. Einstein was in the music room improvising on the piano. The music stopped and Einstein came past them, hair straying in all directions, no shirt or undershirt on, trousers sadly drooping and, I think, barefoot. He walked past them as if in a trance." Blackwood said there was "no sense of embarrassment, no recognition of his mother's presence. He just drifted past and walked upstairs, while Mrs. Einstein clasped her hands and said, 'Oh, Albertle!'" Einstein also had a life-long habit of not wearing socks, and many believed he simply forgot to put them on.

Since Einstein was so famous, just about every move he made appeared in the news and was often seen as a sign of the man's brilliance. So it's not surprising that even his casual clothing—baggy sweatshirt, brown corduroy pants, and sock-free feet—became an iconographic image of his intelligence. The image of the absentminded professor was born; lack of concern with daily appearance became forever linked with genius. But who knows whether Einstein honestly forgot to put on his shirt and socks, or if he just didn't embarrass easily. It's clear that Einstein knowingly toyed with his public image. He took great delight in mocking his own wild hairstyle and sweatshirt-based attire, suggesting that he was very aware of—if not actually cultivating—his distracted persona. In truth, Einstein was just a man like any other, and not a tidy one at that. Perhaps he was absentminded. Or perhaps he just didn't care.

See **Clothes; Hair.**

Anti-Semitism

As a Jew living in pre-World War II Germany, Einstein was subjected to vigorous anti-Semitic attacks, despite the fact that he wasn't religiously observant. As anti-Semitic fervor rose, even his world-famous scientific theories were derided as a "Jewish fraud."

In 1919, the year Germany lost World War I, Einstein lived in Berlin. Germany's financial condition was sinking; inflation and unemployment soared. The country took another blow ten years later when the U.S. stock market crashed in October, sending the world economy into a tailspin. In Nazi Germany, the country's problems were blamed on the Jews, who were said to be responsible for everything from pornography to a Communist plot to take over the world. The immoral Jews, claimed Hitler, were mounting a global takeover, and although he did not become Germany's leader until 1933, his beliefs seeped into the country's culture long before that. Hitler's political party, the National Socialist German Worker's Party, published a leaflet in 1920 stating: "The Jewish big capitalist always plays our friend and do-gooder; but he only does it to make us into his slaves. The trusting worker is going to help him set up the world dictatorship of Jewry. Because that is their goal, as it states in the Bible. 'All the peoples will serve you, all the wealth of the world will belong to you.'"

The year 1919 was also the year that the theory of general relativity was proven, and Einstein became an international celebrity overnight, without a doubt the most famous Jew in the world. His success attracted attention. In 1922 he wrote to fellow German scientist Max Planck (1858–1947), "The trouble is that the newspapers have mentioned my name too often, thus mobilizing the rabble against me." Indeed, being a scientist made him all the more suspect; Hitler saw the physical sciences as materialistic and inferior to the high disciplines of art and music. So, long before World War II began, Einstein became one of the first to suffer from Nazi anti-Semitic propaganda.

Einstein's politics didn't help. He was a confirmed pacifist and spoke out against Germany's behavior in World War I, demanding that the military be scrutinized for war crimes. Einstein believed the best way to achieve world peace was to have a single global government—it was nations themselves that divided society into artificial, and contentious, factions. In a country that licked its wounds after losing World War I by nurturing extreme nationalism, such beliefs didn't endear him to the average German. The country looked for scapegoats, and Einstein was a natural target.

Ad Hominem Attacks

One of the loudest voices to speak against Einstein came from an unlikely source: the president of the German physics society, Philipp Lenard (1862–1947). Lenard won the Nobel Prize in 1905 for his work on cathode rays. His work on the photoelectric effect laid some of the groundwork for Einstein's discoveries. Early in Einstein's career, he corresponded with Lenard and discussed physics, but, as Germany's politics turned dark, Lenard not only joined the anti-Semites, he became a rabid attack dog. His assaults against Einstein, two-sided and contradictory, alternated between denying relativity outright as a "Jewish fraud" and claiming Einstein's theories were too good to be his own; he must have stolen his theories from Friedrich Hasenohrl, a full-blooded German who had died in World War I. Lenard insisted that if accurate "racial knowledge" had been disseminated earlier, everyone would have known relativity was a deception from the beginning simply because Einstein was a Jew.

Joining Lenard in speaking out against Einstein was another German, Paul Weyland. Weyland claimed to be the head of an organization called the Study Group of German Natural Philosophers, though he seems to have been the only member. The sole purpose of his organization seemed to be to entice money out of anti-Semitic financial supporters and then rally against Einstein, the Jewish scientist. (Indeed, it is unclear what motivated Weyland more: anti-Semitism or the search for money. Weyland ultimately lived a life on the run as a professional grifter.)

On August 24, 1920, Weyland and Lenard gathered a large crowd for a lecture against Einstein in Berlin's Concert Hall. Einstein, against the advice of his friends, attended, sitting in the balcony where he seemed to be paying rapt attention and occasionally laughing at the speaker. Weyland claimed that the theory of relativity was merely a mass hypnosis of the public and was anathema to "pure" German thought.

Despite his good humor at the lecture, Einstein was defensive enough to submit an impetuous response, a letter to the editor of the Berlin newspaper, the *Berliner Tageblatt*, which published it on the front page. Einstein cited prominent scientists who did support the theory of relativity and then he pointed out the obvious: had he not been Jewish, or had he been more nationalist, he would never have received such attacks. In an uncharacteristic move, the normally high-minded scientist also personally derided Weyland and Lenard as both ignorant and vulgar. Of course, the letter did nothing to convince the opposition, and merely disturbed Einstein's friends who wished he had kept more distance.

The anti-Semitic attacks continued. In a lecture in Berlin, one of the students stood up and yelled: "I'm going to cut the throat of that dirty Jew!" Days later, groups rallied outside another of Einstein's physics lectures yelling denouncements.

Soon the verbal jousts grew into more dangerous threats. In 1922, the German foreign minister—and Einstein's friend—Walther Rathenau, was assassinated. Rathenau was a thoroughly assimilated Jew who thought of himself as a German first and foremost. He was so confident that this anti-Semitic culture would pass that he dismissed all of his bodyguards, despite repeated threats on his life. On June 24, as he drove through the streets of Berlin in an open convertible, two men with submachine guns and a hand grenade killed him. Einstein was shaken to the core. He attended Rathenau's funeral and was soon informed that his life was also in danger. Einstein wrote to Planck: "A number of people who deserve to be taken seriously have independently warned me not to stay in Berlin for the time being and, especially, to avoid all public appearances in Germany. I am said to be among those whom the nationalists have marked for assassination. Of course, I have no proof, but in the prevailing situation it seems quite plausible." Newspapers in the United Kingdom reported that Einstein was forced to leave the country, but in fact, he merely left Berlin for a time.

A New Cause

Not only did Einstein not think of himself as an observant Jew, but he had always rejected nationalism of any kind. He was well known for making statements that he would never have taken up arms for the German cause in World War I, and that he sought a universal nation free from geographical or political boundaries. However, the intensity of what Einstein perceived to be the evils of fascism and anti-Semitism caused him to rethink his position. He determined that certain acts are so heinous that the right-thinking man may pick up arms to combat them.

The ferocity of the increasing anti-Semitism led Einstein—now in his forties—to join the Zionist campaign to found a Jewish state, led by Chaim Weizmann. To help the Zionists, Einstein accompanied Weizmann on a lecture tour through Europe and America—Einstein's first trip to the United States—seeking support for a nation where Jews could be free from prejudice. While Einstein's efforts to use his fame ultimately did a great deal of good for Jews around the world, some worried that his lectures were hurting the Jews back home. In the 1920s, much of the German Jewish population was integrated into society. They were fiercely loyal to the German government, and fought side-by-side with non-Jews in World War I. These Jews worried that Einstein's call for a separate nation would just make Germans hate them more. Indeed, it had already turned many Germans against Einstein.

In February 1933, Hitler, who had steadily been amassing power, was officially handed the reins to the German government. Einstein happened to be in the United States at the time, and he immediately renounced his German citizenship and spoke out against the Nazi

Party. Nazi revenge was swift. All of Einstein's German property was seized and, in May, Einstein's books were burned at a public bonfire. Einstein's photograph appeared in a list of Nazi enemies with the caption *"Noch Ungehäängt"* (not yet hanged). Einstein also renounced his membership in the Royal Prussian Academy of Sciences, which responded with a public statement: "We have no reason to regret Einstein's resignation. The Academy is aghast at his agitation activities abroad. Its members have always felt in themselves a profound loyalty to the Prussian state. Even though they have kept apart from all party politics, yet they have always emphasized their loyalty to the national idea."

Einstein also had "no reason to regret" his resignation. He worked from the United States to help get Jews out of Germany, and after the horrors of the Holocaust were fully learned, Einstein never once regretted leaving his native country behind.

See **Germany; Hitler, Adolf; Judaism; Lenard, Philipp; Nazism; Stark, Johannes.**

Arms Race

As the United States and the USSR stockpiled weapons during the Cold War that followed World War II, Einstein repeatedly stated his beliefs that amassing weapons was more likely to lead to conflict than to peace.

After the United States dropped two atomic bombs on Japan, it became clear that the devastating effect of nuclear weapons demanded a new theory of military strategy. Instead of using armies to actively defeat a foe, nations could now merely threaten other nations into submission. But if several nations had an equal ability to destroy, such that if one government launched a lethal attack on another, they could be assured of being killed themselves—a concept known as mutually assured destruction—the thinking went, there would be a balance of power throughout the world. Einstein disagreed. He said that building more weapons would never lead to greater peace, and

> As long as armies exist, any serious conflict will lead to war. A pacifism which does not actively fight against the armament of nations is and must remain impotent.
>
> —Einstein, "Active Pacifism," in *Ideas and Opinions*

he often spoke out against what he saw as an excuse for a nation's violent nature. He described the arms race as having assumed a "hysterical character" and that it did nothing more than hasten the chances of mass destruction.

Einstein believed that giving the military too much power created a society addled with distrust of other nations, one that would inevitably go to war simply because they were so overwhelmingly prepared to do so. The only solution Einstein saw to ending the arms race was the development of a strong international government that would keep the power hungry in check and support weaker nations.

Einstein took it upon himself to prod other scientists to speak up against the arms race. In 1955, the British philosopher Bertrand Russell wrote Einstein of his "profound disquiet by the armaments race in nuclear weapons." Einstein suggested that he and Russell organize a public declaration of their pacifist position, signed by twelve other internationally-known scientists. The Russell-Einstein manifesto was signed just days before Einstein died.

See **Atomic Bomb; Russell-Einstein Manifesto; Pacifism.**

Atomic Bomb

Einstein developed the scientific theory—$E = mc^2$—that laid the groundwork for humans to get massive amounts of energy out of the atom, leading to the building of the atom bomb. In 1939, he also helped spur the creation of nuclear weapons by writing to President Franklin Roosevelt encouraging him to build such a bomb before the Germans did.

In 1935, Einstein gave a lecture at the annual meeting of the American Association for the Advancement of Science in Pittsburgh. After his talk, he was asked if it was possible to create a feasible power source by smashing atoms to release their intrinsic energy. He said it was as promising, "as firing at birds in the dark, in a neighborhood that has few birds." Headlines for the local newspaper, the *Pittsburgh Post-Gazette*, said Einstein had wrecked all hope of deriving energy from the atom.

The headlines had it wrong. Einstein did believe it was possible to get energy out of an atom; what he meant was that it wasn't going to be easy or practical in the near future. But as it turned out, scientists just needed to focus on the right kind of atom—atoms of uranium. As early as July 1920, Einstein spoke about uranium to the Berlin newspaper, the *Berliner Tageblatt*, saying that "It might be possible, and it is not even improbable, that novel sources of energy of enormous effectiveness will be opened up." At the same time, Einstein added the hefty caveat, "but this idea has no direct support from the facts known to us so far. It is very difficult to make prophecies, but it is within the realm of the possible. . . . For the time being, however, these processes can only be observed with the most delicate equipment. This needs emphasizing, because otherwise people immediately lose their heads."

Others did appear to be losing their heads: In the same issue of the newspaper, Germany's Privy Councilor declared: "We confidently believe that German science will now find a way [to create energy from uranium]." Germany also seemed to be the first country to conceive of using the energy in an atom for a weapon. Four years later, German scientists recommended that the German Army look into ways to build bombs that used chain reactions. One wrote, "The country that exploits it first will have an incalculable advantage over the others."

Energy from the Atom Becomes a Reality

At the end of 1938, two scientists at Germany's Kaiser Wilhelm Institute discovered that bombarding uranium nuclei with neutrons would split them in two. The information reached the Allies, because one of the scientists, Otto Hahn (1879–1968), wrote a letter to a former colleague, Lise Meitner (1878–1968), who had fled Germany to live in Sweden. That Christmas, Meitner and her nephew, Otto Frisch (1904–1979), wrote a notice about the discovery for the British journal *Nature*. Frisch also told Niels Bohr about the experiment just before Bohr left for the United States to spend a few months studying alongside Einstein at the Institute for Advanced Study in Princeton, New Jersey. Bohr reported the news to American physicists and suddenly the scientific community was abuzz with concern. Everyone was caught up in a frenzy of experimental activity to see whether splitting an atom and reaping its energy truly was possible.

At the time, Nazi Germany was on the rise and the scientific community, quite rightly, believed that Germany was attempting to build an atomic weapon. But while many physicists were studying atomic science, Einstein himself had only a passing knowledge of what was going on. It was far from his more theoretical interests in quantum mechanics and finding a unified field theory. On March 14, 1939, the *New York Times* published an extensive interview with Einstein to coincide with his sixtieth birthday. Einstein speculated about his fellow physicists' latest obsession. He said that so far, none of the science suggested a viable practical application, "However there is no single physicist with soul so poor who would allow this to affect his interest in this highly important subject."

By that summer, however, Einstein had become fully versed in the true possibilities of atomic fission. Einstein had long since left Nazi Germany for his new home in Princeton, and often spent his summers in Long Island, New York. In the middle of July 1939, physicists Eugene Wigner and Leo Szilard—motivated by their growing fears— decided to pay a surprise visit to Einstein's rental house on Great Peconic Bay. Szilard, a Hungarian Jew who had also fled Hitler's Europe, wanted to convince Einstein to use his close relationship with the queen of Belgium to keep uranium out of Germany. At that time, the largest deposits of uranium ore discovered were in the Belgian Congo, and Einstein had continued a lively correspondence with the queen from the time they met in 1929.

Einstein wrote the letter and gave it to Szilard to relay to the queen via the American State Department. But Szilard rethought the idea and, after speaking to presidential advisers, returned to Einstein's beach house. Szilard believed the person who really needed to know about the possibilities of a uranium bomb was the president of the United States. Szilard and Einstein wrote another letter, this one to Franklin Roosevelt. (Actually there were two letters to Roosevelt, one short and one long; Einstein signed both, but told Szilard that he preferred the second one.)

Albert Einstein
Old Grove Rd.
Nassau Point
Peconic, Long Island
August 2d, 1939

F.D. Roosevelt
President of the United States
White House
Washington, D.C.

Sir:

Some recent work by E. Fermi and L. Szilard, which has been communicated to me in manuscript, leads me to expect that the element uranium may be turned into a new and important source of energy in the immediate future. Certain aspects of the situation which has arisen seem to call for watchfulness and, if necessary, quick action on the part of the Administration. I believe therefore that it is my duty to bring to your attention the following facts and recommendations.

In the course of the last four months it has been made probable—through the work of Joliot in France as well as Fermi and Szilard in America—that it may become possible to set up a nuclear chain reaction in a large mass of uranium, by which vast amounts of power and large quantities of new radium-like elements would be generated. Now it appears almost certain that this could be achieved in the immediate future.

This new phenomenon would also lead to the construction of bombs, and it is conceivable—though much less certain—that extremely powerful bombs of a new type may thus be constructed. A single bomb of this type, carried by boat and exploded in a port, might very well destroy the whole port together with some of the surrounding territory. However, such bombs might very well prove to be too heavy for transportation by air.

The United States has only very poor ores of uranium in moderate quantities. There is good ore in Canada and the former Czechoslovakia, while the most important source of uranium is the Belgian Congo.

In view of this situation you may think it desirable to have some permanent contact maintained between the Administration and the group of physicists working on chain reactions in America. One possible way of achieving this might be for you to entrust with this task a person who has your confidence who could perhaps serve in an unofficial capacity. His task might comprise the following:

a) to approach Government Departments, keep them informed of the further development, and put forward recommendations for Government action, giving particular attention to the problems of securing a supply of uranium ore for the United States.

b) to speed up the experimental work, which is at present being carried on within the limits of the budgets of University laboratories, by providing funds, if such funds be required, through his contacts with private persons who are willing to make contributions for this cause, and perhaps also by obtaining the co-operation of industrial laboratories which have the necessary equipment.

I understand that Germany has actually stopped the sale of uranium from the Czechoslovakian mines which she has taken over. That she should have taken such early action might perhaps be understood on the ground that the son of the German Under-Secretary of State, von Weizaecker, is attached to the Kaiser-Wilhelm-Institut in Berlin where some of the American work on uranium is now being repeated.

Yours very truly,
[signed] *A. Einstein*

While the existence of Einstein's letter to Roosevelt is often cited as one of the main reasons Roosevelt began the Manhattan Project, Roosevelt actually received quite a bit of information from all types of scientists before authorizing the project. In fact, Roosevelt was too preoccupied to pay attention to Einstein's letter right away—it was weeks before he read it, and even then it didn't immediately inspire him to action. Frustrated with the delay, Einstein sent Roosevelt two papers from the *Physical Review* describing advancements in science that could lead to releasing the atom's energy.

On September 1, 1939, Germany attacked Poland, and on September 3 World War II began. That same month, scientists in both France and the United States made a crucial discovery. When a uranium nucleus was split by a neutron, the atom's energy was released along with two neutrons. Those two neutrons could then split two more nuclei, releasing more energy, and more neutrons, which would then set off more uranium atoms, and so on and so on. If enough uranium could be induced to split this way—a process called *fission*—then it might set off a chain reaction that could create immense amounts of energy all from that single original atom.

The discovery of the possibility of a chain reaction renewed the scientific urge to get through to Roosevelt. Finally, on October 11, Roosevelt met with his friend and adviser Alexander Sachs. A colleague of Leo Szilard's, Sachs presented Einstein's letter in person, along with background material. According to reports, Roosevelt interrupted Sachs's presentation, "Alex," he said, "what you are after is to see that the Nazis don't blow us up." Sachs replied, "Precisely."

Finally, Roosevelt was ready to take action, and on October 19, 1939, he responded to Einstein's letter, saying he had chosen representatives of the military to investigate the issue. But the wheels of government turned slowly and, even though a committee was formed, five more months went by. In an effort to spur things along, Szilard asked Einstein to write a second letter. That letter, dated March 7, 1940, didn't seem to have much effect, for it wasn't until the Japanese bombing of Pearl Harbor in December 1941 that the top-secret bomb project began in earnest.

Despite his standing as a physicist, and his obvious knowledge about molecular structure, Einstein was not part of the Manhattan Project. On December 19, as requested, Einstein supplied the science adviser to the president with some notes on isotope separation, and he also stated his interest in helping the U.S. war effort. But the FBI and army intelligence had come to the conclusion that Einstein was a security risk—thanks to his association with pacifist societies thought to be Communist fronts. Einstein later expressed relief that he wasn't asked to help.

After Hiroshima

Einstein was haunted by the atomic bomb. When the first one was dropped on the Japanese city of Hiroshima, on August 6, 1945, Einstein reportedly reacted with despair, saying "Oh, weh" (essentially "Alas" or "Oy, vey"). Einstein's secretary, Helen Dukas, made a public statement on Einstein's behalf: "Military expediency demands that he [Einstein] remain uncommunicative on the subject until the authorities release details."

It wasn't until mid-September that Einstein made his first public comments on the new weapon. A *New York Times* reporter tracked him down at a summer cottage on Saranac Lake in upstate New York. In the ensuing article, titled "The Real Problem Is in the Hearts of Men," Einstein said the only salvation for civilization was the creation of a world government: "As long as sovereign states continue to have separate armaments and armaments secrets, new world wars will be inevitable."

Einstein never condemned the use of the bomb on Hiroshima or Nagasaki, and he never condemned the advance of technology, either. He strongly believed that science could not be stopped, even though discoveries could have catastrophic consequences. The trick, thought Einstein, was to make sure humans made intelligent decisions about how to use technology. To keep involved with making such decisions, Einstein became the chairman of the Emergency Committee of Atomic Scientists, a group that included a considerable number of the physicists of the Manhattan Project. The committee eventually disbanded without making a discernible political impact, but Einstein carried on, and up until his death he was the champion of a great number of appeals and proclamations. His last public act, published posthumously, was to sign his name to the Russell-Einstein manifesto, urging the United States and the USSR toward restraint in the arms race.

Despite his horror of a weapon capable of such mass destruction, Einstein did not see the atomic bomb as something fundamentally new—merely a more powerful tool to aid mankind's penchant for war. In a particularly eloquent turn of phrase written in "Atomic War or Peace" for the November 1945 issue of *Atlantic Monthly*, Einstein said that the bomb had "affected us quantitatively, not qualitatively."

Einstein also discussed the complex sense of guilt many scientists, including himself, had about creating such a weapon, when coupled with the simultaneous confidence that the war made it necessary. His attitude was summed up in a speech given on December 10 in New York. Einstein said, "We helped create this new weapon in order to prevent the enemies of mankind from achieving it first; given the mentality of the Nazis, this could have brought about untold destruction as well as enslavement of the peoples of the world. This weapon was delivered into the hands of the American and the British nations in their role as trustees of all mankind, and as fighters for peace and liberty; but so far we have no guarantee of peace nor any of the freedoms promised by the Atlantic Charter . . . the war is won, but the peace is not."

$E = mc^2$

In addition to his letter to Roosevelt, Einstein's most famous equation, $E = mc^2$, was the key that opened the door for scientists to even consider the fact that the mass of an atom might also hold a great amount of energy. But Einstein did not feel that he bore a special responsibility for the atomic bomb because of his theories. Years after the war had ended, when the ban on publication of pictures related to the bombing in Hiroshima and Nagasaki was lifted in 1952, the editor of a magazine in Japan, *Katsu Hara*, asked Einstein about his role. Einstein replied in a letter, "My participation in the production of the atomic bomb consisted of one single act: I signed a letter to President Roosevelt in which I emphasized the necessity of conducting large-scale experimentation with regard to the feasibility of producing an atom bomb."

And yet, because of $E = mc^2$ Einstein's name has been inextricably linked to nuclear weapons. It was a connection he always dismissed. In a 1947 edition of *Atlantic Monthly* magazine he said, "I do not consider myself the father of the release of atomic energy. My part in it was quite indirect. I did not, in fact, foresee that it would be released in my time. I believed only that it was theoretically possible." Einstein believed that it was impossible to predict how science could be applied, and he often commented that it would have been difficult for a lowly patent officer to see how his idea could create a bomb.

While Einstein's contribution to the Manhattan Project comes down to one unintended catalyst, the $E = mc^2$ equation, and an inconsequential one, the letter to Roosevelt, he is nevertheless tied to the atom bomb in the popular imagination. It's an ironic legacy for a man whose strongest connection to nuclear weapons was in speaking out against their being used again.

See **Arms Race; Pacifism; Roosevelt, Franklin D.; Russell-Einstein Manifesto.**

Awards

Einstein received hundreds of awards throughout his life and even after his death. Among the most significant is his 1921 Nobel Prize for Physics, and his being declared—posthumously—the "Man of the Century" by Time *magazine. But Einstein also won a number of offbeat and downright odd awards that pleased him almost as much.*

In addition to the Nobel Prize, the serious accolades Einstein received include the gold Copley medal from the British Royal Astronomical Society in 1926, and the Franklin Medal from the American Franklin Institute in 1935. Einstein also received honorary degrees from, if not quite every university in the world, a startling number of them, including Britain's Cambridge University, Harvard University in the United States, and Kobe University in Japan. In 1929, Einstein received the highest distinction of the German Physical Society—the Planck medal. For this, as well as many of his other awards, Einstein was humble, saying he was "ashamed" to receive such a high honor.

Einstein also received a number of awards for his work on pacifist and Zionist political causes. During the McCarthy communist hearings, Einstein was delighted to receive a membership card from the Chicago Plumber's and Sanitary Engineer's Union after he made a public statement that if he were to do it over in today's circumstances he would, "not try to become a scientist or scholar or teacher. I would rather choose to be a plumber or a peddler in the hope to find that a modest degree of independence is still available under present circumstances."

Einstein's reaction to his awards was to be either humbled or nonplussed at his various scientific honors. He called the corner where he kept his numerous honorary degrees and diplomas the "*Protzenecke*" or boasting corner. He was thoroughly bemused by some of his sillier accolades—in 1933, when Einstein heard that A. V. Fric named a flowering cactus plant, located on the highest mountain peak of the Cordilleras "Einsteinia," the physicist wrote the botanist saying, "you have given me great pleasure by your thoughtful act." Other such honors for Einstein included advertisers who wanted to name a hair tonic after him (he refused) and a certificate from a pipe manufacturer stating that Einstein was an "Honored Pipe Smoker."

See **Nobel Prize in Physics.**

Beauty and Equations

Einstein held his theories up to one subjective ideal to determine if they were true: Were they beautiful?

Einstein wasn't the first to examine the veracity of his equations in a subjective light—the long cherished concept of Occam's razor, attributed to the fourteenth-century philosopher William of Occam, states that if all other things are equal, then one should always embrace the simplest theory. But Einstein took this idea to an extreme degree, experiencing the beauty of an accurate equation as strongly as one might experience the joy of a Mozart opera or a DaVinci painting. He was not alone. To this day, many scientists talk of the profound enjoyment they receive from the simple elegance in some of Einstein's work.

When Einstein talked later in life about his discovery of the general theory of relativity, he described a moment when all his thoughts coalesced, and suddenly the forces of gravitation made sense. As he wrote down the math he knew that it was "too beautiful to be wrong." Even though it would be several years before there was outside proof of general relativity, the beauty of these equations that so simply described the universe was enough to convince Einstein he had found the correct solution. Indeed, the beauty of the equations was enough for him, without proof. When general relativity was confirmed by Sir Arthur Eddington's famed trip to the Principe Islands to measure starlight as it bent past an eclipse, someone asked Einstein what he would have done if his theory hadn't been supported. Einstein scoffed, saying he would have felt sorry for God, because "the theory was correct."

Numerous scientists continue to use the gauge of beauty and simplicity to help guide their work, and many have described the beauty they perceived the first time they learned Einstein's relativity theory. Here is an equation that explains the shape and movement of the entire universe but is short enough to write on your hand. It's easy to understand why that can be perceived to be as beautiful as a perfect Bach concerto, every note in its place. To those who work with math, there is an appreciation akin to aesthetic pleasure for equations that explain a facet of nature so simply and completely.

There is, however, nothing inherent that suggests something beautiful is automatically good or true. In fact, the beauty of equations can be falsely seductive. Physicist Eugene Wigner (1902–1995) lamented the "unreasonable effectiveness of math," and it is too easy to see patterns of numbers as pointing to some fundamental insight as opposed to merely being coincidence. Surely, Newton's mechanics equations and Maxwell's light equations are also beautiful, yet both have been shown to be incomplete. Nevertheless, Einstein said fairly often that he could never accept an equation that wasn't beautiful, and this represents a trust in his physical intuition and innate understanding of math that certainly helped fuel his creativity.

Besso, Michele
(1873–1955)

Michele Besso was a friend, a sounding board, and a bit of an older brother to Einstein. Besso was six years older—and not only did he aid in some of Einstein's scientific theories, but he often became directly involved in Einstein's personal life, as he intervened in Einstein's first marriage, negotiated the terms of his divorce, and offered advice about how to raise his sons.

In 1905 Michele Besso, a trained mechanical engineer, worked with Einstein at the Swiss Patent Office. The two men often strolled through the streets of Bern discussing the philosopher Ernst Mach, debating music tastes, assessing Judaism—and arguing current problems in physics. The modern theories of light and mechanics caused contradictions that kept Einstein up nights, trying to understand how they could ever be reconciled. Einstein went to Besso asking for help, and for seventeen days the two men discussed every aspect of the problem. Then, one night, inspiration struck. Einstein appeared in Besso's doorway the next day and, without even saying hello, Einstein exclaimed, "Thank you. I've completely solved the problem." Einstein had conquered the problems with light—and developed his special theory of relativity. Besso was the first person to hear Einstein's explanation of a theory that changed the very foundations of physics.

At the time, both Einstein and Besso seemed to know the theory was "special." Einstein's paper on the subject was remarkably clear and concise, and Einstein later said that the five weeks it took him to prepare it for publication were a very happy time. While Besso was no slouch, it is clear that the special theory was Einstein's and Einstein's alone—but credit must be given to Besso, who had the listening skills and the technical expertise to absorb this brash young physicist's startling ideas. Einstein thanked Besso upon the paper's publication by writing, "In closing, I wish to say that my friend and colleague, M. Besso, has constantly lent his valuable advice while I was working on this problem, and that I am indebted to him for many interesting suggestions."

A Lifelong Friendship

Besso and Einstein continued to correspond over the rest of their lives, although Besso never collaborated with Einstein on a paper. Instead, the two seemed to have a relationship more like brothers. Einstein often asked Besso for advice and Besso often scolded Einstein for his behavior. The letters between the two men contain a vast amount of personal information about Einstein.

The two men met in 1900 when Einstein was staying at the home of his teacher Jost Winteler for one last year of high school before he entered university. Einstein retained close ties to many people of that time—Winteler's son, Paul, became his first good friend; and Winteler's younger daughter, Marie, became his first girlfriend. Besso lived there too, and he was destined to have a far longer connection to the Wintelers—in 1898 he married the older daughter, Anna.

Once married, Besso settled in Milan as a technical consultant to the Society for the Devleopment of the Electrical Industry in Italy, and he nudged the society to hire Einstein for a small job examining how electricity radiates during alternating current.

Einstein was later able to repay the favor by telling Besso of an opening for an Examiner Second Class at the Swiss Patent Office. At the time, Einstein was an Examiner Third Class and applied for the promotion himself. But he never seemed distraught that Besso was hired instead. In fact, Besso clearly was a welcome addition to Einstein's Bern community.

But over the next decade, Einstein and Mileva's relationship unraveled, culminating with the family's move to Berlin—a move Einstein partly made to be closer to his mistress, Elsa. Not surprisingly, Mileva was miserable in Berlin; she stayed only long enough for Besso to arrive and provide her and her two young children with a proper escort back to Switzerland. Thus it was in June 1914 when Besso became the intermediary between Einstein and his first wife. Einstein and Mileva's divorce was bitter and prolonged, with cruelty on both sides. Mileva was distraught, Einstein was distant, and both cried on the shoulders of their mutual friend, Besso.

But unlike his two charges, Besso, to his credit, seemingly kept his head. He chided Einstein for his poor behavior toward his wife, and protected Einstein from Mileva's more dramatic behavior. At the time Besso was still living in Zurich, and thus he also became a bit of a guardian to Einstein's two sons, Hans and Eduard.

Besso was also there for the Einstein family through a second crisis: the diagnosis of Eduard's mental illness. In 1932 Eduard was admitted to the Burgholzi Psychiatric Hospital. It was the first of many institutionalizations for the troubled young man. And, just as he handled Einstein's divorce, Besso also managed Eduard's illness—keeping Einstein informed of the boy's condition, reprimanding him when he was not helpful enough, and consoling Mileva.

What I admired most in him as a person was the fact that he managed for many years to live with his wife not only in peace but in continuing harmony—an undertaking in which rather shamefully I failed twice.

—March 21, 1955 letter to Anna Besso, after the death of her husband, Michele Besso

Through all of these travails, Besso and Einstein's correspondence almost always included science. The two men discussed Einstein's refusal to accept the edicts of quantum mechanics, the new astronomy discovered at the Mount Wilson Observatory in the United States, and Einstein's later discovery of the general theory of relativity.

Besso died just a few months before Einstein did, and Einstein must have felt the loss keenly after so many years of personal and scientific support. But Einstein used his science as a balm, writing to Besso's wife in March 1955, "He has preceded me a little by parting from this strange world. This means nothing. To us believing physicists the distinction between past, present, and future has only the significance of a stubborn illusion."

Black Holes

So dense and heavy that nothing, not even light, escapes the pull of their gravity, black holes are an astronomical phenomenon that is a natural outcome of general relativity. But they were too weird for Einstein—he never believed they existed.

Black holes first made their appearance in the world of science in 1783, introduced by a British scientist named John Michell (1724–1793). At that point, scientists called them "dark stars," and, to be strictly accurate, they did not resemble black holes as we currently conceive of them. Michell used the Newtonian understanding of gravity and light to theorize about stars of various sizes. Newton believed light was made of tiny corpuscles, little particles that traveled together in straight lines. Just as a ball thrown up into the air will return to your hand, such light corpuscles were subject to the pull of gravity. Light streaming off of a star, therefore, would also feel gravity; if the gravity was weak, the light would easily escape, traveling off into space. But if the gravity was too strong, those light corpuscles would slow down and return to the star just as a thrown ball does to Earth. Michell showed that a star of the right size, with the right amount of gravity—say the size of the Sun, but weighing 500 times more—would never be visible on Earth. The light would be trapped, doomed to remain forever bound to the star's surface.

The dark star theory was popularized by the French mathematician Pierre Laplace (1749–1827) over the course of the next two decades, but it lost credibility when scientists abandoned the notion that light was made of particles. By the beginning of the nineteenth century, light was thought of as nothing more than a wave. If light wasn't made of a physical entity, it wouldn't be able to feel gravity's pull; the idea of dark stars was largely forgotten.

Einstein's conception of light merged the two possibilities: the corpuscle and the wave. Einstein's light was made up of massless objects called photons, but it also traveled as a wave. More important, with the advent of his general theory of relativity, Einstein offered an explanation of how light moved in the presence of gravity.

At first glance, massless photons shouldn't be affected by gravity at all, but Einstein changed the very notion of what gravity is. Instead of envisioning gravity as a force that pulls two masses together, Einstein said gravity is simply the way in which we perceive a curve in space. For example, a person walking on Earth's surface, who may think of himself as walking a straight line, is constrained to walking on a curved line quite simply because he is on a curved surface. A massive object, said Einstein, creates similar curves in three-dimensional space, and something moving through such curves "falls" toward the massive object simply because space itself is curved, like a massive bowl, and the moving object slides down to the bottom. So if what we think of as gravity isn't limited to objects that have mass, then light, too, realized Einstein, would have to travel a curved path through space.

However, Einstein did not connect this idea with the possibility of a "dark star." The first person to tie general relativity to stars was a man named Karl Schwarzschild (1873–1916), a German astrophysicist who in 1915 was serving in World War I for the German army. Schwarzschild wanted to determine just how a given mass would warp space, so he decided to apply the relativity equations to the simplest star he could conceive of: a perfect sphere that didn't spin. Within just a few days, he had described the curvature of space around such an object, and Einstein, who hadn't expected such an immediate application of his equations given the complexity of the math, presented Schwarzschild's solution in Berlin at the Prussian Academy of Sciences in January 1916. A few weeks later, Schwarzschild calculated the shape of space just beneath the surface of the star and Einstein presented this work as well. Schwarzschild died several months later from an illness he contracted while fighting on the Russian front, but his effect on scientists' understanding of the geometry of space was monumental, and other physicists followed up on his ideas. Indeed, it was Schwarzschild's work that first gave rise to the metaphor used earlier— the idea that a star bent space into the shape of a bowl.

The more massive and compact an object, it was agreed, the more severely space would warp around it. But Schwarzschild's geometry went further, showing that if an object was dense and heavy enough— if a particular mass reached some critical radius—space would be so warped that light couldn't escape. Even more, time itself would stop at the surface of such a body, and deep inside the star, all the laws of physics that govern the rest of the universe would become meaningless.

Einstein's Rejection of the Theory

While Einstein was alive, this odd beast was known as a "Schwarzschild singularity" and it was considered fanciful enough that few people truly believed it existed. Unlike a dark star, a black hole doesn't get its odd attributes because gravity's pull keeps the light from escaping. In a black hole, the gravity is so strong that it results in a dramatic slowing down of time—a natural outcome of Einstein's theory of relativity. In normal cases, such as the minute time dilation that occurs outside a body the size and mass of the Sun, light simply appears to us as if it slowed slightly, resulting in longer wavelengths and a redder appearance. This is known as redshifting and was a phenomenon well-studied in Einstein's day. But Schwarzschild singularities—if they existed—resulted in space so warped that time itself came to a stop, space was infinitely long, and light quite simply didn't move.

In modern times, black holes have been so popularized that society is fairly knowledgeable with all that is odd about them. Even a casual viewer of science fiction movies or television shows has heard that time slows down around a black hole, and if one gets too close one can get sucked into its inescapable gravitational clutches. Another well-known idea is that the space inside a black hole is so nonlinear that if one could survive the trip, the black hole might spit you out on the opposite side of the universe. (It is, in fact, impossible by any known means today to survive a trip through a black hole, but the idea that it could be a portal between two very different parts of space is nonetheless credible.) But being so cavalier about black holes is a very modern attitude—the conclusions drawn are so amazing that one cannot blame physicists of the 1920s for rejecting them. The math of relativity might be in agreement with such fantastic creatures as black holes, but many claimed that was no reason to think they actually existed.

But over time physicists addressed the issue with a little more detail, and after a while, there were some who thought the Schwarzschild singularity deserved more respect. In 1939 Einstein still resisted, writing a paper illustrating why he believed such absurd things could not exist. Einstein reasoned that while the relativity of a black hole might indeed result in the exact scenario discussed, there simply was no way a black hole could ever be created. In envisioning a mass of particles pulled together via gravity, increasingly condensed, shrinking over time toward the critical Schwarzschild radius, Einstein noted two impossibilities: first, as this mass diminished and approached the critical size, gravity would cause the particles swirling on the outside to move faster than the speed of light; second, the internal pressures needed to keep the body from collapsing would in fact be infinite.

Of course, today scientists say that this is the point—since the surface cannot move faster than the speed of light and the internal pressures are not infinite, such a body will collapse due to gravity, forming an object so dense that a black hole is created. Under the right conditions, gravity is so strong that nothing can withstand its pull. But Einstein couldn't conceive of a body collapsing in on itself in this way. The very notion of so-called implosion, in which a structure lost its integrity and shape to this drastic a degree, was one that Einstein rejected out of hand.

How to Make a Black Hole

Over the 1930s, 1940s, and 1950s, the life and death of stars became better understood. Scientists applied relativity theory to stars in more and more detailed ways, and the concept of implosion became an inherent part of astrophysical theory. Stars shine because the atoms deep in their hot cores are constantly merging together into larger atoms, releasing energy and light in the process. However eventually this stellar fuel runs out and can no longer create the internal pressure needed to counteract the force of gravity pulling the atoms together. Without this repulsive force, the star's heavy outer layers crush the center in an enormous cosmic vice, and the center implodes, collapsing in on itself. Depending on its size and mass, the resulting remnant could end up a neutron star, which has enough internal pressure from its neutrons to resist collapsing even further. Although they're dim and dark and small, neutron stars can nevertheless be detected because they send pulses of radiation out into the universe. But if the remnant is three times heavier than the Sun, there is no internal force that can resist the crushing weight of gravity. The neutron star collapses even further—into a black hole.

The American theoretical physicist John Wheeler (1911–) first coined the term "black hole" in 1967, by which time their existence was fairly well accepted theoretically. Einstein died in 1955, and he went to his grave rejecting the possibility of black holes, but theorists today believe that black holes—in all their strangeness—are an inherent consequence of Einstein's theory of relativity and are a logical outcome of the way the universe works.

By their very nature it is impossible to see black holes and thus prove they exist by direct observation. If no light escapes from them, we'll never be able to "see" one. However, the evidence for black holes has accumulated, and today most astronomers accept their existence. For example, astronomers believe that a gigantic black hole—two million times the mass of the Sun—lives at the heart of the Milky Way.

Bohr, Niels Henrik David
(1885–1962)

Niels Bohr was one of the founders of twentieth-century physics, most widely remembered for developing what's known as the Copenhagen interpretation of quantum mechanics. As intellectual equals, Bohr and Einstein had a warm friendship, filled with lively conversations and scientific debates. The two men live on in scientists' imaginations as the twin pillars of modern physics, one representing relativity, the other representing quantum mechanics.

A Danish physicist, Niels Bohr made a name for himself in 1913 when he published the first description of what a hydrogen atom looked like—complete with a nucleus and the newly discovered electron. Bohr's model of the atom had taken the strictly classical model produced by Ernest Rutherford (1871–1937) and added in the new idea that energy might come in discrete packets called quanta. This cobbling together of an old theory with a new one did not turn out to be the perfect solution, but it was the first step on the path toward understanding atomic physics and it launched Bohr onto his lifelong quest to understand the behavior of atomic particles. Einstein was immediately captivated by this work. He was only six years older than Bohr, and also just beginning to make his name; the two men were natural colleagues, and they followed each other's work closely.

Over the next decade, both Einstein and Bohr rose in fame and stature. Einstein became world famous when his general theory of relativity was proven in 1919, while Bohr's name landed him a job as a professor at the University of Copenhagen. In 1920 the university even founded the Niels Bohr Institute. (The institute received a great deal of its funding from the Carlsberg brewing company, prompting many modern scientists to wonder what they need to do to get more support from their local beer proprietors.)

Mutual Respect . . .

The first meeting between Bohr and Einstein occurred in 1920 in Berlin. As if they'd known each other all their lives, the two talked about relativity and atomic physics, about Einstein's growing concern that quantum physics was abandoning the laws of cause and effect, about whether light was a particle or a wave, about all that was occurring in modern scientific thought. Shortly after meeting they wrote letters of how profound an experience it had been—Einstein to Bohr: "Not often in life has a human being caused me such joy by his mere presence as you did." And Bohr to Einstein: "To meet you and to talk with you was one of the greatest experiences I ever had."

The two men always held each other in high esteem and cared for each other deeply. Within a few years, however, they fell into an intellectual conflict that would dominate their relationship for the rest of their lives. Bohr and Einstein both contributed to the world of atomic physics. Some of their papers turned out to be correct, others woefully off, but in general, Bohr continued in a direction that Einstein disdained. As Bohr formulated his theories, he was not distracted if they seemed to throw off the mantle of causality. Atoms, he began to accept, didn't behave in perfectly predictable ways. On the contrary, at any given moment there was merely a range of probabilities that a particle might move in a certain direction or at a certain speed.

In 1924, Bohr put forth a theory along with Hendrik Anton Kramers (1894–1952) and John Clarke Slater (1900–1976) that briefly captured the imagination of contemporaries as a possible explanation for how light and matter interacted. The BKS theory, as it is known, turned out to be incorrect, but it was notable for two reasons. First, it rejected the existence of light particles, insisting that light was a wave and only a wave. At that time, most of the physics community had come around to the idea that light was made up of quanta of energy packets, as Einstein had predicted in 1905. Bohr would be one of the first to promote the idea that light was simultaneously a wave and a particle (Einstein himself was the very first) but it's intriguing to note how long he rejected the corpuscular nature of light. It's remarkable that Bohr was both one of the last to accept light particles, and yet once he accepted them, he jumped on the bandwagon wholeheartedly. He promoted, more fervently than anyone, the seemingly absurd concept that light was both wave and particle, depending on how you measured it. That kind of intellectual dogma change is rare, whether one is a scientist or not. Einstein wrote of Bohr decades later in 1954, "He utters his opinions like one perpetually groping and never like one who believes to be in the possession of definite truth." Bohr's ability to keep such an open mind is quite stunning.

The second interesting note about the BKS theory is that it was the first time Bohr and Einstein came down decisively on opposite sides of the fence. Like so many of the current theories, BKS abandoned causality and Einstein wouldn't accept it—which put a great many other scientists in a dilemma. So many of them respected Einstein's intelligence as well as his leadership that they found themselves hard put to embrace a theory he rejected. In an ideal world, such personality conflicts shouldn't play a part in determining what scientific theory is objectively "correct," but even scientists are human. To have two of the greatest physicists of the day in conflict left many of their colleagues discomfited. Many of them refused to comment on which scientist they thought in the right, and those who did were unhappy about it. Einstein biographer Abraham Pais tells of a story about how Paul Ehrenfest literally shed tears when forced to choose between Bohr and Einstein—and found himself having to choose Bohr.

... and a Mutual Disagreement

But soon everyone in the community had taken sides. The fifth Solvay conference, held in October 1927, has gone down in history as one of the most momentous intellectual dialogues in modern times. Everyone, including Einstein, saw the new quantum mechanics as a powerful mathematical tool to predict how atoms and subatomic particles functioned. But there was disagreement on the implications of that mathematical tool. Some, led by Bohr and the German physicist

Werner Heisenberg (1901–1976), believed that quantum mechanics was the final word: if the math said that an atom's future wasn't completely precise, then it quite simply wasn't. On the other side, with Einstein and Erwin Schroedinger (1887–1961) leading the charge, there were those who said that quantum mechanics was a lovely statistical tool, but that in reality atoms did behave with absolute precision and someday, somehow, scientists would develop all new theories to represent that.

The discussions occupied the scientists day and night. One of the participants, Otto Stern (1888–1969), offered a famous vivid description of the conference, describing how every morning Einstein came to breakfast with a new counterargument and every evening Bohr came up with a new refutation. These discussions have been raised to the level of physicist lore, and are referred to as the Bohr-Einstein debates. Indeed, even the participants seemed in awe of what took place at this conference. In 1949, Bohr wrote an essay, "Discussion with Einstein on Epistemological Problems in Atomic Physics" for the book *Albert Einstein, Philosopher-Scientist,* in which he credits Einstein's ingenious thought experiments as being the catalysts that helped him truly understand just what was going on in the tiny atomic world. While these debates between Einstein and Bohr are often described as contentious, Bohr himself remembered them as fairly pleasant. In the essay, he refers to Einstein's "humorous" new thought experiments, and that Einstein "mockingly" asked if the "providential authorities took recourse to dice-playing."

Over the course of the conference, the tide turned against Einstein completely. While their contemporaries might have been hesitant to commit to either position before, by the end of that Solvay conference, almost every scientist accepted Bohr's version of quantum mechanics. This version became known as the Copenhagen interpretation, since Bohr was from Copenhagen.

Einstein, however, never accepted the Copenhagen interpretation, and the debates between Einstein and Bohr continued for decades. At the sixth Solvay conference, in 1930, Einstein presented his latest thought experiment: if a box filled with radiation was set up so that it sat on a scale, and a clock timer was set to let out a single photon at a specific point in time, one could perfectly measure the change in weight of the box. Simultaneously, therefore, one would be able to measure the time and the amount of energy of that photon—a violation of Heisenberg's Uncertainty Principle stating that one couldn't know both those attributes of a photon simultaneously. Bohr was stumped for a full twelve hours or so, and he said that "it would be the end of physics if Einstein were right." But by the next morning Bohr had come up with a refutation: because Einstein's own laws of relativity stated that as the box recoiled due to the moving photon, time itself for the box's reference frame would be affected. Time couldn't be measured definitely after all.

The two men continued their discussion, but that was Einstein's last Solvay conference, since he left for the United States in 1933, never to return to Europe. They did encounter each other in the United States when Bohr visited Princeton, and Bohr was also responsible for refuting another of Einstein's famous thought experiments—the EPR argument that Einstein developed in an attempt to discredit the Uncertainty Principle. But, while many scientists held out hope that Bohr would one day convince Einstein, it never happened. It saddened Bohr, as it saddened so many of their colleagues, that Einstein refused to accept the Copenhagen interpretation. Einstein was a legend even in his own time, and to have had his approval on what they considered to be their grandest lifetime achievement would have meant a great deal.

Lifelong Friends

Although Bohr was Christian, he had Jewish relatives on his mother's side, and so, when the Nazis occupied Denmark in 1940, his life became difficult. Bohr escaped to England in 1943 where he began to work on creating a nuclear bomb. After a few months he went with the British team to the United States where he continued to work on the project, in Los Alamos. And so, both Bohr and Einstein were refugees from Nazism and, although Bohr's efforts in creating a bomb were clearly more direct, both helped create the nuclear age. And like Einstein, Bohr actively worked to keep such weapons under control after the war. In 1950 Bohr wrote a public letter to the United Nations saying, "Humanity will be confronted with dangers of unprecedented character unless, in due time, measures can be taken to forestall a disastrous competition in such formidable armaments and to establish an international control of the manufacture and use of powerful materials." Due to his work speaking out against the arms race, Bohr received the first U.S. Atoms for Peace Award in 1957.

Despite Einstein's resistance to Bohr's Copenhagen interpretation, he clearly thought the development of quantum mechanics and atomic physics was a stunning achievement—one that would surely be incorporated into whatever "true" theory was due to come along soon. Einstein thought Bohr's contribution to quantum mechanics stunning as well. In a 1949 essay, in *Albert Einstein, Philosopher-Scientist*, Einstein wrote: "That this insecure and contradictory foundation [of modern physics] was sufficient to enable a man of Bohr's unique instinct and tact to discover the major laws of the spectral lines and of the electron shells of the atoms together with their significance for chemistry appeared to me like a miracle—and appears to me as a miracle even today." Despite a lifelong opposition about quantum mechanics, the friendship between the two men remained true, helped along by a strong admiration for the other's genius.

Books about Einstein

As Einstein is one of the most famous people ever, it's not surprising that there are innumerable biographies of the man. Of course, like most biographies of the famous, these books range from the simplistic and factually questionable, to incredibly detailed works documenting not only Einstein's greatest discoveries, but also what he had for breakfast.

Einstein himself wrote extensively about his beliefs on peace, science, even jokes and bawdy limericks. As was the fashion at the time, Einstein kept up an extensive correspondence—writing letters to everyone from the queen of Belgium (a dear friend) to the fifth grade class of Farmingdale Elementary School in New York in 1955.

Einstein only once wrote what could be called an autobiography. In 1949 he wrote a chapter titled "Autobiographical Notes" that was the beginning of the book *Albert Einstein, Philosopher-Scientist*. Edited by Paul Arthur Schilpp, the book collected twenty-five critical essays from scientists and philosophers to comment on both Einstein's science and his world views. In the "Notes," Einstein rarely delved into his personal life, or even commented on critiques of his world philosophy. Other than a brief mention of his childhood, Einstein kept his comments to descriptions of how he developed his scientific theories. Nevertheless, this autobiography is a fantastic first source for information about the man.

As for others who've written about Einstein, early biographies were often limited, no matter how good the author's intentions, since not only was Einstein reticent to talk about his life, but Einstein's secretary, Helen Dukas, and his friend, Otto Nathan, worked to maintain an idealized image of Einstein during his later years and after his death. They were so successful that the first collection of Einstein's writings was delayed for over two decades after his death. Titled *The Collected Papers of Albert Einstein*, it encompasses a tremendous number of documents and is often cited as one of the most ambitious attempts at documenting the history of science. When complete, the *Collected Papers* will span twenty-five volumes, and that still represents just part of the 40,000 papers from Einstein's personal collection and 15,000 additional papers discovered by the editors.

The *Collected Papers* are far from complete. Volume 7 was published in 2002 and Volume 8 in 1997—they're being published in a fairly loose chronological order. In addition, even now after the reign of Dukas and Nathan, the release of the *Collected Papers* is a tightly controlled matter embroiling both Princeton University and the Hebrew University in Jerusalem, both of which lay claim to them. As a result, new volumes are released only every few years, and because they're organized chronologically, Einstein historians are still waiting for the publication of letters and documents that will shed light on events that occurred in Einstein's later years. The timed release of the *Collected Papers* also ensures that every few years there will be a flurry of activity surrounding the man—keeping the flame of his fame alive.

The first biography of Einstein came as early as 1921. At the time Einstein was only forty-two, but he had already achieved worldwide fame. The biography was titled *Einstein: Einblicke n seine Gedankenwelt* (Einstein: insights into his world of ideas) and was published by the Berlin literary critic Alexander Moszkowski. It consisted of a long series of dialogues with Einstein. Many books about Einstein have been from his friends or relatives, including both of the men who could call Einstein their father-in-law. Rudolf Kayser (1889–1964) married Einstein's stepdaughter Ilse Einstein and under the pen name Anton Reiser he wrote one of the first biographies of Einstein. Published in 1930, it was one of the few that had Einstein's blessing. The situation was quite different with Einstein's other son-in-law. The book, titled *Einstein: An Intimate Study of a Great Man*, was a tell-all written by Dimitri Marianoff after he had divorced Einstein's younger stepdaughter, Margot. Marianoff dragged out as much dirty laundry as he could about the scientist, and Einstein went out of his way to discredit the book.

Other biographers include Einstein's sister, Maja, as well as, after his death, his longtime secretary, Helen Dukas, who cowrote an insightful book with Banesh Hoffman called *Albert Einstein: Creator and Rebel*. Having as an author the woman who spent thirty years living under Einstein's roof ensures that this book is full of great personal anecdotes that are hard to find anywhere else. On the other hand, Dukas's propensity for portraying her employer in the best possible light means one must be aware of her bias.

Other colleagues of Einstein also wrote of their experience with him. Einstein's friend and fellow physicist Phillip Frank wrote a biography that had Einstein's blessing, titled *Einstein: His Life and Times*, published in 1947. But while Einstein agreed with the portrayal, Einstein's son Hans Albert complained bitterly that the book provided a poor portrayal of his mother, Mileva. And scientists often complain that the book isn't the best at explaining Einstein's science.

For those looking for an exhaustive look at Einstein's science, and how he arrived at his ideas, the excellent book *Subtle Is the Lord . . .* published in 1982 by Einstein's friend and fellow physicist Abraham Pais is in order. Pais left no stone unturned in his quest to describe how and why Einstein pulled together his theories, touching on far more than simply the relativity and $E = mc^2$ that most other books stop at. Pais has a second book more focused on Einstein's personal life titled *Einstein Lived Here*, published in 1994. Both of Pais's books are improved by the fact that they were published after the first volume of Einstein's *Collected Papers* was published.

The release of Einstein's papers held a treasure for Einstein biographers, as well as some time bombs, including, among other things, the information that Einstein had a propensity for affairs and that his first wife, Mileva, had a child born out of wedlock. Such information led to a new crop of "exposé" books about Einstein. *The Search for Lieserl*, by Michele Zackheim, describes the birth of Einstein's first child and her disappearance—all record of her existence has been lost to history. *Einstein in Love* by Dennis Overbye gives a complete account of Einstein's often contentious relationship with his first wife, and his ambiguous relationship with his second.

This is, of course, but a fraction of the books about Einstein. New biographies are released constantly and there are hundreds of books that describe his scientific theories. In addition, Einstein's popularity and prominence in popular culture has led to his name being added to just about any book that had a passing acknowledgment with science—thus, there are books like *What Einstein Told His Cook*—a book about science in the kitchen—and an entire series of books for preschoolers titled Baby Einstein Books. Einstein's fame assures there will be many more to come.

Born, Max
(1882–1970)

The German physicist Max Born was, alongside Niels Bohr, Max Planck, Werner Heisenberg, and Einstein, one of the founders of quantum mechanics. Born and Einstein were lifelong friends who maintained an extensive correspondence for decades; the letters between the two famous scientists are a fantastic source for historians and researchers.

The first meeting between Born and Einstein came two months after Einstein quit his job at the Patent Office in 1909. Einstein gave a renowned lecture at a conference in Salzburg, saying that scientists would soon show that light could be thought of as both a beam of particles and a wave. Einstein himself had first predicted light was made up of particles—quanta of energy that would eventually be named photons—but he knew too well that the wave description of light also seemed accurate. Creative thinker that he was, he easily accepted that light might turn out to be both. Born met Einstein after this lecture, and excitedly discussed this new "quantum" view of light—but Einstein could not have predicted the direction his ideas would go once they fell into the hands of others.

Within fifteen years, Niels Bohr (1885–1962), Born, and others fully accepted this wave-particle duality, and took quantum mechanics even further, describing a universe that was ruled by other such vagaries. There were many interpretations of just how light could be both a wave and a particle—Born's personal view was that light was made of particles but that their movement was guided by a wave. Those who accepted traditional quantum mechanics viewed the world as filled with such quirks; the new science also insisted that all fundamental particles were ruled solely by laws of probability and chance, no more predictable than making a bet on a roulette wheel or at a craps table. It was a view Einstein could not accept. He wrote Born in 1925: "Quantum mechanics is certainly imposing. But an inner voice tells me that it is not yet the real thing. The theory says a lot, but does not really bring us any closer to the secret of the 'Old One.' I, at any rate, am convinced that He is not playing dice." As Einstein voiced this opinion more emphatically over time, Born worried that Einstein was alienating himself from the scientific community.

Living in Berlin at the same time, Born and Einstein had similar experiences in Germany. In 1918, after World War I ended, revolutionary students at the University of Berlin took over a building and took hostages. Einstein, believing—correctly—that he held some sway with the students, asked Born to join him in negotiating for the hostages. Einstein had a reputation for having extremely liberal, almost Communist leanings, and the students were surprised that their beloved professor was not with them. In his autobiography Born wrote: "I can still see before me the astonished faces of these eager youths when the great Einstein, whom they believed wholeheartedly on their side, did not follow them blindly in their fanaticism." Together the two scientists helped bring about a peaceful resolution; the hostages were freed.

After World War I, growing nationalism in Germany led to a rise of anti-Semitism that affected both Einstein and Born, also a Jew. Finding their native land hostile, Born eventually immigrated to Scotland, while Einstein moved to the United States. They continued to write to each other to the end. It was to Born's sadness, however, that Einstein rejected every attempt Born made at convincing him of the validity of quantum mechanics. Einstein argued against every paper and every letter Born wrote and never accepted the new science.

Bose-Einstein Condensate

In the 1920s, Albert Einstein expanded on the ideas of the Indian physicist Satyendra Nath Bose (1894–1974) to predict that at extremely cold temperatures, atoms would coalesce into a new phase of matter—different from liquid, gas, or solid—known as Bose-Einstein condensate.

In 1924, Bose was living in Calcutta and having a hard time getting attention for his work in the European community. Bose wrote to Einstein, sending him a paper that used a new form of counting statistics to arrive at Planck's law—the famous equation that represents how energy radiates from a dark cavity, claiming that radiation always comes in discrete packets. Einstein was impressed with Bose's paper, calling it "a significant advance." He personally translated it into German and arranged for it to be published in the *Zeitschrift Fur Physik* in 1924.

Bose's new statistics offered more information on how to understand the behavior of photons. Bose showed that if one photon went into a specific quantum state (a general collection of attributes including the amount of energy the photon has), then there was a slight bias that the next one might go into the same state. It's as if every time you shot a billiards ball it was more likely to go into a pocket that already had a ball in it.

Bose had applied his counting statistics to a "gas" of photons. This inspired Einstein to consider the application of Bose's statistics to an ideal gas of atoms or molecules; Einstein wanted to see what happened when one was dealing with actual matter. Building on Bose's work, Einstein came up with a set of statistics to predict how atoms in a gas should behave that turns out to be correct for certain kinds of particles—including protons and neutrons—that are now, appropriately, referred to as bosons.

One of the most intriguing ideas that came out of this work was the prediction of what would happen to atoms at freezing cold temperatures. In 1925, Einstein made the remarkable discovery that if a gas was lowered to a temperature of almost absolute zero—the point at which atoms barely move at all—they would all fall into the exact same quantum state.

Going back to the pool table, one can imagine dropping twenty balls on the table and watching them roll into various pockets. This kind of random rolling is what happens at normal temperatures—each atom falling into a certain energy state. But at absolute zero, those dropped balls would all, one by one, follow each other into the same hole. At absolute zero, the atoms lock into the same quantum state and trail along after one another unquestioningly. Then they coalesce into a whole new phase of matter—not liquid, solid, gas, or even the esoteric fourth state of matter, plasma—that became known as the Bose-Einstein condensate. All the atoms in the Bose-Einstein condensate have lost their individual identity. They march in lockstep, acting for all intents and purposes as if they were a single superatom. Indeed, a Bose-Einstein condensate interacts with another Bose-Einstein condensate as if it was a particle unto itself—they might repel each other or attract each other just as individual atoms do.

Einstein published this work in 1925, when he was forty-six years old. It's rare for a scientist to contribute something completely new to a field when in his forties, and indeed this was Einstein's last great addition to physics. Seventy years would pass before a Bose-Einstein condensate was observed. In 1995, a team led by physicists Eric Cornell and Carl Weimen at JILA Institute at the University of Colorado coaxed a dilute gas of roughly 2,000 rubidium atoms into a Bose-Einstein condensate at a chilly −459.69E °F (−273.15E °C). Einstein's last great prediction was finally realized. For their efforts and early studies of the condensates, Cornell, Wieman, and Wolfgang Ketterle of MIT were awarded the 2001 Nobel Prize in physics.

Brain

Chunks of Einstein's brain are now sealed in wax, some pieces have been sliced up and put on microscope slides, and other bits are floating in jars of formaldehyde. His brain has been part of a museum exhibit, it was the main subject of a popular nonfiction book, and it has been studied by numerous scientists to see what made it so special. So far, there's no conclusive evidence that Einstein's gray matter was any different than anyone else's.

At Einstein's birth, his head was so misshapen and oversized his mother openly worried her first born son was *zurckgeblieben*—German for mentally retarded. The fact that Einstein didn't start talking until he was three years old did nothing to ease her fears. Of course, as he got older, Einstein was a normal child, and went on to show that he was incredibly gifted at math and science. No one knows if Einstein himself believed these gifts came from a brain that was physically different from anyone else's. (Though we do know he did believe in genetically fated dispositions, as he often wondered if his younger son's mental problems were genetically linked to his first wife's melancholy.) Regardless, Einstein thought it an interesting enough question to donate his brain to science after his death.

Despite the fact that Einstein appears to have agreed to it ahead of time, the removal of his brain was immediately contested. Einstein's friends and family told reporters they were shocked and upset at the procedure as doctors and hospitals squabbled over who should own the organ. And yet, or maybe because of all the controversy, the man who took the brain out of Einstein's head disappeared with most of it for over forty years.

The strange saga of Einstein's brain and the pathologist who removed it, Thomas Stoltz Harvey, is documented in the book *Driving Mr. Albert* by Michael Paterniti. In it, the author and Harvey travel across the United States—with most of Einstein's brain in the trunk of their car.

Harvey was the pathologist on duty at Princeton Hospital on April 18, 1955. He came to work at 8 A.M. that day, and found the body of the world-famous physicist on his cold metal table. What happened next depends on whom you ask. Harvey, Einstein's family, and the officials and staff members at Princeton Hospital all have wildly different accounts of the autopsy. Hospital officials contend that Einstein's remains were handled with the utmost respect. Harvey and other hospital workers say that people were dropping by the morgue all day long to take a peek. Family members and friends of Einstein say they didn't know that Einstein's brain was removed for study, but Harvey contends he had a letter of permission from Einstein's son and that Otto Nathan, Einstein's friend and executor of his will was in the room during the procedure. What clearly did happen was the following: After peeling back Einstein's mane of wild, white hair, Harvey, using a buzz saw, cut off the top of Einstein's head and removed his brain. It weighed 2.7 pounds and looked perfectly normal. The pathologist washed and soaked the organ in paraformaldehyde and injected it with sucrose to preserve it. After taking a series of black and while pictures, Harvey then cut up the brain into about 240 pieces.

The pathologist continued his preparation of Einstein's brain, sealing some of the pieces in paraffin to preserve them, others were left floating freely in formaldehyde, and a few bits were cut into very thin slices and put onto slides for further study. As these preparations continued, the firestorm over who should own Einstein's brain erupted.

Doctors at New York's Montefiore Medical Center said that Harvey had promised the organ to them and it had to leave Princeton University immediately, while Einstein's son, Hans Albert, threatened a lawsuit, saying he never gave permission for the autopsy in the first place.

Harvey held a press conference saying he intended to study the brain for science. He was no academic slouch, but he also wasn't a neuropathologist, and so others in the field questioned his ability to study the brain. Leading brain researchers of the day held a meeting. They invited Harvey, and many of them, including Webb Haymaker, an army doctor who had studied Mussolini's brain, tried to cajole, persuade, and finally threaten Harvey into giving up the brain. He refused.

The greatest brain of the century sat in Thomas Stoltz Harvey's Princeton office for years. As the hubbub died down over Einstein's organ, Harvey's career died too. Ultimately, he left the hospital and moved to Lawrence, Kansas, working for a plastic extruder company, E & E Display Group. But when Harvey went west, he quietly took the brain with him.

After all the media attention and threatened lawsuits faded away, the location of Einstein's brain became a true urban legend, bubbling up through pop culture every now and then. Famed American writer, Joyce Carol Oates wrote a poem about the autopsy titled "Love Letter, Static Interference from Einstein's Brain," and the BBC developed a documentary. Einstein's brain, gathering dust in someone's garage, entered modern myth, right up there with Hitler being alive and well in Argentina, and the location of Jimmy Hoffa's body.

Then, in the 1980s, for reasons he has never made clear, Thomas Harvey began to send out portions of the brain to scientists and researchers around the world. Those who have studied Einstein's brain include Japanese researcher Haruyasu Yamaguchi, Jorge Columbo in Buenos Aires, the Australian Charles Boyd, Britt Anderson at the University of Alabama, and Marian Diamond at the University of California at Berkeley.

Finally, after taking care of the brain for forty years, Harvey gave the remains to Elliot Krauss of Princeton University. As documented in Paterniti's book, the brain made the trip from Kansas to California in the trunk of a car, sloshing around in formaldehyde inside two glass cookie jars.

As for those who studied the brain, one of the most widely reported studies was by the Canadian Sandra Witelson. She claimed that Einstein's brain lacked a particular small wrinkle (the parietal operculum) that most people have. Perhaps in compensation, other regions on each side were a bit enlarged—about 15 percent larger than normal. Because the inferior parietal lobe is often associated with mathematical ability, it offers an intriguing explanation for why Einstein was so smart. But a vast number of scientists who have reviewed these studies remain unconvinced, saying there aren't any physical differences in Einstein's brain that would account for his revolutionary ideas. In fact, many scientists believe the study of Einstein's brain is a waste of time—they say that although the brain was preserved the best way scientists knew how, studying a dead organ will not show any insights into Einstein's thought processes. Today there are many ways to study a "live" thinking brain, yet many neurologists dismiss the idea that even under ideal conditions there would be any physical evidence in Einstein's brain that would grant us insight into his intelligence.

Yet, almost everyone finds it fascinating that Einstein's brain is still here. People have long searched for physical anatomical reasons for intelligence. Scientists and charlatans have focused on everything from the silly, like studying bumps on the head, to the serious, like counting the number of neurons in brain matter, all to try to understand what makes humans intelligent. To learn that there may not, in fact, be any smoking gun associated with Einstein's brain that predestined him for scientific greatness is perhaps as interesting a discovery as any.

Brownian Motion

The same year that Einstein published special relativity, he also published a groundbreaking paper on the random movements of molecules, an occurrence known as Brownian motion. Since moving particles aren't as exciting as changes in time and space, Einstein's explanation of Brownian motion has been completely eclipsed by his sexier theories—but there are those who say that had he not published anything else, Einstein would have still deserved a Nobel Prize for explaining just how particles move about.

In 1828, Robert Brown (1773–1858) studied how grains of pollen moved in liquid under a microscope and discovered that they moved randomly and of their own accord. Others had noticed this motion before, but no one else examined it so extensively, proving that the grains didn't move because they were alive, and that bits of glass and granite exhibited the same behavior. Today, the idea that grains might switch places with the molecules in a liquid and thus move around does not seem so odd, but in Brown's day scientists didn't know of the existence of atoms or molecules. By the time Einstein began to study science, physicists and chemists had begun to incorporate the idea of atoms into their theories, but they were by and large split on whether they truly existed. Perhaps, some thought, atoms and molecules were simply a mathematically convenient way to describe certain phenomena, but did not offer a true picture of reality.

Einstein was not torn on the issue. He believed in atoms, and many of his early papers made the assumption that matter could be divided into discrete particles. He wrote his dissertation on how to determine the size of molecules by measuring their Brownian motion in a liquid. A version of his dissertation was published in the German journal *Annalen der Physik* in April 1905, and it is one of the first papers to show definitively that molecules are not just mathematical constructs, but real entities.

Eleven days later, Einstein published a paper on Brownian motion itself. The paper was called "On the Motion of Small Particles Suspended in Liquids at Rest Required by the Molecular-Kinetic Theory of Heat," and Einstein didn't state that it was about Brownian motion per se. He simply stated in his opening paragraph that he was going to describe the movement of molecules suspended in liquid, and that perhaps the phenomenon was identical to that chemical occurrence he'd heard of, Brownian motion. From that start, he went on to show that he could use current heat theories to describe how heat—even room-temperature heat—would make liquid molecules move around. The moving liquid would result in the jostling of any grains suspended in the liquid. Einstein had just offered the first explanation of what caused Brownian motion.

Next, Einstein wrote up the mathematical description of how the grains in the liquid will move. He used statistical analysis to calculate the average path of any such particle. While the particle movement might be random, flitting briefly to the left and then to the right, Einstein showed that you could determine a basic direction for the movement. It's not unlike the way a drunk walking down the street might collide with the wall, bounce into another pedestrian, and then bump into a parked car all while heading in the general direction of the corner. One can see the basic area where the drunk is headed and make predictions about how long it will take him to get there even without knowing exactly how many foreign objects he's going to smash into along the way. Indeed, the math for how particles move in Brownian motion is called "a random walk"—as one can overlook the randomness on short time scales to make predictions about what will happen in long time scales.

Einstein's paper offered an explanation for Brownian motion, but it was other scientists who performed the experiments showing that molecules did indeed exist, and that it was heat transfer that caused their movement in a liquid. The foremost experimenter in the field was Jean Babtiste Perrin (1870–1942) who was awarded the Nobel Prize in Physics in 1926. All of this research into Brownian motion solved a problem confronting all physicists and chemists of the day as to whether nature was fundamentally continuous or made up of particles. With his dissertation, his Brownian motion work, and his photoelectric effect paper, Einstein was a crucial force in the growing acceptance of the existence of atoms and molecules. Einstein, however, rarely worked with anything related so directly to molecules again.

See **Miracle Year.**

Career

Einstein began his career forced to take a job in a patent office since he couldn't get a job in science anywhere—and ended with universities all around the world courting him to join their faculty.

Einstein graduated from university in Zurich with undistinguished grades and a host of professors who thought he was argumentative and confrontational. He had hoped to be offered a job at his alma mater right out of school but found that, without the support and recommendations of his professors, he couldn't get an academic position there—or anywhere, for that matter. For a year, Einstein wrote letters to other physicists, imploring them for assistant positions. It was quite possibly the most trying year of his life, as at the same time his college sweetheart, Mileva Maric, whose grades were just a smidgen worse than Einstein's and hadn't graduated, announced she was pregnant.

The impending family and Einstein's parents' utter dismay with his prospects led him to grasp at straws, so when a job at the Patent Office in Switzerland was suggested by the father of Einstein's college classmate Marcel Grossman, Einstein jumped at the chance. He moved to Bern even before the position was officially offered.

Despite its inauspicious beginnings, the Swiss Patent Office suited the young Einstein. He worked there for seven years—from 1902 to

> *I decided the following about our future: I will look immediately for a position, no matter how humble.*
> *My scientific goals and my personal vanity will not prevent me from accepting the most subordinate role.*
>
> —Einstein to fiancée Mileva Maric
> on July 7, 1901

1909—and even remained on the job, receiving modest promotions while he gave lectures at conferences for the world's eminent physicists. Later in life he called the Patent Office the most satisfying appointment of his career. The pay was reasonable, he had found friends in Bern who satisfied both his intellect and his playful manner, his young bride arrived (without the baby, who presumably was put up for adoption), and his work stimulated his mind while also giving him the free time to develop his own theories. The combination of relative calm in his personal life, and being surrounded by smart company, resulted in Einstein's astounding "Miracle Year"; he published five groundbreaking physics papers in one year and Einstein's star began to rise.

The fame was not enough to land him a job, however. In 1907 he applied to be a *privatdozent* at the University of Bern, a nonfaculty, unsalaried teaching position where each student paid a small fee to attend. The job application required that he include an unpublished paper that he was about to submit to a journal. At this point Einstein had already published the special theory of relativity, his famous $E = mc^2$ equation, and theorized the existence of the light quanta for which he would win the Nobel Prize, but none of this mattered in the face of the bureaucratic requirement to have a new paper. It took Einstein another year to bother to furnish them with the necessary article, but he finally landed that first teaching job in 1908. The following year, Einstein accepted his first official faculty position as an associate professor at the University of Zurich. That year he was also awarded his first honorary doctorate from the University of Geneva. And, in 1919 Einstein received his first nomination for the Nobel Prize in physics; clearly the world had taken notice.

In 1911, Einstein began a series of jumps, never staying in one place too long for several years. He accepted his first full professorship at the German Karl-Ferdinand University and moved his family—Mileva and their two young sons—to Prague. But Einstein only stayed in Prague for a matter of months. Einstein hated the city, finding it dirty, cold, and pretentious all at once. So when Grossmann offered him a professorship back at his alma mater, Einstein quickly accepted. It was a triumphant return since just eleven years earlier the institution had barely let him graduate. And yet, despite Einstein's connection to Grossmann, Einstein stayed in Zurich for only a year. The lure of a nonteaching position at the newly formed Kaiser Wilhelm Institutes in Berlin (and the occasion to be closer to his mistress, Elsa) was too much for Einstein, and he left Zurich in 1913.

Finally, Einstein found a job he wanted to hold on to. He remained at the Institute for nearly twenty years. During that time Einstein became the most famous scientist in the world, accruing honorary degrees and expanding his influence beyond science into the politics of Zionism, racism, and world peace. But as his international popularity and scientific stature grew, the opinions of his fellow countrymen fell. As a famous Jew he was a prime target for anti-Semitic persecution; he knew it was time to begin searching for a new home and a new job. Einstein had ties to a number of other universities. Many Zionists, especially Einstein's former companion in the cause, Chaim Weizmann, felt it was Einstein's duty to go to the Hebrew University in Palestine. Einstein had championed the creation of the university for many years, but he had a previous falling out with the school's administration. Although Einstein had made public statements about his problems with the university, Weizmann still petitioned the scientist, in private and in public, to make his home there, but Einstein continued to refuse. Einstein had also spoken frequently at the California Institute of Technology and was in negotiations with the administration there for a job as well. But it was Princeton University that finally lured him away from Germany in 1932. The brand new Institute for Advanced Studies simply was the best fit—with the most money and the least teaching work for the now fifty-seven-year-old scientist.

On the whole, Einstein was quite happy in Princeton, where he spent the last twenty-two years of his life. Shortly after his arrival, his second wife, Elsa, passed away, and with her went the driving force behind Einstein's lecture travel. He settled into the Institute befriending such other greats as the mathematician Kurt Godel (1906–1978), Robert Oppenheimer (1904–1967), and Wolfgang Pauli (1900–1958). He retired in 1945, though this "retirement" came with no change in his salary, nor did he lose his office. Even in his last days, he regularly made the short trip from his house to continue working on his latest physics theories.

See **Miracle Year; Patent Office; Princeton.**

Causality

Einstein believed that everything in the universe followed the laws of cause and effect: a ball that's thrown up will fall down; a car moving at a certain speed will arrive at a predictable time. Causality, also known as determinism, means that if one knows enough about any given situation, any given system, then one should be able to foretell with certainty what will happen next. Quantum mechanics, however, chucked causality out the window.

For hundreds of years, scientists assumed that the rules of cause and effect governed the universe. For example, when Isaac Newton discovered how gravity made planets move, astronomers predicted their orbits for thousands of years into the future. If one knew the initial situation, then one could surely describe its destiny perfectly. But in the twentieth century, the advent of quantum mechanics turned this predictable world upside down. Quantum mechanics insists that the most fundamental laws of nature are random. And even though Einstein's early work led directly to the development of the new science, Einstein always refused to accept this randomness.

When physicists developed quantum mechanics, they felt an uncontainable excitement because they were devising the tools they needed to describe the just-discovered world of subatomic particles. Einstein shared in the excitement. But the field of quantum mechanics took a turn that frustrated Einstein: the equations scientists developed were only able to predict the probabilities of how an atom would act. If you knew, say, the position and speed of an electron, one couldn't say exactly how long it would take to get somewhere. Instead, the math of quantum mechanics would give imprecise answers such as: "There is a 25 percent chance the electron will be here, a 50 percent chance it will be over there, and a 25 percent chance it will be somewhere else entirely." Quantum mechanics was chipping away at the lovely laws of causality that Einstein embraced.

As the field developed, Einstein held on to the hope that scientists would find additional information, or additional tools, that would finally allow everyone to understand what was truly going on. With more information, scientists surely would be able to put causality back into their descriptions; they'd be able to determine *exactly* how an electron, a photon, or an atom would move. But instead, the new science gave up on causality completely. In 1927, the German physicist Werner Heisenberg developed his Uncertainty Principle, a theory that said one could never precisely measure certain attributes of a particle. If a scientist measured a particle's speed, that meant he couldn't simultaneously measure its position. This was not due to limits on one's tools, but was due to an inherent limitation of the particle itself: when the speed was precise, the position simply wasn't, and vice versa.

If such basic things in the universe as speed and position can only be measured to within a "range" of values, then there is no way to make accurate predictions about anything. In 1927, Heisenberg phrased it this way: "In the sharp formulation of the law of causality— 'if we know the present exactly, we can calculate the future'—it is not the conclusion that is wrong but the premise." Because reality at any single moment is imprecise, due to the Uncertainty Principle, the future is inherently unpredictable as well. A photon whizzing by could travel willy-nilly, since at any given moment it could be in a whole sweep of places. (Quantum mechanics does put limits on how particles can move, but particles are nevertheless governed by possibilities and probabilities, not assigned to definite paths.)

Einstein hated all that the Uncertainty Principle implied. He and his fellow physicist, Niels Bohr (1885–1962) had epic, but civilized, arguments over uncertainty versus causality. In his attempt to bring back causality, Einstein often stated he couldn't accept that "God played dice with the universe." After hearing this statement time and time again, Bohr finally became enraged, saying: "Stop telling God what to do!"

In that, Bohr summed up quite neatly the opposing position. Einstein felt strongly that one could never accept a science that summarily dismissed causality—but the key word there is "felt." There was no concrete evidence to support Einstein. Indeed, quantum mechanics seemed to predict how particles moved—albeit only with "ranges"— so successfully that almost everyone else in the scientific community accepted it completely. Today, most scientists believe that the rules of the game are quite different when dealing with subatomic particles. While the laws of cause and effect may reign in the macroscopic world, causality has abandoned the world of particles, and most scientists now believe that Einstein's instinctual clinging to determinism clouded his understanding.

Childhood
(1879–1896)

Growing up, Einstein was a fairly typical, well-adjusted child, who was already showing glimpses of his adult personality: stubbornness and persistence, frustration with authority, and a love for science.

Einstein was born on a sunny Friday, March 14, 1879, at 11:30 in the morning at his parent's home on Bahnhofstrasse in Ulm, a quiet town on the Danube River. His birth certificate identifies his parents, Hermann and Pauline, as "belonging to the Israelite faith."

Family legend holds that when Einstein was born, his head was so big and so angular that his mother thought he was deformed. Einstein was also quite slow to speak during his first three years, throwing his mother into fits of fear that her son was mentally slow. Decidedly later, Einstein described how he skipped the step of babbling baby talk. He said that some of his earliest childhood memories, back when he was two or three years old, were of first trying out an entire sentence in his head, then speaking it aloud when he got it right. One of Einstein's first such sentences was in 1881, when he was promised a toy upon the birth of his sister. When Einstein saw Maja for the first time, he exclaimed, "But where are its wheels?"

As he grew older, young Albert continued to be quiet and uncommunicative. Up until the age of seven, he had the habit of softly repeating to himself every sentence he uttered; even at nine years old, Einstein wasn't a very fluent speaker. He did, however, have unusual concentration for a small child. One of his favorite activities was building houses of cards, at times up to fourteen stories high.

In 1880, Einstein's family moved from Ulm to Munich where he spent much of his youth. He avoided the rough and tumble games of other kids. But he also had a persistent, even stubborn nature. Like many children, Einstein was prone to tantrums, at times his face would go completely yellow and the tip of his nose turned white. But he learned to control these rages, and by his elementary school years they subsided.

Einstein always seems to have been fascinated by science; in his *Autobiographical Notes* he fondly described an early memory. When he was about five years old, he was tremendously excited by the behavior of a compass his father gave him. Einstein's mother, possibly because she realized her child had a thirst for knowledge, or possibly just because she had high aspirations for her only son, hired a private tutor for him even before he entered elementary school.

In 1885, Einstein started school at the nearby Volksschule, where he did well. A letter from his mother to his grandmother in August 1886 boasted that seven-year-old Einstein had been placed at the top of the class "once again" and had received a "splendid" school report.

Bavarian law required all children to receive a religious education, and at the Volksschule, only Catholicism was provided. Einstein was the only Jewish boy in the class, and so a distant relative taught him the elements of Judaism at home. When he moved up to middle school, the Luitpold Gymnasium, this instruction continued at school. Possibly as a result, Einstein went through an intense religious phase when he was eleven years old. Later in his life, when he was living in Berlin, he told a close friend that during this period he refused to eat pork as mandated by Jewish dietary laws and had composed several songs in honor of God, which he sang enthusiastically to himself on the way to school. This interlude came to an abrupt end a year later; Einstein attributed his return to secular life to his exposure to science; with facts to answer questions about the universe, Einstein became disdainful of what he now decided were simply the fanciful stories of religion.

Aside from the influence of his mathematics teacher, Josef Zametzer, much of Einstein's love of science was developed at home. His father and uncle were in the telecommunications and electronics business, so young Einstein was surrounded by adults involved in what was the cutting-edge technology of the time. Einstein's uncle Jakob introduced him to geometry and algebra by having Einstein hunt for an animal "x, whose name we do not know." Another great source of information was a family friend, Max Talmud (who later changed his name to Max Talmey), a medical student who introduced Einstein to some of the great science books of the day.

In primary school, Einstein rebelled against what he saw as the strict instruction by his schoolteachers, possibly because he was used to so much adult attention outside of school. He complained bitterly about his formal schooling, writing, "The teachers in the elementary school appeared to be like sergeants and the gymnasium teachers like lieutenants."

One solace for Einstein was music. He began violin lessons at the age of six, and his instrument accompanied him his entire life. At first, the lessons were forced upon him by his mother, part of her drive to create a perfect son. But Einstein fell in love with the violin, and he needed the comfort for the difficult times ahead. When Einstein was fifteen, his father's business went under, and the family was forced to move from the idyllic villa that had been Einstein's childhood home. It was sold to a developer, and before Einstein's eyes, the stately trees that surrounded the house were cut down. His mother, father, and younger sister moved to Milan to try again the electrical business with Jakob. Einstein, however, was left behind. His mother didn't want to interrupt his schooling, and so the plan was for him to live with relatives for a year until it was time to go to college.

But Einstein was miserable. In his sister's 1924 biographical sketch, she wrote that Einstein's solitary existence made him depressed and nervous. Only six months into the experiment, he dropped out of the Luitpold Gymnasium and surprised his parents by showing up on their doorstep in Italy.

The impetuous decision also had implications for his citizenship. Leaving before the age of seventeen, Einstein became a voluntary exile, resulting in Germany automatically absolving him from military service without categorizing him as a deserter. (While that was a bonus for the pacifist-leaning young Einstein, the decision to leave Germany as a teenager probably had more to do with homesickness than a desire to avoid the military, because Einstein did appear for his Swiss military examination, only to be marked unacceptable due to flat feet.)

With her son suddenly in Italy, Einstein's mother decided he was ready for college. Pulling strings, she got Einstein the opportunity to test for early acceptance to the Swiss Federal Polytechnical School, later to be known as the Eidgenössische Technische Hochschule, or the ETH. Einstein was allowed to take the test, and passed the science and math sections, but failed the rest. And so Einstein was sent to the cantonal school in Aarau, a small town located on the bank of the Aar River. When he arrived in 1895, Aarau had less than ten thousand people, most of them German-speaking Protestants. Einstein boarded with the family of Jost Winteler, who taught at the school. Einstein, then sixteen years old, became good friends with Jost's son, Paul. In Switzerland, Einstein had his first romance, with Marie, Winteler's daughter. The affair was intense at first, but lost steam after a year.

In the fall of 1896, Einstein passed his final exams and finally enrolled at the ETH, one of only five students in the physics and mathematics group. The other four were Marcel Grossmann, Louis

Kollros, Jakob Ehrat, and Mileva Maric. Still only seventeen years old, Einstein was the youngest of the group.

But Einstein was headstrong and confident, despite his age. The boy who could travel to Italy all by himself had no problem making his personality felt at the ETH—and the relationships he made there would have an effect on his adult life. Grossman became his best friend and Maric his first wife.

Children

Einstein had three children with his first wife—one before they were married—and he was the stepfather to his second wife's two children. Einstein had what could only be called complicated relationships with all of them: he never met his first child, he was often distant or confrontational with his two sons, he proposed marriage to one of his stepdaughters, and lived the last of his days overly dependent on the other.

Lieserl (1902–?)

Einstein's first child was born in 1902. Known only as Lieserl, Einstein's only biological daughter was born before Einstein and his first wife Mileva were married. We only know of Lieserl's existence through Einstein and Mileva's letters, and it seems that in the beginning, they planned to keep the child. But a subsequent letter, from Mileva to Einstein, describes the baby's bout with scarlet fever. Einstein's reply includes asking how the child was registered so that there would be no problems for her later, which suggests she might have been given to others to raise. It's unknown whether some member of Mileva's family adopted Lieserl, or if she died young. Regardless, Einstein never laid eyes on his daughter, and the paper trail of Lieserl's life stops in 1903.

Hans Albert Einstein (1904–1973)

Mileva and Einstein did marry and went on to have two sons. Their older son, Hans Albert, was born on May 14, 1904. He had a conflicted relationship with his famous father, beginning with Einstein's undeniably harsh treatment of Mileva. Hans's early childhood, by many accounts, was happy, but as Einstein's career began to take off, his relationship with his wife soured, and they were separated in 1914.

Hans Albert later said his mother took the break very hard, and that the whole family suffered when Mileva took her sons away from where they'd been living in Berlin back to Zurich. For a time, Mileva, Hans, and his little brother, Eduard, lived a vagabond existence, renting rooms in a lodging house while Mileva waited to see if the marriage could be revived. It could not.

The boy's distrust of his father emerged very early in his parents' separation, and Einstein seems to have sensed it. A letter written in late 1915 from Einstein to Hans, who was then 11, illustrates the gap that opened between them. Einstein wrote, "Yesterday I received your dear little letter, I was already afraid you didn't want to write to me at all anymore." Despite leaving Hans's mother, Einstein did want to stay in his son's life. Einstein's letter continues, "In any case, I shall press for our being together every year for a month so that you see that you have a father who is attached to you and loves you." But the relationship didn't improve. Einstein formally asked Mileva for a divorce in 1916 when he arrived in Zurich in April for the Easter holidays. Mileva objected bitterly when Einstein wanted to take Hans alone for an outing, and the boy took his mother's side. He ceased to write to Einstein for several months thereafter, and Einstein was furious with what he saw as the boy's betrayal.

Mileva collapsed physically after the visit, and Eduard soon became so sick that he went to a sanitarium to regain his health. In 1917, Hans was essentially left alone. Family friends, the Zanggers, took Hans in temporarily, but Einstein saw the accumulating crises as yet one more opportunity to repair his relationship with his son. Perhaps at last this was the time to bring his older son to Berlin, despite Mileva's desires. But this plan was thwarted because in February Einstein also fell ill, taking months to recover. In July, he finally felt well enough to go to Zurich and pick up Hans for a visit with Eduard, who was recuperating from his own illness in the Swiss village of Arosa.

On February 14, 1919, a district court in Zurich formally ended Einstein's marriage to Mileva Maric, and Mileva was awarded custody of the children with visitation rights for Einstein. For a while, Hans managed to have a genial relationship with his father. But in 1922 Einstein won the Nobel Prize, and according to his divorce decree with Mileva, the prize money was hers. This might be seen as generous on behalf of the physicist, but the funds, approximately 180,000 Swiss francs, were deposited in an inaccessible trust account, with only the interest at Mileva's disposal. This greatly upset Hans. In a letter to Paul Ehrenfest, on July 20, 1923, Einstein said that Hans had "on the occasion of the arrangement of the N. Pr. [Nobel Prize] written such an ugly and arrogant letter that I cannot meet with him this year." Family friends Heinrich Zangger and Hermann Anschütz intervened in this delicate family matter and managed to settle the dispute. At the end of August 1923, Einstein and both his sons were Anschütz's guest at the Lautrach Castle in Southern Germany. A bit later, the reconciled father spent two weeks in September with Hans in Kiel in a small apartment Anschütz provided. In another letter to his friend Ehrenfest, Einstein wrote on September 12, 1923, "I am again completely reconciled with Albert . . . I am . . . in my hidey-hole here with him at the Anschütz factory, where we are having a wonderful time and are able to make music together and sail."

But the two would clash again, this time over Hans's marriage. In fact, Einstein opposed Hans's bride in such a brutal way that it far surpassed the scene that Einstein's own mother had made about Mileva. It was 1927, and Hans, at age 23, fell in love with an older and—to Einstein—unattractive woman. He damned the union, swearing that Hans's bride was a scheming woman preying on his son. When all else failed, Einstein begged Hans to not have children, as it would only make the inevitable divorce harder. But despite his father's objections, Hans married Frieda Knecht on May 7, 1927, in Dortmund, where Hans worked for some time as a steel designer.

Einstein so objected to the marriage that not only did he mobilize his friends Zangger and Anschütz to dissuade Hans, he also had the medical history of the mother of his unwanted daughter-in-law investigated: after a hard life, she had at one time undergone psychiatric treatment. Einstein was firmly convinced of the hereditary nature of mental illness, and he worried about the effect of mental illness on both sides of the family. That may explain Einstein's ambivalence about his first grandchild, Bernhard Caesar Einstein, known as "Hardi." Writing to Ludwig Hopf, after Hardi's birth in 1930, Einstein said Hans had "very disrespectfully promoted him to grandfather." A second son of Hans and Frieda died at the age of six.

It was well into the 1930s before Einstein accepted his son's marriage. During those years, Hans was the caretaker for his mentally disturbed younger brother, who was institutionalized in a psychiatric hospital. The mental and financial strain of taking care of Eduard clearly was a point of contention between Hans and his father. In

1933, Hans wrote Einstein a nasty letter blaming Einstein for not securing the material future of Mileva and his children.

Three years later, Hans received his Ph.D. in technical sciences from his father's alma mater, the ETH, and decided to move to the United States. The *New York Times* was there to record the meeting of father and son when Hans arrived in New York on October 13, 1937. The *Times* reported Hans came in on the Holland-America liner *Veendam*, and Einstein was at the pier to welcome him. The account read, "His son said it was his first visit to the United States. His wife and two children remained in Europe, pending his decision to make America his permanent home."

Hans did decide to make America his permanent home, and soon after the New York trip, Hans and his family immigrated to the United States. Hans became a naturalized citizen in 1943, and he joined the faculty of the University of California, Berkeley.

With Hans on the West Coast, and Einstein in his Princeton enclave, even in their new country, father and son were apart. When Einstein became gravely ill in 1955, it took two days for his step-daughter and caretaker, Margot, to inform Hans that his father was hospitalized. As soon as Hans heard, he came immediately. He arrived at Princeton Hospital on April 16; two days later Einstein died.

In Einstein's will, Hans was awarded very little. However, Einstein did bequeath his beloved violin to his first grandson, Bernhard Caesar.

Eduard (1910–1965)

Eduard Einstein was Einstein's youngest son, born on July 28, 1910—right when his father's scientific career began to take off. The boy was nicknamed "Tete," thanks to the inability of his older brother to pronounce the word "Dete," which means "child" in Mileva's native Serbian. The nickname stuck with Eduard all his life.

As a boy, Eduard was exceptionally bright and musically talented. He learned to read early and started school in the spring of 1917. Two years later, at the age of nine, Eduard was reading the German classics of Goethe and Schiller.

He was a smart but sickly child. When he was nine, he spent a significant amount of time in a sanitarium for headaches and severe pain in his ears. On February 14 of that year, his parent's divorce became final. The next year, 1920, doctors diagnosed Eduard with schizophrenia, but for a time the illness subsided and he continued his studies.

Throughout high school, Eduard seemed to have a steady hand on his mental health, but things took a turn after graduation. Eduard enrolled in the University of Zurich to study medicine, hoping to specialize later in psychiatry, but as he got older the manifestations of his schizophrenia became more pronounced. In 1930, Eduard wrote a spate of angry letters to his father, blaming him for having ruined his life. Einstein's "desertion" had cast a "shadow" over everything, he said. This was the first Einstein and Mileva realized their son was truly suffering a total breakdown. Einstein rushed from Berlin to visit his son, but was unable to bridge the gap. Numerous psychiatrists studied Eduard, and he openly acknowledged that his depression stemmed from sickness, but he did not recover.

While Eduard's mental problems were clearly psychological, it's unclear what, if any, catalyst caused a breakdown at this time. Friends at college suggested that Eduard had suffered a serious rejection from an older medical student, and heartbreak may have triggered his depression. Whatever the reason, it was while at the university that his symptoms flared. Eduard covered the walls of his room with pornographic pictures of women, began to obsessively write nonsensical stories, and had attacks of rage so violent he had to be taken to Burghölzi, a psychiatric institution near Zurich. Thereafter, a male nurse discreetly accompanied Eduard at college. After only three semesters, Eduard withdrew.

> *It is a thousand pities for the boy that he must pass his life without hope of a normal existence . . . I have no further hopes from the medical side. I think it better on the whole to let Nature run its course.*
>
> —Letter from Albert Einstein to Michele Besso, concerning his schizophrenic son, Eduard, November 11, 1940

The year before, the Nazis had driven Einstein and his second wife, Elsa, from Berlin. They immigrated to the United States, settling in Princeton. For all of Eduard's life, the cost and strain of taking care of him fell on the shoulders of Einstein's first wife, and Mileva frequently complained that Einstein did not help enough. Even when friends intervened—such as Michele Besso, who took on the role of surrogate father to young Eduard—asking Einstein to pay more attention to his son, Einstein demurred, using his busy schedule as an excuse.

Einstein did not lay eyes on Eduard after 1933. This is partly because Einstein moved to the United States and partly because Einstein seems to have been unable to deal emotionally with his son's illness—a sickness he blamed squarely on his ex-wife. Mileva's mental state was not always steady, and there is no doubt that Mileva's sister was certifiably insane. Einstein always believed his son's insanity came from his ex-wife's family. In a letter to Hans Mühsam dated June 4, 1946, Einstein wrote that he would have been spared the pain of having a mentally disturbed son if he had never married Mileva. "Perhaps there is something benevolent in the wasteful sport that nature, seemingly blind, places on its creatures. Still it can only be beneficent if we try to persuade young people how critical that decision [marriage and reproduction] is, taken at a moment when nature leaves us in a kind of drunken sensual delusion so that we least possess our power of judgment when we most need it. I had to experience this drastically in myself and in my son."

After Mileva's death, Eduard lived at the Burghölzi Sanitarium for another seventeen years. He died on October 25, 1965, and was buried in the Hönggerberg cemetery. His brother, Hans Albert, and stepsister Margot signed the newspaper announcement of his death. The notice makes no mention of the mother who spent her life caring for him, but it does mention that Eduard Einstein was the "son of the deceased Professor Albert Einstein."

Ilse (1895–1935)

Einstein's stepdaughter, Ilse, was the daughter of Elsa Einstein, and her first husband, Max Lowenthal. Since her mother was Einstein's cousin, it is quite possible that Ilse met the man who would be her stepfather early in her childhood, but their lives did not become entwined until 1908, when Einstein and her mother began their affair. At the time, Ilse was thirteen years old, and described as a headstrong, swan-necked beauty.

In 1918, after years of legal battles with Einstein's first wife, and Einstein's own reluctance to commit to a second marriage, the way was finally clear for Einstein and Elsa to marry. But Einstein, who was already living down the hall from Elsa and her two children, created one last crisis. Einstein proposed that he marry either Elsa or Ilse, and he left it up to the two women to choose which one.

The proposition shocked Ilse. She wrote letters asking for advice to family friend, and her former lover, Georg Nicolai. But the question remains if Ilse was truly surprised, since she had close contact with Einstein at his office. She had been hired as his secretary when

Einstein's Institute for Theoretical Physics was founded. In her letters to Nicolai, Ilse denied that having sex was involved in Einstein's request, but in a later letter, Ilse mentions that Einstein was interested in having children. In 1918, Einstein was thirty-nine, Ilse was twenty, and Elsa was forty-two years old. It is possible that Einstein was, in his own mind, just being rational; he loved both women, and Ilse was of child-bearing age. Yet, Einstein also had a history of sexual affairs throughout his life. Simply by reading Ilse's letters it's impossible to know whether Einstein's suggestion was lecherous, logical, or even misunderstood. Regardless, Einstein distanced himself from the question so completely that Ilse believed he truly did not care one way or the other; he left the decision as to whether he marry mother or daughter up to the women.

Because the entire sordid suggestion only came to light in 1998 when a cache of Einstein family wartime correspondence was unsealed, there's no record of Einstein or Elsa's opinion of what happened. According to Ilse, she made the choice, in her words, "to step aside and let Mama marry." The episode became a closely held family secret, and it was Ilse's little sister Margot who kept the letters out of the public eye for eighty years. Again, because Einstein historians must rely on just a few short letters, it's difficult to know if Ilse and Einstein's relationship was strained after this or not—certainly, Ilse did continue working closely with Einstein at the Institute for six years. Nevertheless, when she left to marry a writer by the name of Rudolph Kayser in 1924, a few short notes to her friends hint that she was relieved to be out of the Einstein household.

About Ilse's rather quiet married life, little else is written. She, like her younger sister, remained exceptionally close to her mother, but according to notes to Ilse's friends, she seems to have kept her distance from her world-famous stepfather for the rest of her life. When Einstein and Elsa moved to the United States in 1933, Ilse went to Paris to stay with Margot and her husband, but shortly after, Ilse became terribly sick and died. Her mother returned to Europe to tend to her sick daughter, but Einstein refused to come, believing it too dangerous for someone so famous to visit war-torn Europe.

After Ilse's death, Elsa returned to Princeton but died one year later of heart disease. Einstein's personal secretary, Helen Dukas, wrote that she always believed Elsa died as the result of the shock of losing her oldest daughter.

Margot (1899–1986)

Unlike Ilse, Margot was dedicated to her stepfather. From the beginning the two seemed to have a quirky bond. As a child, Margot was artistic and exceptionally shy. Many of her mother's friends told stories of how the child would hide under the table when company called, and Einstein went along with the game, sometimes covering her with the tablecloth and joking if she made a sound.

Margot was only eleven when the romance between her mother and Einstein began. As she grew older, Einstein encouraged her career as a sculptor, and she vigorously nagged her stepfather, in private, over his manners and sloppy dressing. In 1930, Margot married Dimitri Marianoff, but their marriage failed within four years. Seven years later, Marianoff wrote one of the first tell-all books about Einstein, *Einstein—An Intimate Story of a Great Man*. When the book was published Einstein spoke out about the account, calling Marianoff incompetent and without the moral right to comment on his life.

Margot never remarried and instead seems to have dedicated all her energy to the doting Einstein. She may have been overly close to her mother and stepfather: in his albeit biased account, Margot's ex-husband described her as having, "that shyness pussy cats have who rarely leave their mother's side." When the Einstein household left Berlin for Princeton in 1933, Margot stayed behind in Europe for only one year. After her sister's death, Margot moved from Paris to Princeton, making her one of the women, along with Einstein's devoted secretary, Helen Dukas, whose lives revolved around Einstein in the little white house at 112 Mercer Street, Princeton. Even before the move to the United States, Margot had taken over her mother's role as Einstein's traveling partner when the famous scientist went around the world talking science. But after Elsa's death, Margot went from Einstein's traveling companion to his gatekeeper. To get to Einstein, friends, family, and the press had to go through her or Dukas.

Margot's emotional support for Einstein allowed him the distance he always sought from others. Margot protected him even from his own family—she was often the go-between for his son Hans, and she kept Einstein from knowing exact details about the deteriorating physical and mental health of his youngest son, Eduard.

When Einstein collapsed in 1955 and was taken to the Princeton hospital, Margot was already there, being treated for sciatica. She was wheeled to his bedside, where he greeted her with cheerful comments—yet he looked so different due to the pain and internal bleeding from a ruptured blood vessel that she claimed she did not recognize him at first.

Margot had positioned herself closer to Einstein than either of his sons. His eldest, Hans Albert, only found out about his father's collapse because Margot telephoned, and even then, it was over two days after the event. Margot was one of the few who saw Einstein during his last days. She wrote, "As fearless as he had been all his life, so he faced death humbly and quietly. He left the world without sentimentality or regrets."

Margot and Dukas continued to be adamant protectors of Einstein's legacy. In his will, Einstein left $20,000 and his house, furniture, and household goods to his stepdaughter. She said one of his last requests was to not let the house become a museum, and the two women lived there for over twenty-five years. Although they discouraged visitors and biographers, they also left Einstein's rooms untouched, like shrines to his memory.

Margot also continued to stand in between Einstein and his sons. In 1958, she supported a successful lawsuit in Switzerland to prevent the publication of a sensational book by Hans's wife, Frieda, although the book would have helped pay for Eduard's hospital bills.

Margot lived in Princeton until her death at the age of ninety-seven, and yet, even after her death, she protected "Herr Professor." She sealed the early letters her mother and Einstein exchanged, nearly five hundred of them, for over a decade, to be released after her death. Because of Margot's protection, it wasn't until 1998 that the world at large learned of Einstein's rather shocking marriage proposal to Elsa's older daughter, Ilse, as well as many of his other infidelities.

Others

And infidelities, he certainly did have. It is not believed that any of these resulted in offspring, but as Einstein became a famous figure, many women either claimed to be, or claimed to have given birth to, his children. One of the most famous of these claims was that of Grete Markstein, a Berlin actress, who claimed to be his daughter. Her claim does seem unlikely, and the fact that acquaintances of Einstein at the time confirm suspicions that the two had an affair means she was possibly just trying to connect herself in any way to the world-famous scientist. However, that the existence of Lieserl was held an absolute secret until decades after Einstein's death proves that Einstein knew how to keep a confidence—so it is possible that the famous physicist had other children we will never discover.

As for Einstein's legal heirs, Hans had one adopted granddaughter, two grandsons, and five great-grandchildren.

Clothes

Einstein was a famously sloppy dresser; in fact, he pretty much created the stereotype of the bedraggled scientist—one too caught up in science to worry about appearances. But Einstein didn't always dress like a bum. Well, he probably would have, if only his wife, Elsa, would have allowed it. When Einstein's fame and scientific renown was fresh and new, it was Elsa who made sure the scientist was ready for his close-up.

By all accounts Elsa Einstein was very concerned about appearances. As the notoriety of Einstein's theories spread in the 1930s, the famous physicist was in great demand, and through Elsa's insistence, the couple was wonderfully well-appointed as they traveled in style to Japan, California, Brazil, and all around the world. In photographs of the time Einstein is well-dressed, even dapper.

Dear Elsa,

But if I were to start taking care of my grooming, I would no longer be my own self. . . . So, to hell with it. If you find me so unappetizing, then look for a friend who is more palatable to female tastes.

> —*Einstein to his second wife on December 2, 1913, during the first years of their courtship*

At home it was a different story. Even in the proper parlor room of his Berlin home, Einstein would receive visitors in slacks and a sweater, something other German professors would never have dreamed of doing. Some have made the claim that Einstein's unstarched shirts and scuffed shoes were a rebellion, showing his lifelong disdain for German society. After suffering through the indignity and depression following World War I, Germany on the whole was very concerned with its pride, and just as Einstein denounced his country's militaristic leanings, he also rejected its sartorial pretensions.

After Elsa passed away, Einstein made fewer and fewer public appearances. Without her watchful eye his indifference to his appearance became all the more evident. Einstein wasn't unaware of how he looked, just uncaring. In a 1942 letter to his friend, Hans Mühsam, Einstein wrote, "I have become a lonely old chap who is mainly known because he does not wear socks and who is exhibited as a curiosum on special occasions."

However, there may have been more to Einstein's sockless feet than just a curious habit. When Einstein was judged unfit for military service in Switzerland in early 1901, the doctors recorded that he had varicose veins and flat, sweaty feet. The term varicose veins can refer to anything from minor blemishes to painful distended blood vessels. So it is possible that Einstein's legendary habit of not wearing socks wasn't just because he was a quirky, cerebral scientist, but possibly because they were physically uncomfortable.

Regardless of his reasons for his style—or lack thereof—the image of the unkempt Einstein is the one we often associate with him today, his clothes representing the man as much as his science does.

See **Absentmindedness; Hair.**

Communism

Einstein had specific political views and was very outspoken about them. He was not afraid to lend his voice to any cause he deemed worthy, and yet he wasn't typically a joiner, often staying on the fringe of any group he advocated and criticizing it as often as praising it. As such, he was never a member of the Communist party, but his liberal politics landed him in the company of numerous communist-leaning groups.

Einstein carefully stepped his way through political philosophies. He's known to have refused to join certain organizations specifically because they were ruled by what he perceived to be a Communist agenda, and yet it's clear that he found himself, at least later in life,

*I have never been a Communist. But if
I were, I would not be ashamed of it.*

—Einstein in a letter to Lydia Hewes
on July 10, 1950

in line with a generally Marxist view of the world. In Germany in the 1930s, Einstein often signed appeals by the Worker's Red help party Rote Arbeiterhilfe, and he spoke to the Marxist Worker's College, which was managed by the Communist Party. (Of course, his lecture was titled "What a Worker Should Know about the Theory of Relativity"—not exactly a political topic.)

After Einstein moved to the United States, he continued his leftist leanings. In May 1949, he wrote for the *Monthly Review* an article entitled "Why Socialism?" outlining the problems, from racism to poverty, that he saw existing in the world. He stated:

I am convinced there is only one way to eliminate these grave evils, namely through the establishment of a socialist economy, accompanied by an educational system which would be oriented toward social goals. In such an economy, the means of production are owned by society itself and are utilized in a planned fashion. A planned economy, which adjusts production to the needs of the community, would distribute the work to be done among all those able to work and would guarantee a livelihood to every man, woman and child. The education of the individual, in addition to promoting his own innate abilities, would attempt to develop in him a sense of responsibility for his fellow-men in place of the glorification of power and success in our present society.

It was not, in a time of patriotism during the fervent Cold War, an article destined to please American society.

It certainly attracted the attention of the FBI, which already had a growing file on Einstein's Communist-related activities. The FBI file had been opened in 1932, with an attack from a U.S. organization, the Women Patriot Corporation, even before Einstein had moved to the United States. Written by Mrs. Randolph Frothingham, the letter was mailed to the State Department. Well written and intelligently organized into a legal brief—but filled with dubious information—it accused Einstein of belonging to more anarchist-communist organizations than Stalin or Trotsky, and that he wished to destroy the U.S. government as well as the American church. While the description of

Einstein was both faulty and overly dramatic, it came at a time in history when the potential damage of Soviet espionage was very real, so the letter caught the attention of the FBI. From then on they kept their eye on the possibility that Einstein was a Communist spy.

That Einstein was not a spy is certain, but his leftist politics were clearly a reality. He thought the arms race, if left unchecked, would ultimately annihilate mankind, so he sought to improve relations between the United States and the USSR—and he certainly went on record as sympathizing with Soviet interests. He was a product of his times and history, and to Einstein the one great evil was Fascism; he spoke out venomously against Hitler and against any practice he saw as Fascist, such as the surveillance of his home and mail that he experienced while living in the United States. He also defended those who were publicly attacked as Communists. With so many of such public statements he gave one who was looking to suspect him of being a Soviet supporter quite a bit of ammunition; the April 5, 1949, issue of *Life* magazine showed a picture of Einstein, among others, under the headline "Dupes and Fellow Travelers Dress Up Communist Fronts."

His association with American Communists did not imply that he thought the Soviet Union's policies per se were not problematic. Stalin's attacks on human rights did not go unnoticed by the aging scientist—and the distressing state of Jewry in Russia was additionally upsetting. On the other hand, for some reason he continued to perceive the Soviet government as a lesser evil than Hitler's. Numerous colleagues were shocked and dismayed by this, wishing Einstein to see Stalin's ways as comparable to the Nazi regime Einstein hated. For whatever reason—whether because they were legitimately different or merely perceived to be so by Einstein because he had seen German Fascism up close, but had no such personal knowledge of the reality of Russian life—he never equated the two regimes in his mind.

The FBI cites that Einstein was affiliated with thirty-four Communist fronts between 1937 and 1954 and was honorary chairman for three of them. While FBI agents during the Cold War probably had more expansive criteria for what constitutes a Communist front than one might today and the numbers may not have been truly that high, Einstein clearly had affiliations with organizations that in turn had affiliations with the Communist Party. However, it does not seem to have been more so than other similarly political celebrities had at the time.

See **FBI; McCarthyism.**

Correspondence

Einstein was a prolific letter writer—writing family, scientific colleagues, and even the queen of Belgium. Einstein also devotedly responded to the numerous letters he received from those he didn't know, offering everything from advice to the lovelorn to explanations of his theories.

For the last thirty years of his life, Einstein's immense volume of correspondence was dutifully opened, read, replied to, and collected for posterity by his secretary, Helen Dukas. Dukas also screened Einstein's letters to keep him from being exposed to anti-Semitic diatribes. As the physicist received hundreds of letters a month, and used the mail as his main way of contacting both his friends and scientific colleagues (they were often one and the same), Dukas had her hands full. She once wrote to the Einstein biographer Carl Seelig in the early 1950s, "What I hate most is the filing of letters, especially because I have so little space. I have filing cabinets even in the hallways and there are books everywhere, innumerable crates in the basement. I have often wished that Gutenberg had never lived!"

Much of what we know about Einstein's personal and scientific life is through his letters. For as much as Dukas complained, she was rather possessed by efficiently collating his documents—so much so that after Einstein's death, she and the co-trustee of Einstein's estate, Otto Nathan, succeeded in tripling the size of the Albert Einstein Archives.

Today, much of this correspondence is being catalogued and published by the Hebrew University in conjunction with Princeton University. *The Collected Papers of Albert Einstein* will ultimately contain twenty-five volumes containing Einstein's scientific papers, his speeches and political writings . . . and, of course, his poetry. In his letters Einstein was often taken with writing rather bad verse. An example is the poem that he wrote to the queen of Belgium on his first stay at the White House on January 25, 1934:

> In the Capital's proud glory
> Where Destiny unfolds her story,
> Fights a man with happy pride
> Who solution can provide
>
> Of our talk of yester night
> There are mem'ries bright;
> In remembrance of our meeting,
> Let me send you this rhymed greeting.

Indeed Einstein was often playful in his letters, and some of his favorite pen pals were children to whom he explained everything from whether we would live if the sun expired, to how to succeed in life.

Einstein spent inordinate amounts of time on his extensive correspondence, devoting much of each afternoon to its pursuit. Historians owe a huge debt to his prolific writing; it has afforded the world invaluable details about the thoughts and stumbling blocks he encountered over decades of creating scientific theories.

See **Dukas, Helen.**

Cosmological Constant

Believing unquestionably in a static universe, Einstein introduced an ad hoc term, the cosmological constant, *into the general theory of relativity to describe an unknown force that would counteract the forces causing the universe to expand or contract. The cosmological constant is one of the most legendary of Einstein biographical facts—often referred to as his "greatest mistake."*

Einstein added what was essentially a "fudge factor" into his equations of general relativity in 1917. Known at the time as lambda, this has since been named the cosmological constant and it had one job: to keep the universe from collapsing in on itself. After all, thought Einstein, everyone knows the universe is stable. Conventional scientific wisdom of the time was that the universe had been around an infinite amount of time and that it had existed forever in essentially the same state as it is now. Einstein's relativity equations suggested a universe that could expand or contract, so he decided to add the constant to counteract this movement.

Einstein didn't know what the cosmological constant was, or what kind of mysterious force it represented. His best guess was that this constant represented some force within the very nature of vacuums themselves, a force that caused space to repel against itself, working in opposition to gravity, the force that constantly brings objects together. Incorporating the constant was so arbitrary that Einstein wrote to Paul Ehrenfest (1880–1933) on February 4, 1917: "I have again perpetrated something relating to the theory of gravitation that might endanger me of being committed to a madhouse." Einstein knew only that something had to be added to make his equations fit the universe he believed to exist.

Einstein was wrong. The universe has changed dramatically over time, expanding ever outward, and no such fudge factor was needed. Indeed, the cosmological constant doesn't solve the problem of a changing universe, anyway. In 1922, Alexander Friedmann showed that the cosmological constant would not actually keep the universe's movement at bay. There was no way around it: Einstein's relativity equations guaranteed a nonstatic universe.

Einstein resisted this concept for as long as he could, even writing letters to scientific journals attacking Friedmann's mathematics, but by 1929, when Edwin Hubble's careful observations of receding galaxies showed that the universe was indeed expanding, it was clear the cosmological constant had been a mistake.

This mistake, by the seemingly all-knowing physicist, has captured the imagination of writers for years, and they've pounced on the idea that Einstein once called the constant "my biggest blunder." But, like so many statements attributed to the famous, it is possible that Einstein never said those words. The phrase "my biggest blunder" only appears in an autobiography by the scientist George Gamow—it's not from any of Einstein's written letters, speeches, or scientific papers. In fact, Einstein's writings do not maintain such a strong standpoint. Nonetheless, Einstein certainly prided himself on keeping an open mind and challenging authority, so this bowing to conventional assumptions—that the universe was static—was atypical for the physicist.

The Cosmological Constant Today

While it's known that the cosmological constant was a mistake, it is an inherent part of Einstein's relativity equations and has never been removed; it is merely assumed to be zero. Yet again and again there are times when the science community considers including a nonzero constant.

In the 1980s and 1990s, when scientists were trying to determine the age of the universe, the cosmological constant often reappeared. Cosmologists who found the age of the universe using cosmology theories came up with an age of roughly 10 billion years. Astronomers insisted that some stars were much older than that, closer to 20 billion years old. One of these two "facts" had to be wrong. Some cosmologists tried to resurrect the cosmological constant as one way to adjust cosmology theory and get the numbers to agree. (Over time astronomers have lowered their estimates for the age of the stars, while new information about the universe helped cosmologists increase their estimates for the universe's age, so the discrepancy between these two numbers is not as great as it once was. These days, scientists agree that the universe is close to 14 billion years old.)

In the mid-1990s, the cosmological constant reared its head for an all-new reason: observations of extremely distant supernovae suggested the universe was rapidly inflating. Previously, scientists thought the expansion of the universe was slowly winding down. Instead, this new data suggested that everything was in fact accelerating; the universe was growing at ever-increasing speeds. If this is true—and many modern cosmologists believe it is—then there clearly is some force at work—a repulsive force like Einstein first imagined, linked to the vacuum of space itself.

But the fact that there may turn out to be a nonzero cosmological constant should not imply that Einstein had some incredible prescience. Einstein's introduction of lambda was not because his genius ensured that somehow he simply knew in his bones that it should be part of his equations. Einstein chose to add the extra term for nonscientific reasons, and he happily tossed his constant in the trash upon realizing his assumptions were wrong. On a postcard to the physicist Hermann Weyl (1885–1955) in 1923, Einstein wrote: "If there is no quasi-static world, then away with the cosmological term." If the universe changed size and shape, then Einstein saw no place for this extra force; and the fact that scientists today may now incorporate it once again is more due to happenstance than Einstein's foresightedness.

See **Cosmology.**

Cosmology

Cosmology is the study of the formation of the universe: how it began and what it looks like now. For most of history, theories on the creation of the universe were solidly the purview of religion and philosophy. So when scientists took the theory of general relativity and used it to explain how the universe began, they were traveling into a world that had always been dominated by mysticism and faith—a place no self-respecting scientist who relied on logic was expected to go.

The stories of how the universe began have historically been quite beautiful and fanciful. Some cultures describe a world created out of silt or golden eggs, or even phoenix-like universes that die and get reborn endlessly through time. The classic religious tale of modern Western civilization, of course, is that God formed everything in the seven days of creation. Initially, it was almost to Einstein's chagrin that his theories of relativity opened the door for legitimate scientific study into the origin of the universe. Einstein knew his equations would have implications for understanding the size and shape of space, and he certainly proposed different kinds of models for the universe over the years. But back in 1915, when he published his general theory of relativity, Einstein could never have foreseen, or indeed have desired, that it would spark an entirely new branch of science.

Cosmology got its start from relativity, since the equations of relativity describe how a massive body warps the space around it. Previously, according to Newton's theories of gravity, space was expected to more or less stay straight. Send a rocket ship off in a straight line and it will continue forever in a straight line, at least until some other force acts upon it. Einstein claimed this wasn't quite right. Instead, gravity actually bends or warps the rocket's path. So, for example, the space shuttle in orbit around Earth isn't so much being "pulled" toward the planet as much as being "forced" to travel in a curved line. It's fairly similar to the way we don't feel pulled in toward Earth as we walk across its surface—and yet we are most definitely walking along a curved path.

Other scientists soon jumped into the fray, applying the relativity equations to the entire universe. When he created his theory, Einstein foresaw that certain consequences of relativity might affect the size and shape of the universe. Namely, the equations corresponded to a universe that changed shape, a universe where gravity might someday cause the whole shebang to collapse like a falling soufflé. To counteract this problem, Einstein inserted an extra bit into his equations: the cosmological constant. Whether this was antigravity or some repulsive force inherent in a vacuum was unclear. It was something that Einstein readily admitted had no correspondence to any known force of the time, but it acted in the opposite direction of gravity. The constant had no basis in rational thought other than this single one: Einstein believed, as did just about all scientists at the time, that the universe was perfectly stable, unchanging throughout time. By putting the cosmological constant into the equations, Einstein managed to keep the universe from collapsing.

Einstein's assumption that the universe was stable was incorrect, however, and several other theorists soon created models showing this. Within several years, Alexander Friedmann (1888–1925) in Russia, and Willem de Sitter (1872–1934) in Holland both devised simplistic models that jettisoned the cosmological constant and allowed for an expanding universe. De Sitter's model had no matter in it whatsoever, while Friedmann's had an even distribution of matter. Indeed, de Sitter would go on to show that regardless of whether one incorporated the cosmological constant, one could never come up with a stable universe. While Einstein was initially dismissive of these men's work, clearly there was nothing mathematically wrong with it. The only issue was that it flew in the face of his assumptions that the universe was unchanging.

In 1929, Edwin Hubble showed that the galaxies around us were indeed sliding away, receding, thus offering the first experimental proof of the expansion of the universe. Now Einstein had to accept that his initial assumptions had been incorrect, and he began working with de Sitter to create a model of the universe that incorporated this expansion. Once expansion was accepted, a Belgian named Georges Lemaître took cosmology a step further. He suggested that an ever-growing universe must have been smaller in the past—infinitely smaller. Lemaître theorized that the universe had begun in what he named a "primeval atom"—a tiny, incredibly dense point that expanded into the universe we see today. Physicists, including Einstein, reacted poorly to this at the time, since most of them associated such a cosmogenesis tale with religion. One of the reasons so many held onto the idea that the universe had existed just as it is for all time, was because it didn't coincide with religious stories.

Scientific theories aren't just accepted or rejected based on one's gut feelings, however, they are tested experimentally, and observations over the last seventy years have supported at least a version of these early ideas. Cosmologists now believe that the universe did begin with a tiny point, billions of years ago, that exploded in a big bang. They believe that black holes exist, and the universe expands, and that there is mysterious, unseen, dark matter that gives the universe its shape. Modern science has even shown that perhaps some version of Einstein's cosmological constant does indeed exist, because even though Einstein once described the constant as one of his biggest blunders, the constant would explain why parts of the universe are expanding more quickly than we could otherwise explain.

Observational techniques have improved so dramatically, from incredibly powerful tools like the Hubble Space Telescope to multi-lensed telescopes like the Very Large Array in New Mexico, that the science of the creation of the universe has expanded exponentially in the last few decades. Cosmology now relies heavily on many new areas of physics, like particle physics, since understanding how particles form is necessary to understand how they formed during the big bang. Cosmology also incorporates modern string theory and new astrophysics theories on how stars and galaxies form, but ultimately, cosmology always comes back to the same questions about how the universe is shaped, what it looks like, how it curves, and how it was created—questions proposed for the very first time by Einstein and his theory of relativity.

See **Black Holes; Cosmological Constant.**

Curie, Marie
(1867–1934)

Marie Curie, a diminutive Polish physicist who lived most of her life in Paris, is one of the world's most famous scientists—not only was she a female pioneer in a male-dominated field, but she was the first scientist to be awarded two Nobel Prizes. Curie and Einstein did not have an extremely close relationship, but their simultaneous fame ensured that they met often.

Marie Curie won her first Nobel Prize for physics in 1903, and the second for chemistry in 1911. Working in collaboration with her husband, Pierre Curie (1859–1906), Curie won the Nobel Prizes for discovering the radioactive elements polonium and radium, and essentially founding the science of radioactivity. The couple was awarded their first prize together, but Pierre was killed in a coach accident before Curie won the second prize.

Einstein met Curie not long after she'd been awarded the second Nobel. Both were invited to the First Solvay Conference in Brussels. Shortly after the conference, Curie wrote a professional recommendation for the brash thirty-one-year-old physicist. She said, "I have greatly admired the works that were published by M. Einstein on questions concerning modern theoretical physics . . . in Brussels, where I attended a scientific conference in which M. Einstein took part, I was able to appreciate the clarity of his mind, the breadth of his documentation and the profundity of his knowledge. If one considers that M. Einstein is still very young, one has every right to build the greatest hopes on him and see in him one of the leading theoreticians of the future."

Einstein and Curie remained friendly after the conference, even taking their children on a hiking trip through an alpine pass of Switzerland near Engadine in 1913. The two physicists also briefly agreed on world politics. In 1922, Curie was instrumental in convincing Einstein to join the newly formed International Committee on Intellectual Cooperation, at the League of Nations. Curie wrote, "My feeling is simply that the League of Nations, although still imperfect, is a hope for the future." For a time, Einstein agreed, but less than a month after he joined, Einstein's political views were shaken by the assassination of Germany's Jewish foreign minister, Walther Rathenau. Dismayed that he was standing for Germany on the committee, Einstein wrote Curie, "I have felt that a very strong anti-Semitism reigns in the milieu that I am supposed to represent to the League of Nations and . . . I cannot agree to this role of representative or mediator. I think you will understand perfectly." Curie did not understand. She tried to change his mind, and eventually Einstein did go back for another stint with the league.

However, despite political disagreements, Einstein was one of many prominent figures who came to Curie's aid when she was attacked in the press for an affair she began with the married scientist Paul Langevin. Although history has shown that it occurred, Curie always denied the affair. Einstein believed Curie and called the rumors of her affair nonsense. "She is not attractive enough to become dangerous for anyone," he declared—an interesting statement from a man who tended to have problems relating to women (and who more than once succumbed to such "dangerous" affairs). It holds a clue to Einstein's and Curie's long intellectual friendship. That Curie was a woman didn't seem to enter into Einstein's head.

After years of exposure to radiation through her work, Marie Curie died on July 4, 1934. A year later, Einstein wrote a glowing tribute for the Curie Memorial Celebration on November 23, 1935, at the

Roerich Museum in New York. "It was my good fortune to be linked with Mme. Curie through twenty years of sublime and unclouded friendship. I came to admire her human grandeur to an ever-growing degree. Her strength, her purity of will, her austerity toward herself, her objectivity, her incorruptible judgment—all these were a kind seldom found joined in a single individual."

Death

Einstein died at the age of seventy-six of a burst aneurysm in Princeton, New Jersey, on April 18, 1955. He was not well for the last few years of his life, but he made the choice to live his final days without any extra medical attention or surgery.

In the summer of 1950, Einstein's doctors found that an aneurysm—a weak blood vessel—on his abdominal aorta was getting larger. When it was found, doctors had few treatment options and wrapped the inflamed blood vessel with cellophane hoping to prevent a hemorrhage. Einstein seemed to take the news as well as could be expected and refused any additional attempts at surgery to correct the problem.

On March 18, 1950, he signed his will. It appointed his secretary, Helen Dukas, and friend Otto Nathan as his literary executors; left all his manuscripts to the Hebrew University, the school he helped found in Israel; and bequeathed his violin to his first grandchild, Bernhard Caesar Einstein.

Einstein also organized his funeral affairs. He wanted a simple ceremony and no gravestone. He chose not to be buried since he didn't want to have a gravesite that could be turned into a tourist site and, contrary to Jewish tradition, asked to be cremated. His last few days were relatively peaceful. Early in 1955, at the age of seventy-five, he still walked to the Institute for Advanced Study at Princeton every morning. He saw the fiftieth anniversary of the theory of relativity, but wrote to his fellow physicist Max von Laue on February 3, 1955, that, "age and sickness make it impossible for me to participate."

That February he described death to his colleague Gertrud Warschauer as "an old debt that one eventually pays. Yet instinctively one does everything possible to postpone this final settlement. Such is the game that nature plays with us. We may ourselves smile that we are that way, but we cannot free ourselves of the instinctive reaction to which we are all subject." He knew death was near but continued to interact with others just as he always did. On April 11, a few days before his death, Einstein signed a paper drawn up by Bertrand Russell against the arms race, a paper that would come to be called the Russell-Einstein Manifesto. That afternoon, Einstein received the Israeli ambassador Abba Eban to discuss a planned radio address on the seventh anniversary of the establishment of Israel. None of his visitors suspected the end was near, but on Wednesday, April 13, strong pains set in.

On Friday, April 15, Einstein was hospitalized. His doctor feared there was a small perforation of the aneurysm, but Einstein resolutely rejected surgery. Later that month, Helen Dukas would tell Einstein's friend and biographer, Abraham Pais, that Einstein said, "I would like to go when I want to. To prolong life artificially is tasteless."

> *I have to apologize to you that I am still among the living. There will be a remedy for this, however.*
>
> —Einstein, in a letter to Tyffany Williams, a young girl who'd written to say she was surprised Einstein was still alive

Friends arrived to be with Einstein. His oldest son, Hans Albert, came from California, and Otto Nathan from New York. On Sunday it seemed that Einstein might recover; his condition improved so much that he asked for his papers on calculations on the unified field theory and for the draft of his radio broadcast for his "Israeli brethren." However, late that night, shortly after 1:00 A.M. Monday morning, he became restless, spoke a few words in German, which the night nurse could not understand, and passed away. Einstein died on April 18, 1955, at 1:15 A.M. at Princeton Hospital.

A brief autopsy showed that the aneurysm had indeed finally ruptured. According to his wishes, his brain was removed and set aside. Einstein's body, however, was cremated at 4 P.M. the next day at the Ewing crematorium in Trenton, New Jersey.

That afternoon, twelve close friends and family held a simple ceremony. Otto Nathan gave a short address and recited the epilogue *Epilog zu Schillers Glocke*, which Goethe had written for Schiller's funeral. Einstein's ashes were scattered, but his friends never told anyone where.

See **Brain**.

de Sitter, Willem
(1872–1934)

Willem de Sitter was a well-respected Dutch astronomer and physicist who contributed to the formation of modern cosmology. He was one of the first theorists who interpreted general relativity as it applied to the universe as a whole, bringing Einstein's new theory of gravity to the sciences of astronomy and cosmology.

De Sitter was an astronomer in Leiden in the Netherlands, first as the chair of astronomy at the University of Leiden and later the director of the Leiden Observatory. He studied the solar system extensively and recalculated the motions of Jupiter and Earth. However, he is most remembered for his work in cosmology, a science that got its start through the work of early pioneers like himself.

From the first moment he heard of it, de Sitter wanted to apply Einstein's work to astronomy. In 1911, after studying how the special theory of relativity was explained in Einstein's 1905 scientific paper, de Sitter showed that, if true, Einstein's theory would radically alter all astronomical understandings based on the simpler Newtonian gravity. Specifically, the motions of the planets in the solar system would not, in fact, match the predictions so long held to be true.

From 1916 to 1918, Einstein and de Sitter corresponded extensively on exactly what kind of universe best fit the relativity equations. De Sitter initially developed a model of a spherical universe, in contrast to the cylindrical one Einstein had envisioned. De Sitter also tried to map out the shape of that spherical universe in the absence of all matter. Einstein's reaction to de Sitter's model was strong and negative because it flouted several assumptions that Einstein held dear. For one thing, de Sitter's sphere described a universe that changed in size instead of remaining nicely constant. Einstein's objections ranged from the scientific to the emotional. On a scientific level, what kept the universe from wildly flying apart? On a gut level, an expanding universe meant that going backwards in time, the universe had been smaller and smaller—beginning as nothing. This meant that the universe hadn't always existed. At some point in time, the universe somehow *began*— a point of creation that smacked of the superstitious and religious.

The lack of matter in de Sitter's model also rubbed Einstein the wrong way. Einstein saw matter—and its corresponding gravitational field—as what inherently created the shape of the universe. He cited what he dubbed "Mach's principle," a tenet that came from the Austrian physicist Ernst Mach (1838–1916). The principle states that the movements of any object throughout the universe were determined by the distribution of all the other bodies in the universe. Because how a body moves through space is tantamount to what shape space is, the concept of "shape" without matter, Einstein insisted, was meaningless.

Einstein and de Sitter discussed their models in person and through letters. Einstein initially claimed that there must be some mathematical deficiency in de Sitter's model, a sentiment he announced loudly as well as published. Eventually, however, through correspondence with de Sitter as well as with others, Einstein had to admit that de Sitter's math was sound. There were no objections to the model other than that it described a nonstatic world, a world that seemed inherently impossible to Einstein. Of course, Einstein was wrong about this, and the fact that the universe is expanding would soon be shown by Edwin Hubble in 1929. But none of this was known at the time and Einstein stuck to his belief that the universe never changed size. So, while Einstein conceded that there was nothing mathematically wrong with de Sitter's static spherical model, he still did not accept it, nor did he ever publish a retraction to his previous criticisms.

Of course, de Sitter's model was always meant to be a simplified version of the universe—the universe does clearly have mass in it—and current cosmological models deviate substantially. De Sitter's model did, however, become incorporated into the Steady State theory of the universe. This theory describes a model in which there is no beginning and no end to the universe. While the universe does keep expanding, according to the theory, new matter is always created to replace it, thus maintaining a universe that does not change in density over time.

In the decades after Einstein published his theory of general relativity, the flurry of models and competing theories on the origins of the universe was almost overwhelming to a cosmologist trying to keep up. In 1931, de Sitter looked back on the past twenty years of science and wrote, "Never in all the history of science has there been a period when new theories and hypotheses arose, flourished, and were abandoned in so quick succession as in the last fifteen or twenty years." But, of course, none of them managed to tell the whole story. At the January 1930 meeting of the Royal Astronomical Society, de Sitter spoke about how no current models were able to completely represent the universe.

Even more hypothetical models of the universe were to follow. After Hubble had published his findings on the expanding universe, Otto Heckmann showed that if a universe is both expanding and has matter, it doesn't require curved space. Various other scientists like Georges Lemaîtres (1894–1966) and Alexander Friedmann (1888–1925) publicized additional models. Einstein and de Sitter published a joint paper in 1932 in the *Proceedings of the National Academy of Sciences*, in which they described what is known as the Einstein-de Sitter model of the universe. It was still a fairly simple solution of Einstein's general relativity equations, but the model does include universe expansion, matter, and even dark matter. Their model describes a Euclidean space; that is, a "flat" space where light travels in straight lines instead of the curved path as described in both Einstein's and de Sitter's previous models. In their new model, the universe has an infinite total volume and begins in a big bang scenario from some tiny initial point. It also allows the universe to expand, although the rate of that expansion slows down over time so that someday the universe will coast to a complete stop.

Alongside the publication of the Einstein-de Sitter paper, Richard Tolman wrote a commentary pointing out that there was not, as of yet, enough information about the density, rate of expansion, or kinds of matter in the universe for scientists to be able to choose one winner of all the proposed models of the universe. Now, decades later, there is substantially more data on the subject and scientists are converging on an answer. But still, no one can definitively say whether the universe is flat, as Einstein and de Sitter suggested together, or curved, as each had thought previously.

Dukas, Helen
(1896–1982)

Dukas was Einstein's devoted secretary, working with the scientist for over thirty years. She zealously guarded Einstein's schedule, his day-to-day affairs, and his public image—even after his death. As co-trustee of his literary estate and archivist of his papers, she earned the ire of many of Einstein's biographers by not only often refusing to answer questions about the man, but in her actions to actively suppress or contain almost every document he left.

Dukas entered Einstein's life following one of his many bouts of poor health in 1928. While working in Zuoz, Switzerland, Einstein collapsed due to overexertion—he was diagnosed with an enlargement of the heart and ordered to bed for four months. Back in Berlin, Einstein's wife, Elsa, hired Dukas to become his secretary beginning Friday, April 13.

Dukas clearly suited the occasionally cantankerous physicist and became his trusted associate. Dukas rounded out the little world of women who surrounded Einstein. His wife was the social butterfly who made Einstein presentable to the world and kept him on an often rigorous travel schedule to make sure the world did not forget his importance. Dukas, on the other hand, was Einstein's scheduler and transcriber, making sure all his various lectures and speeches on physics and politics were duly recorded, in addition to helping the man answer his at times overwhelming correspondence.

Dukas was irreplaceable by the time the Einsteins moved to the United States in 1933, so she moved with them to Princeton. After Elsa's death, Dukas stepped up her role in protecting Einstein from the outside world—even shooing away passers-by at their clapboard house at 112 Mercer Street.

Some visitors to Einstein's Princeton home commented that he treated Dukas dismissively. While he did often speak to Dukas brusquely, a more complete view shows that Einstein and Dukas were much the same as an old married couple, expressing their affection through—at times, pointed—barbs. Their mutual friend and frequent house guest Thomas Bucky said that Dukas devoted her life to Einstein. Einstein also called Dukas "Madame Dictionary" for her knowledge of trivia. Bucky recalls, "She knew the whole world, everything that went on in the movies and on the radio which, of course, he was completely above."

Dukas, along with Einstein's dear friend Otto Nathan were coexecutors of Einstein's estate. And after Einstein's death in 1955, Dukas and Nathan devoted themselves to preserving, and even burnishing, Einstein's legacy. Many Einstein scholars who worked with Dukas were amazed at her ability to take any scrap of writing from the famous physicist and place it immediately into the chronology of his life. But as useful as Dukas was in chronicling Einstein's achievements, she was equally good at stonewalling those who wanted to dig deeper into Einstein's private affairs. Nathan and Dukas banded together to gather all of Einstein's writings to keep them from the public eye. They even went so far as to sue Einstein's own son, Hans, to keep him from publishing his father's letters. Their tactics were so successful that the first volume of *The Collected Papers of Albert Einstein*, titled *The Early Years: 1879–1902*, was not published until 1987—thirty-two years after Einstein's death, and five years after Dukas's.

When Einstein's letters were finally viewed in 1986, scholars were surprised to discover mention of Einstein's first child, a daughter who was born out of wedlock before Mileva and Einstein were married. As very little is known about what happened with the child, nicknamed in his letters Leiserl, speculation abounded that Dukas was in actuality Einstein's daughter. While intriguing, this myth is highly unlikely. Although Dukas was the right age to have been Leiserl, give or take five years, most of the evidence given to support the idea is Einstein's naming Dukas so prominently in his will, not on any true evidence. There have also been rumors that Dukas and Einstein were having a romantic affair, but these too are based solely on circumstantial evidence, such as the fact that she remained unmarried all her life and that Einstein had a history of having affairs with his secretaries. More than likely, however, the relationship was exactly what it appeared to be—a close friendship and working relationship between two people who had grown to be incredibly dependent on each other.

E = mc²

E = mc² is by far the most famous equation in the world. The equation means that energy is equal to mass times the square of the speed of light—in other words, energy and mass are equivalent and related in a straightforward way.

Einstein wasn't the first to suggest that energy and mass might be related. In 1905, physicists already understood that the energy of an electron gave it "electromagnetic mass." But Einstein was the first to suggest that this equivalence was a general rule, applicable to all masses and not just special cases. Einstein discovered this connection from a thought experiment—what he called thinking hard—about his earlier idea on the special theory of relativity. At its heart, the theory of relativity insists that the laws of physics must be the same in any reference frame (i.e., whether you are moving or standing still). In addition, the theory says that those laws are the same no matter how they are perceived from any other reference frame. Einstein calculated that a body giving off light, which is the same as energy, as observed from a second moving reference frame, would appear to slow down and lose momentum. Looking at it from that second reference frame, the only explanation for how it lost momentum is if it lost mass. Since the laws of physics must be the same in all reference frames, then if this is what is happening in one reference frame, it must be what's happening in all of them. It must be true that when the body loses energy, it is also losing mass—and the amount of mass as related to energy is specifically given by the $E = mc^2$ equation. Einstein wrote: "The mass of a body is a measure of its energy-content."

In that first paper, Einstein did not write the equation in exactly this form, referring to energy instead as "L" which is short for Lagrangian, and is the difference between kinetic and potential energy for any given object. It was not until a few years later that the equation was molded into its famous format. Indeed $E = mc^2$ is a simple version of the full equation, since it relates only to the rest mass of an object—the mass and energy it contains when sitting still. When an object is moving, additional terms get added, and the full equation reads: $E^2 = (mc^2)^2 + (pc)^2$ where p is the momentum of the object.

Einstein discovered the $E = mc^2$ equation because the math led him there—the equivalence equation naturally popped out of understood laws of physics. But Einstein knew that his conclusion was startling, and he wrote in a note to his friend Conrad Habicht, "I cannot know whether the dear Lord doesn't laugh about this and has played a trick on me." Moreover, he wasn't sure that the idea could ever be tested. At the end of that first paper Einstein suggested that perhaps studying the energy emitted when radioactive radium salts decayed might be a way of proving the prediction.

How Do You Prove It?

As it happens, the technology to measure such precise changes in mass and energy simply didn't exist when Einstein came up with the idea, so the first experimental test of $E = mc^2$ ultimately came from a very different method—and not until 1932. John Cockcroft (1897–1967) and Ernest Walton (1903–1995) were two physicists at Cavendish laboratories at Cambridge in the United Kingdom. In the early 1930s they built what was essentially the first particle accelerator and began studying collisions between particles. They sent a proton at high speeds into a lithium atom and studied the results, which turned out to be two alpha particles. The initial lithium and proton weighed more than the final alpha particles did, but those resulting particles were moving a lot faster. Using their brand-new accelerator technology, Cockcroft and Walton made precise measurements and determined that the energy of the moving alpha particles when added to their mass did indeed add up to the total mass plus energy of the original lithium and proton. So, while mass all by itself was not conserved, mass and energy definitely were. Mass and energy were truly two sides of the same coin.

One year later, in Paris in 1933, Irène (1897–1956) and Frédéric Joliot-Curie (1900–1958) studied the phenomenon in the opposite direction, examining how energy could convert into mass. That year, they took photographs of particles moving through a cloud chamber and showed a massless photon of light changing into particles with mass and energy equivalent to the amount of energy of the photon.

This does not mean simply that mass can be converted into energy, or that energy can be converted into mass; a better description is that they are two aspects of the same concept. Moving objects, in fact, get heavier as they move, since all that extra energy gives them weight. A jet, for example, traveling at 600 miles per hour is 0.0000000001 percent heavier than it is when standing still. Objects that are at rest have energy too: the mass of a 1-kilogram (2.2-pound) brick could keep a 100-watt bulb illuminated for 30 million years. (The problem is that extracting this energy would take heat and pressures greater than what's at the center of the sun; it would take far more energy to extract a brick's energy than you'd get out at the end. So it's hardly a worthwhile power source.)

E = mc² Meets the Real World

While large objects such as marbles, baseballs, or even buildings contain inherent energy even though they are sitting perfectly still, it is in small particles where the equivalence of mass and energy is most interesting. When atoms break apart—a process called "fission"—or when they bind together—a process called "fusion"—the final mass never adds up to the original; some of that mass is released as energy.

Fusion is what keeps stars shining. At the heart of a star like the Sun, hydrogen atoms fuse under the incredible pressure they experience. Four hydrogen atoms that bind together become one helium atom—but one that isn't as heavy as the original hydrogen atoms. The extra mass has been radiated off as energy, and the fusion process sends out a pulse of light into space. The continual fusion of atoms—100 million quadrillion quadrillion times each second—creates so much light that the Sun can illuminate the Earth from 92,961.4 miles away. And, as it loses that energy, the Sun gets lighter—every single second light is lost through radiation translates to the sun's losing four million tons of mass.

Fusion is a naturally occurring process. Fission doesn't seem to be. It is solely a manmade occurrence and can be created fairly easily in a lab by bombarding a large atom with a smaller one. The larger atom splits apart into various components like a car in a big accident. Again, the final particles don't weigh as much as the original ones, and the extra mass is dispersed as energy. (This is what Cockcroft and Watson saw in their particle accelerators in 1932.)

During World War II, physicists realized that if enough atoms could be made to undergo fission at the same time, such that the energy from one fissioning atom would cause another atom to fission and so on, it would create an immensely powerful bomb. Inducing simultaneous fission like this was not an easy process; it took the scientists several years to create bombs that induced a chain reaction of fission in either uranium or plutonium, thus giving off more destructive energy than had ever been seen before in a weapon. After the United States built such weapons during World War II and dropped two atom bombs on Japan, the equation $E = mc^2$ became inextricably linked to the power—and destruction—of nuclear weapons.

Of course, such chain reactions are not used only for destruction. Nuclear power plants use the same principle in very controlled ways to create energy for electricity. And the $E = mc^2$ equation applies to many situations besides a fission chain reaction. Nonetheless, Einstein's mild equation has become, for many, solely correlated with the devastation of nuclear war.

See **Miracle Year; Relativity, Special Theory of.**

Eddington, Sir Arthur
(1882–1944)

Sir Arthur Eddington was a true believer in Einstein's theories, and it was his results in investigating the solar eclipse of 1919 that provided the scientific proof of the general theory of relativity—more than ten years after it was first published. The extensive news coverage of Eddington's experiment pushed the theory of relativity—and Einstein himself—to an unprecedented level of fame.

Sir Arthur Eddington is considered one of the greatest modern English astronomers, and he specialized in interpreting observations of star movements at the Greenwich Observatory. In 1913, he was one of the first English-speaking scientists to hear of Einstein's general theory of relativity, and he immediately believed in its precepts, becoming one of its strongest supporters.

When Einstein first began publishing on the general theory of relativity, Eddington, like many other scientists, were convinced it was true; it simply made so much sense they felt it had to be correct. But that doesn't mean they didn't want to see some concrete, experimental proof. Since general relativity revolves around the idea that gigantic masses—things as big as the earth, the sun, and the moon—bend the very shape of space itself, the only way to test the theory was to rely on the heavens. Scientists wanted to measure whether a star's light bent as it passed the immense gravity of the sun. The problem was that one couldn't measure such a thing with the blinding power of the daytime sun's light obscuring the faint beam from a distant star. What was needed was an eclipse.

And so in 1912, 1914, and 1916, expeditions set off to various locations around the globe to track down solar eclipses. But each and every one of those three expeditions was inconclusive; the first was rained out, and the others were unable to continue thanks to world politics—World War I began in 1914. As it happens, this turned out to be a good bit of luck, since although Einstein's theory was correct, one detail was off. In his publishing of the theory in 1911, Einstein had calculated the wrong value for how much light bends because of gravity; he had neglected to include all the effects of curved space. Had the eclipse data disagreed with Einstein's predictions, the theory might have been erroneously discarded.

In 1915, Einstein corrected his theory, coming up with the correct value for the arc of bent light. There was brief momentum in the United States to test the theory against an eclipse in 1918, but the results were inconclusive.

During all of these attempts, Eddington simply accepted the theory of general relativity, without needing more proof, but the director of the Greenwich Observatory, and British Royal Astronomer, Frank Watson Dyson, wanted to see the results of a conclusive test. Einstein's theories were upsetting the apple cart of Newtonian physics—Sir Isaac Newton was British so it became a point of national pride for an English scientist to validate Einstein. So Dyson commissioned two expeditions for 1919. He chose the Royal Observatory's Andrew Crommelin to lead one of the expeditions to the town of Sobral, Brazil. The other expedition he assigned to Eddington—thanks to a deal Eddington had made in 1917 with Dyson to get out of mandatory military service. In 1917, the British government began a draft, and while Cambridge University had pulled strings to exempt their pro-fessor from service, Eddington's Quaker upbringing led him to formally denounce the war. Dyson stepped in and convinced the British Army to exclude the outspoken scientist, but the deal with Dyson demanded that, instead of being sent with other war objectors to a detention camp, Eddington was to lead an expedition that would ensure the British legacy of being on the forefront of physics so Newton would not be tarnished. Eddington would lead the expedition to test Einstein's theory on Principe Island, a Portugese-held island in the Gulf of Guinea, in the crook of Africa. (Sending Eddington away would also keep him from making any more embarrassing anti-war statements.

In 1919, with World War I over, Eddington's group battled rainy Brazilian skies and technical glitches to measure starlight during a solar eclipse. They found that the bent light exactly matched the pre-dictions Einstein had made in 1915—they had confirmed evidence for Einstein's general theory of relativity.

As soon as he heard of the British scientists' success, Einstein sent a postcard to his mother. It read, "Dear mother, joyous news today. H. A. Lorentz telegraphed that the English expeditions have actually demonstrated the deflection of light from the sun." Scientists also immediately cheered the positive results—and possibly thanks to a deep desire for forward thinking after the catastrophic First World War—the rest of the world rejoiced as well. The sister expedition, although it faced some technical problems, came up with positive results as well. Eddington presented the results to a joint meeting of the Royal Society and the Royal Astronomical Society, and newspa-pers jumped on the story. Science had triumphed! Einstein became suddenly quite famous.

The *London Times* trumpeted the headline on November 17, 1919, "Revolution in Science—New Theory of the Universe—Newton's

Ideas Overthrown." And even before the news caught on in Europe the fledgling *New York Times* in the United States ran six articles, all with eye-catching headlines including, "Lights Askew in the Heavens. Men of Science More or Less Agog; Einstein's Theory Triumphs."

The spotlight also shone on Eddington. His lectures overflowed and he spoke often about relativity. In 1920, Eddington published a popular work, *Space, Time and Gravitation* that popularized Einstein's theory among the English-speaking public.

See **Relativity, General Theory of.**

Education

Contrary to popular tales, Einstein was in fact a good student. On the other hand, he was frustrated with the conventional educational system and his rebellion may have helped him think creatively. Einstein famously railed against any type of instruction that he saw as authoritative or dictatorial, and always believed minds had to be kept open to be able to explore. Many of the people who tried to teach Einstein found themselves faced with an intelligent but very argumentative young man.

Before Einstein even started school, his mother, in a push to better her son, hired a private tutor. Einstein found the lessons boring and, still in his tantrum stage, threw a chair at the young woman. She never returned, and another tutor had to be hired.

Einstein seemed to get along better at the Volksschule, his grade school, and despite stories that he failed math, he was a very good student. Things changed a bit when he attended secondary school at the Luitpold Gymnasium. In later years he would complain of the teachers' dictatorial nature; one teacher, he said, complained that even Einstein's smirking smile seemed to show disrespect. But, besides the fact that he, like many quiet, intellectual children, hated athletics, Einstein got along fairly well in high school.

He did, however, get a great deal of his intellectual stimulation outside of class. His uncle Jakob entertained the young boy by teaching him algebra. And Einstein wrote in his autobiography that at twelve years old he'd experienced the wonder of what he called his "sacred little geometry book." Another family friend, Max Talmey (originally Max Talmud), spent many dinners at the house, lending Einstein books on medicine, math, and philosophy. Einstein credited Talmey, a twenty-one-year-old medical student, with first exciting his love of the sciences.

Einstein's education took an odd turn in 1885. His father's business failed, so his parents pulled up stakes and took his sister to Italy with them where another job was waiting. Einstein was left behind to finish his last year of secondary school. Einstein found himself rudderless without his family and even more miserable at what he saw as his teachers' military rigidity. So he left school and surprised his family by showing up at his parents' doorstep in Italy. His mother, possibly at a loss as to what to do with her wayward dropout, pulled strings to get Einstein permission to take the entrance exam for the Eidgenössische Technische Hochschule, or the ETH, then known as the Swiss Federal Polytechnical School. These were not easy strings to pull—family friend Gustav Maier did persuade the Polytechnic's director, Albin Herzog, to let Einstein take the test, but Herzog was not enthused. In his letter to Maier, Herzog writes sarcastically of "this so-called child prodigy."

Einstein took the test, and despite being two years under the normal age of eighteen and lacking a secondary-school certificate, he passed the math and science sections, but he failed his other subjects. Thus Einstein ended up at school in Switzerland to finish up high school. He passed his courses and was finally accepted to the ETH.

Einstein was one of five physics students at the university. One, Marcel Grossmann, would become Einstein's lifelong friend. Another, Mileva Maric, the only woman in the class, would become Einstein's first wife.

Einstein joined Department VI, the "School for Specialized Teachers in the Mathematical and Science Subjects" of the ETH, while still six months younger than the official minimum age. The Poly-

My plans for the future.

If I should have the good fortune to pass my examinations, I would go to the Zürich polytechnical school. I would stay there for four years in order to study mathematics and physics. I see myself becoming a teacher in these branches of the natural sciences, choosing the theoretical part of these sciences. Here are the reasons that led me to this plan. Above all it is my individual disposition for abstract and mathematical thought. . . .

And then there is a certain independence in the scientific profession which greatly pleases me.

—From an essay Einstein wrote during his last year of secondary school in Aarau, Switzerland

technic was founded in 1855, and at the time of Einstein's enrollment, it was considered slightly inferior to other schools, particularly those in Germany, if only because it could not award doctoral degrees. When he first started, Einstein got along fairly well. His examination scores put him near the top of the class, but as he neared graduation, his contrariness against authority reasserted itself.

During Einstein's third semester he threw himself into working in the physics laboratory of his professor, Heinrich Friedrich Weber (1843–1912). At first, Einstein worshipped the professor, but as he continued outside reading into the more profound theories of gases proposed by Ludwig Boltzmann (1844–1906), and the electromagnetic work by Heinrich Hertz (1857–1894), Einstein became disillusioned by Weber's teachings. Weber discouraged his young student from conducting a particular experiment, and Einstein later told his biographer Carl Seelig that Weber said, "You are a smart boy, Einstein, a very smart boy. But you have one great fault: you do not let yourself be told anything." As with previous instructors, once Einstein decided that Weber was dogmatic and closed to any "higher" thought, he treated the professor with disdain.

By this point Einstein had begun a love affair with Mileva Maric, and she joined him in his dislike of the professors. Together the pair developed a reputation for surliness. Einstein and Mileva spent the spring break of 1900 together, working on their diploma essays. They did fair to middling. The highest grade was a 6—Mileva received a 4, Einstein a 4.5. In addition, Einstein's final exams were quite poor. According to their advisers, who weighed individual grades and examinations and papers, Einstein passed, the fourth in his class of five with an average of 4.91. His sweetheart did not, however; Mileva received only a 4.0.

Einstein had believed that after graduation he would be able to return to the ETH for a salaried assistantship, Mileva would retake the exams, and they would continue on to both become shining stars in the scientific world. However, the next two years did not go according to plan. As university position after position failed to come through, Einstein became convinced that his former professor, Herr Weber, was working against him. The headstrong young physicist became disillusioned with the academic world, but he did continue to work on his doctoral dissertation. The ETH did not offer Ph.D. degrees, but one could be obtained simply by sending a thesis to the University of Zurich. In September 1901 Einstein sent off his thesis on the topic of the kinetic theory of gases. It was either not accepted or Einstein voluntarily withdrew it. Historians have been unable to find the university's response.

As Einstein struggled to find a job—generally making money by tutoring—he continued to work on a second thesis. The topic was on a way to use Brownian motion, the movement of atoms, to measure an atom's size. He submitted this thesis to the University of Zurich in April 1905. At the same time, Einstein sent a version of the paper to the premier German journal, *Annalen der Physik,* and it was published almost simultaneously with the university's acceptance of the thesis. Einstein finally had his Ph.D.

Of course, 1905 was the year Einstein published some of the greatest physics papers of his life—he certainly thought of himself as a full-fledged physicist long before the University of Zurich gave him the stamp of approval. So it is typical of his nature that Einstein was not only unimpressed but also dismissive of his degree. Einstein told Seelig in the summer of 1952 when the degree arrived it was mailed to his workplace in Bern. Einstein recalled, "One day I received a large envelope at the Patent Office, containing an elegant sheet of paper with some words in picturesque print (I even believe in Latin) which seemed to me impersonal and of little interest, and therefore landed at once in the official wastepaper basket." Only later did he learn that it was his announcement of the degree and an invitation to the graduation celebration.

Ehrenfest, Paul
(1880–1933)

Austrian physicist Paul Ehrenfest was a close friend of Einstein. He was a man with an effusive personality—given to talking in exclamation points—and fairly emotional. He became extremely upset when Einstein refused to accept certain aspects of modern science, and ultimately he was destroyed by personal tragedies.

Einstein spent less than two years teaching at the German university in Prague, but it was during this time that he met Ehrenfest and many of his future colleagues in the physics community. As a young physicist Ehrenfest, like Einstein, had a difficult time securing an academic position, and so Ehrenfest was on a tour of European universities when he began his friendship with Einstein.

The two men met on the Prague train platform one February day. In his diary, Ehrenfest recorded his impressions: "At last arrival in Prague—gray. get off. Einstein (cigar in mouth) there, with wife. Straight to a café. . . . Talk about Vienna, Zurich, Prague. . . . On the way to the institute first argument about everything. Rain in the street—mud—all the time discussion. Institute: lecture hall—up the stairs into theoretical physics. Continued arguing with Einstein."

Those arguments helped Einstein formulate his groundbreaking general theory of relativity—and each of the two sharp-tongued men relished having someone to quarrel over physics with. Ehrenfest stayed with the Einsteins, and, according to Ehrenfest's diary, spent a lot of time in "discussion." "Tea. From 12–2:30 Argued with Einstein. Very late to bed." The next day, "We start arguing at once. . . . Late Einstein tells me about his gravitation paper."

Both Ehrenfest and Einstein were also greatly affected by, and built on the ideas of, the two old masters in physics at the time, the French mathematician Henri Poincaré (1854–1912) and the Danish physicist Hendrik Antoon Lorentz (1853–1928). Ehrenfest's "world tour" ended successfully when he was offered Lorentz's position in mathematical physics at Leiden University in 1912.

Just a few months before, Einstein had accepted a new professorship created for him at the ETH back in Zurich. Einstein wrote at the time that he was relieved he had already accepted the Zurich position before hearing of Lorentz's retirement, and perhaps being forced to take that job. But it's quite possible that Einstein was saving face—as it seems the two men were a bit competitive with each other, and it was a surprise to the entire physics community that Ehrenfest won the prestigious Leiden chair.

Despite being in separate towns, Ehrenfest and Einstein wrote and saw each other often. In 1913 Ehrenfest and his wife, the Russian mathematician Tatyana Alexeyevna Afnassjewa Ehrenfest, visited Zurich and, while it was to be a vacation, Ehrenfest spent almost every hour deep in discussion with Einstein. Only once did he record in his diary: "A day without Einstein."

Einstein and Ehrenfest's rigorous correspondence provides insight into the development of general relativity. As Einstein was preparing to submit the theory to Germany's scientific association, he wrote Ehrenfest that his new theory of gravitation might well get him interned in a lunatic asylum. "I hope you don't have one in Leiden," he wrote, "so that I may visit you again in safety." Einstein needn't have worried. The general theory cemented his role as one of the world's leading physicists, and shortly thereafter Ehrenfest attempted to lure his old friend to join him at Leiden University. Writing in a 1919 letter, "We are suddenly, all of us, agreed that we have to tie you down in Leiden," and closing with the postscript, "It really is a nuisance that you should have any say in a matter which we are in much better position to judge than yourself!" Without waiting for Einstein's reply, he sent another letter, writing, "Here we have nothing but people who love *you* and not just your cerebral cortex."

Einstein declined however, and the two men continued their jesting letters discussing theoretical physics and, at times, religion. Like Einstein, Ehrenfest was Jewish, and so in him Einstein found not only someone to discuss physics but also Zionism. Ehrenfest was a compassionate ear that Einstein was not finding in Berlin. He wrote: "You don't berate me because of my Zionist escapades. Here there is considerable outrage, which, however, leaves me cold. Even the assimilated Jews are lamenting or berating me."

And as two of the world's leading physicists, Ehrenfest and Einstein often discussed the biggest controversy in physics at the time—that of quantum mechanics. The field arose from Einstein's own theories, and Ehrenfest held the first conference in Leiden on quantum mechanics, during the commemoration of the fiftieth anniversary of Lorentz's doctorate on December 11, 1925. While both men understood relativity in a similar way, they were destined to be on opposite sides of the fence when it came to quantum physics. Ehrenfest embraced it wholeheartedly; Einstein had reservations. That he had to choose to side against his friend in this matter was painful for Ehrenfest, and is reported to have actually brought tears to his eyes at times. In vain did Ehrenfest point out to Einstein that he had once presented a brand new theory—special relativity—and he too had had to convince the older physicists of its veracity. Einstein, now in the role of the more mature scientist, refused to accept the new theories.

Sadly, however, Ehrenfest was not to be part of the controversies over quantum mechanics for long. Einstein and Ehrenfest seemed to live parallel lives, sharing similar tragedies. Einstein's son Eduard developed schizophrenia and spent his last days in a sanitarium. Ehrenfest's son, Vassik, was born with Down's syndrome. When Ehrenfest was distraught over having to put his son in an institution, Einstein tried to console his friend, sharing with him the cold reason he applied to his own tragedy: "Valuable individuals must not be sacrificed to hopeless things, not even in this instance."

And yet, Ehrenfest was inconsolable. He wrote a letter to his colleagues in September 1933.

> My dear friends: Bohr, Einstein, Franck, Herglotz, Joffé, Kohnstamm, and Tolman!
>
> I absolutely do not know any more how to carry further during the next few months the burden of my life which has become unbearable. I cannot stand it any longer to let my professorship in Leiden go down the drain. I must vacate my position here. Perhaps it may happen that I can use up the rest of my strength in Russia. . . . If, however, it will not become clear rather soon that I can do that, then it is as good as certain that I shall kill myself. And if that will happen some time then I should like to know that I have written, calmly and without rush, to you whose friendship has played such a great role in my life.
>
> . . . Forgive me.

The letter, and another one to his students, was never sent. Deep in depression, Ehrenfest shot his son dead in a doctor's waiting room, and then shot himself.

In an obituary for his friend, Einstein wrote, "He was not merely the best teacher in our profession whom I have ever known; he was also passionately preoccupied with the development and destiny of men, especially his students. To understand others, to gain their friendship and trust, to aid anyone embroiled in outer or inner struggles, to encourage youthful talent—all this was his real element, almost more than his immersion in scientific problems."

Einstein, Elsa Löwenthal
(1876–1936)

Elsa was Einstein's cousin—and his second wife. She and Einstein had a good life together—not, perhaps, because they were so close, but because she was tolerant of his philandering and odd ways. Elsa was extraordinarily patient with his eccentricities and affairs, and threw herself into shaping Einstein's appearance, fame, and career, relishing her position as Frau Professor.

Born in 1876 in Hechingen, Hohenzollern, Elsa's father was the first cousin of Einstein's father, and her mother was the sister of Einstein's mother. Upon hearing about Einstein and Elsa's relationship, Einstein's mother, the same woman who threw such heated vitriol at Einstein's first wife, cheered his choice and had a clear hand in convincing Einstein to marry Elsa after seven years of courtship.

Elsa Einstein changed her name to Elsa Löwenthal when she married a Swabian merchant named Max Löwenthal in 1896 at the age of twenty. Their first child, Ilse, was born one year later, followed within two years by another daughter, Margot. A son was born in 1903; he did not survive infancy and Elsa was divorced after twelve years of this early marriage on May 11, 1908. She changed her and her daughters' last names back to her maiden name and moved into an apartment above her parents in Haberlanstrasse.

Einstein met Elsa again when he left his wife and children in Prague in the spring of 1912 to visit his mother in Berlin. Elsa was then thirty-six, three years older than Einstein, and their affair began immediately; Einstein wrote to Elsa in April 1912, "I must love somebody . . . and this somebody is you." Elsa would have looked to Einstein to be the complete opposite of his current wife, Mileva. She had corn-silk blonde hair and clear blue eyes, and she reveled in social encounters, while Mileva was dark-eyed, swarthy, bookish, and brooding. Elsa played the part of the gay divorcee in Berlin, with friends in artistic, literary, and political social circles. Or perhaps Einstein was so quickly taken with Elsa because she had been a childhood friend and reminded him of younger days in Munich. We don't know all the details since much of their early correspondence is lost—Elsa told Einstein to burn his letters so his wife would not discover their affair. A few survived, however; in December 1913, Einstein wrote Elsa, telling her not to worry about his current wife, Mileva, saying, "I treat my wife as an employee I cannot fire."

In March 1914, Einstein moved to Berlin to work with Fritz Haber at the new Kaiser Wilhelm Institute for Physical Chemistry. When he received the offer, Einstein wrote Elsa, "one of the main things that I want to do is to see you often." By that time, the two lovers had been in steady contact for two years. Mileva, for reasons that can be easily surmised, was miserable after the move to Berlin and stayed only for three months. After one last meeting with Einstein on July 29, 1914, Mileva and the boys left Berlin, the beginning of the separation that would lead to divorce.

But although his wife was now safely out of the picture, Einstein did not fall into Elsa's arms as he had promised. In fact, when Einstein returned from seeing his family off at the train station, he returned not to Elsa's comfortable flat, but to his own apartment. The next day, Einstein wrote Elsa that Haber told him Elsa was the right kind of wife for him, and he daydreamed of their marriage, "How much I look forward to the quiet evenings we shall be able to spend chatting alone, and to all the tranquil experiences that lie ahead. . . . Now after all my thought and work, I shall come home to find a dear little wife who will receive me cheerfully and contentedly."

And yet, Einstein had cold feet about getting married for a second time. In a letter to Elsa a month later, he made excuses, saying it was not that he didn't love her: "It is not a lack of true affection that scares me away from marriage again and again." For the next three years, Einstein kept Elsa at arm's length, shipping most of his furniture to Mileva before the end of the year, and then moving, not in with Elsa, but into a still smaller apartment near the middle of town. Elsa's apartment was a ten-minute walk away. Einstein kept his relations with his cousin as casual as she would let him. Elsa, however, was clear on where she stood in the matter: she intended to become Einstein's wife, and she was willing to be patient.

Her waiting paid off. In this period of relative calm in his personal life, Einstein developed his general theory of relativity, culminating in years of work from October 1915 to the late winter of 1917. This flurry of mental achievement led to a sudden drastic turn in Einstein's health. Elsa nursed her reluctant lover back from a year of sickness and, ultimately, for what seemed more like convenience than romance, Einstein moved into an apartment next to hers.

As Einstein recovered, Mileva slowly acquiesced to a divorce, clearing the way for Elsa. Discussions began between Elsa and Einstein about where and when they would finally make their affair legitimate, but there was one last sudden crisis: Elsa's older daughter, Ilse.

In October of 1917, Einstein employed Ilse as a clerk at the newly formed Institute of Theoretical Physics at the Kaiser Wilhelm Institute. While it is not entirely clear what happened between them, and Ilse herself denied that sex specifically was involved, Einstein clearly wouldn't have minded. A distressed Ilse wrote to Georg Friedrich Nicolai in May 1918, that suddenly "the question was raised whether A. wished to marry Mama or me." Einstein said he brought up the idea because he was in love with both women, but wanted to have a child with Ilse. He left the decision up to them. There's little recorded about how Elsa felt about the idea; it seems to have been Ilse herself who made the decision, saying Einstein should marry her mother. The episode became a closely guarded family secret, revealed only in 1998 when the family's wartime correspondence was published.

While Elsa and Einstein struggled over this last hurdle to their marriage, they were waiting out the legal formalities in Einstein's divorce to Mileva. Procedures began in Zurich in mid-1918 with Einstein acknowledging in court documents that he had told his wife of his adulterous affair. After five years of separation, Einstein and Mileva were divorced on February 14, 1919. Three months later, on June 2, Einstein and Elsa married at the Registry Office in Berlin. This marriage, long in coming, flouted the law because, as punishment for his adultery, Einstein was ordered by the Swiss court not to marry for another two years.

Einstein's mother, Pauline, greatly approved of her son's second wife, and she moved in with the couple six months after their marriage to spend her last days—she was terminally ill with abdominal cancer. Einstein's first family—Mileva, Hans Albert, and Eduard—on the other hand, not surprisingly had a poor opinion of Elsa and her bourgeois ways. Evelyn Einstein, Hans Albert's adopted daughter, typically referred to Einstein's second wife as "that social-climbing bitch."

Nevertheless, Einstein and "Frau Professor" did make a well-appointed couple, ready for Einstein's burgeoning fame. Elsa took it upon herself to reform the professor's image; in photographs with Elsa, he is dapper, even elegant. At home it was a different story—Einstein continued to dress very informally, seeing strangers in slacks and a sweater, highly unusual for the times. Keeping up appearances in the public world, while ceding to Einstein's many oddities and dalliances in private life, was Elsa's code.

The Einsteins's domestic life certainly included various oddities. They had separate bedrooms—the bedroom next to Elsa's was her daughters', while Einstein's was further down the hallway. (Elsa however, always contended this arrangement was due to the professor's loud snoring.) In addition, Elsa was not allowed to enter her husband's study without permission, and the attic, a storeroom for Einstein's papers, was not allowed to be cleaned.

This untidiness carried into Einstein's personal life. Dmitri Marianoff, the man who was briefly married to Elsa's younger daughter, Margot, wrote that Elsa and Einstein would toy with amorous women. When women sought audiences alone with Einstein, Elsa would agree, smile knowingly, leave them alone in his study, and then Einstein would grant them nothing but a lengthy lecture on physics. Marianoff said that everyone in the household understood that Einstein's suitors were merely "the worthless emphases of fame."

But Elsa wasn't always in on the joke. After Ilse left her position as the secretary to the Physics Institute, Einstein hired Betty Neumann, and continued on with his tradition of being romantically entangled with the person in that position. They began an affair—this time sexual as well as emotional. When that ended, Einstein followed it with a series of affairs throughout his remaining years in Berlin, often it seems Elsa purposefully left the house to allow Einstein time for his dalliances. For reasons unknown, Elsa seemed to accept this arrangement—perhaps because it didn't infringe on the unique emotional relationship the two of them had. In 1929, an article in the *New York Times* stated, "Mrs. Einstein's attitude toward her distinguished husband is that of a doting parent towards a precocious child . . . his home showed little of his personality."

However, Elsa would fight if she felt publicly humiliated. There are many accounts of arguments between the two, but the arrangement between them never changed. In fact, once Elsa complained bitterly to her daughters about Einstein's affair with an Austrian actress. They pointedly told her she had a clear choice: leave Einstein or put up with the affair, because she had known what she was getting into.

As the Einstein household went through rest and rages, the world outside intruded. It became clear in the years leading to World War II that the Einsteins would have to find a safer place to live. Rumors abounded that Einstein's fame made him a target of assassination, and in 1932 they moved to the United States.

Elsa's time in the United States was destined to be short and difficult. Only a year after leaving Europe, Ilse died at the age of thirtyseven in Paris after a painful illness. In a move that likely hurt both women, Einstein refused to return to Paris with Elsa to nurse Ilse, claiming safety precautions. After Ilse's passing, Elsa returned with Margot to Princeton. Despite now having at least one daughter close by, Elsa is said to never have recovered from Ilse's death.

Shortly after, in 1935, Elsa herself became gravely ill. She had kidney and circulatory problems, and her health deteriorated as winter arrived. To her pleasure, Einstein seemed crushed by the idea of her death—Elsa told her friend Antonina Vallentin, "He wanders about like a lost soul," and "I never thought he loved me so much, and that comforts me." Elsa Einstein died on December 20, 1936, of heart disease. Without the woman who pushed him into the spotlight, Einstein became increasingly solitary, writing his friend Max Born that he was hibernating, and "this bearishness has been accentuated still further by the death of my mate, who was more attached to human beings than I."

Einstein, Mileva Maric
(1875–1948)

Mileva Maric, commonly known as Mila, was Einstein's first wife. Their relationship was emotionally intense from beginning to end. It began as a college fling, fueled by a mutual love of physics, the disapproval of their friends and family, and the lust of youth. It ended with a bitter, protracted divorce, physical and mental breakdowns on both sides, and lifelong estrangement.

Mila was born in Hungary in 1875. Most women in Eastern Europe at that time simply didn't attend school, but through luck of location and her father's political pull, Mila was one of the few to have that luxury. Upon graduating with high honors from secondary school, Mila moved to Zurich, Switzerland, then a haven for educated women. Mila entered the University of Zurich Medical School but after one year, jumped across the Ramistrasse River to study physics at Federal Polytechnic, the finest technical university in Central Europe. It was there that she met Albert Einstein.

Einstein certainly noticed Mila's arrival at Polytechnic; she was the only woman in their entering class of five students. There are few records of their first year at college, but they developed a close friendship that soon blossomed into romance. As Mila and Albert became closer, their friends began to voice disdain for their relationship. Mila's friends thought the little German disheveled and distant. Albert's friends brought up the fact that Mila was not "absolutely sound"—she had a pronounced limp from her hip that seems to have been a birth defect, since Mila's sister, Zorka, had the same problem.

Einstein's mother, Pauline, was equally disenchanted with Mila. It was fine for her son to have a college dalliance with this sullen girl, but she was outraged by their protracted romance. Mila was Serbian, Christian, dark and brooding, four years older, and walked with a limp. As a middle-class German Jew, Pauline Einstein thought Mila was completely unattractive and unsuitable for her Albert.

But, as in many young love affairs, disapproval only strengthened the couple's resolve. Einstein was happy to have found, as he wrote in a letter to Mila, "a creature who is my equal and who is as strong and independent as I am," and he wasn't about to let her go. The love between the couple continued to grow. Later, during much darker periods of her life, Mila would look back wistfully to those college days full of coffee, sausage, and physics.

Their studies weren't going so well, however. The pair had managed to alienate one of their professors, Heinrich Weber. Initially they had thrown themselves into his classes, reveling in Weber's teachings of the classical theories of heat, gases, and electricity. But over time, Einstein—and therefore Mila—became disenchanted with the professor's teachings. Weber was too traditional and closed-minded for two headstrong students who constantly questioned accepted theories. Professor Weber's dislike of the outspoken couple was evident, and Einstein and Mila were both feeling downtrodden by the time final exams came around. It was 1900 and supposed to be their last year in school—Einstein managed to pass his exams, coming in fourth in a class of five. That was good enough for a diploma, and Einstein went home to his parents' house for the summer. Mila, on the other hand, came in last in the class and so was required to continue her studies.

> *I am so lucky to have found you, a creature who is my equal, and who is as strong and independent as I am!*
>
> —Einstein to Mileva Maric in a letter on October 3, 1900

After he graduated, Einstein told his mother that Mila had failed her exams. Pauline asked, "What's to become of her?" and he casually replied, "My wife." Pauline screamed out in dismay and began to sob, yelling at Einstein that he would be destroying his life. Over the next few months she did all she could to discourage her son from marrying the quiet Mileva, going so far at one point as to mourn Einstein as if he were already dead to her. Einstein seems to have handled his mother badly, alternating between arguing with her and agreeing to her wishes. Mila, who received regular letters from her fiancé updating her on the state of affairs in the Einstein family, became distraught, both over her mother-in-law-to-be's acrimony and the fear that Einstein might actually acquiesce and leave her.

Both Einstein and Mila hoped that when they returned to Zurich everything would improve, but Einstein's job there fell through, and Mila's return to classes was long delayed by illness. Ultimately, Einstein chose to live with his parents in Milan, leaving Mila to finish her studies. After applying for other jobs, and a continued feeling that Professor Weber was sabotaging him, Einstein finally found a job teaching mathematics at a school outside Zurich. Thrilled at the idea, Einstein cajoled Mila to join him on a holiday in the Swiss Alps. It was a fateful trip—unknown to the young lovers, Mila became pregnant during the four-day vacation.

Mila resumed her studies under Professor Weber. In the spring of 1901 she still had hopes of earning her Ph.D. and becoming a scientist, but soon she was quite obviously pregnant. As the reality of their situation set in, the two lovers began to assess their fate. Mila's parents seemed to take the news of her pregnancy rather well, but they chose not to tell Albert's parents. Pauline, after all, was still convinced Mileva was a conniving hussy, and Albert's father, Hermann, was having financial trouble because he had just lost his business.

Albert was called upon to support the Einstein family, as well as his pregnant sweetheart, all while working in a temporary teaching job, unable to get a permanent physics position. Feeling the weight of the gloomy situation, Albert noticeably pulled away from Mila, who was naturally distraught. As a compromise between avoiding the vicious Pauline and the need to reassure herself, Mila secretly traveled to a town near where Albert was teaching. As her letters attest, she was incredulous when he made excuse after excuse as to why he could not visit, and ultimately Mila returned home without the reassurances she wanted.

The letters Einstein sent shortly afterward, however, show the couple reconciled. In late July, three months pregnant, Mila retook the graduation exam for the Polytechnic. Given the pressures the young woman was under, it was no surprise when she failed for the second time. Effectively, Mileva Maric's academic career was over; with her failing grades she wouldn't even be able to get a job as a secondary school teacher. She went home to her parents, where she could have her illegitimate child in secret. While Pauline Einstein didn't know Mila was pregnant, she certainly knew her son still planned on getting married. Pauline mailed a vicious letter to the Maric family, accusing the "older" woman Mila of seducing the younger Einstein.

Finally, a ray of hope for the young couple appeared: Einstein was offered a full-time position at the Swiss Patent Office in Bern. It was a job that Einstein later called his salvation. But the job apparently wasn't enough to solve the problem of the impending birth—in fact, if the office found out about Mila's condition, he might lose the offer. So, when Einstein traveled to Bern where he planned to teach and tutor until the patent job began, Mila stayed in Hungary. She gave birth to a daughter nicknamed Lieserl in February 1902.

A few months later, Mila joined Einstein in Bern. She was darkly depressed, and had left their daughter behind. No one quite knows whether Lieserl was left behind simply because of the stigma of an illegitimate daughter or if there were other issues such as the child's health. It was six years into their relationship, and Einstein's affection for Mila seemed to be dwindling—he was not enthused at her arrival.

Nevertheless, out of "a sense of duty," as he later said, the couple was married in a civil ceremony on January 6, 1903. They couldn't afford a fancy affair, or a honeymoon. The full extent of their celebration was to take their two witnesses, friends Conrad Habicht and Maurice Solovine, out to dinner.

Shortly thereafter, Mila visited her parents and her daughter for a month. All that is known about the fate of baby Lieserl is contained in two letters, discovered in 1987, exchanged by the couple during these weeks. In one, Mila writes a short postcard saying, "It's going quickly," and she misses Einstein. In the second, Albert writes that he worries over Lieserl's scarlet fever, what could be a life-threatening malady. He also writes, "As what is the child registered?" and "We must take precautions that problems don't arise for her later." These words seem to suggest that Lieserl ultimately was adopted, possibly by Helene Savic, Mila's best friend, or her family. Historians have scoured private papers, government records, even Yugoslavian gravestones, but no clues to Lieserl's fate have been found. Other suggestions have been that Lieserl died shortly thereafter, or that she had a severe genetic disorder and was given to foster care. Regardless, it's certain that Einstein never met his baby daughter—Mila returned to Bern without her.

In the fall of 1903, the couple moved to the most famous of their seven apartments in Bern (the Kramgass has been turned into a museum, the Einsteinhaus, by local scholars) and things looked up a bit for the couple. They were happy, if under quite a bit of stress. Einstein was working busily on four new theories that would all be published the next year and, on May 14, 1904, Mileva gave birth to a boy they named Hans Albert, or Albertli for short.

Mila made a triumphant return home with Einstein and Hans Albert in the summer of 1905. This was the first time Albert met his parents-in law, and Mila's father, Milos, was charmed with him. Einstein played up his popularity, proclaiming Mila "solves all my mathematical problems for me."

It was statements like this, and Mila's own early promise as a gifted mathematician, that led scholars in the 1980s and 1990s to suggest that she was the true author of Einstein's relativity theories, or at the very least, a significant contributor. But while Mila's intellectual prowess certainly provided inspiration and support for Einstein's deep thoughts, historians now believe Albert Einstein developed his own theories.

Indeed, Mila seemed to lose more and more contact with science and math over the years, much to her dismay. Mila's last involvement with science seemed to be her work on building a machine in the fall of 1907. This device would generate a high voltage by using a series of rotating metal strips. Einstein and the Habicht brothers prepared a patent application for the machine. And, while Mila's name wasn't included on the application, many accounts suggest that Mila was instrumental in developing its circuit diagrams and electrical formulas.

Indeed, Mila's scientific career had long been surpassed by her husband's. During the fame that followed Einstein's Miracle Year of five brilliant physics papers in 1905, Mila began to slide into what became an engulfing depression. As early as December 1906, Mila wrote wistfully to her friend Helene of how happy she'd been during her poverty-stricken student days. By 1909, photographs of Mila show her with deadened eyes, a lined faced, and she seems tired and weary.

Einstein and Mila did apparently have a nice vacation that year, going back to the same Swiss Alps where they conceived Lieserl. They discussed having another child, and in the summer of 1910 Eduard, or Tete as he was called, was born. But the happiness wasn't to last. Over the next few years, the couple moved to Prague, back to Zurich, and finally to Berlin. Mila was increasingly miserable in each city, while Einstein traveled, worked longer hours, and generally avoided coming home.

As the marriage spiraled downward, the now-famous Albert Einstein flirted with other women. Hans Albert later remembered that it was around his eighth birthday, in 1912, when he noticed the tension between his parents. It was that year that Einstein's cousin Elsa caught his eye, and they began an affair. The affair wasn't lost on Mila, she may not have known for sure, but she certainly suspected her husband's infidelity.

By the time the troubled couple moved to Berlin, Mila had had enough. After all those years, she still wasn't accepted by Einstein's family, and she believed correctly that Einstein's mother was conspiring to bring Elsa and Albert together. Pushed by her discontent and Einstein's increasingly bad behavior, Mila demanded that Einstein move out. The move was most likely meant simply as a threat, to remind Einstein that she controlled access to his two boys, but if so, it backfired on her. The separation was the beginning of what became a fantastically protracted divorce.

First, Einstein developed a list of conditions under which he would return to the family. The list included clauses and subclauses of irritable instructions: "1. You expect no tenderness from me nor do you make any accusations of me. 2. When you direct your speech at me you must desist immediately if I request it," and so forth. The impossible document was designed to be just that—he wanted to force Mila to divorce him.

She acquiesced to a formal separation and family friend Fritz Haber drew up the papers. Mila moved with her children back to Zurich where Hans Albert immediately began to disengage from his father, refusing to see him and only writing brief letters when forced. This broke Einstein's heart, and he unleashed his fury at Mila, accusing her of turning the boy against him.

In February 1916, Einstein proposed divorce, but the prospect sent her into hysterics. He visited Zurich to hurry things along but he didn't get anywhere. Shortly after he left, Mila had a complete emotional and physical breakdown; at the age of forty-one she had a series of heart attacks. Einstein's family, never able to sympathize with their disliked daughter-in-law, proposed the idea that she was "sick in the head." Mila finally improved—when Einstein stopped talking about the divorce.

For all intents and purposes, however, the marriage was over. Einstein moved in with Elsa and her girls, and then, almost two years after his first attempt at divorce, he tried again. In a letter he demanded another list of concessions; again Mila refused. But both Einstein and Mila poured their hearts out to intermediaries, the

Bessos, and soon Mila began to understand, finally, that her marriage was over. Einstein, in turn, stopped the lists of demands, and for the first time wrote of his sympathy for his wife. Now that both saw the end, their correspondence became almost friendly. Mila wrote, "I am curious to see what will last longer: the World War, or our divorce." He wrote, "They both began essentially at the same time, this situation of ours is still the nicer of the two."

In the end, their divorce did last longer than World War I. Einstein and Mila were officially divorced on February 14, 1919. In their settlement, it was agreed that should Einstein ever win the Nobel Prize, he would keep the medal but give the money to Mila, which is indeed what happened. (This monetary arrangement is yet another reason why some historians have suggested that Mila was at least partially responsible for his physics theories, though again, there seems little proof that she was more than a knowledgeable sounding board.)

Mila lived in Zurich and settled into the role of a dowager; her presence was more than once described as stern and frightening. By most accounts, however, her mental state had calmed, and she was a doting mother to her two sons. The fame that Einstein achieved later in life did not seem to shine upon her, and she kept quiet about their divorce and her earlier distraught relationship with the physicist who had, by then, captured the world's attention.

Einstein's two sons lived with Mila as their father started a new family with Elsa—whom he married within months of his divorce—and her two daughters. Einstein, off and on, was conflicted about his estrangement from his sons, at times continuing to blame Mila. He did, however, occasionally still exchange scientific ideas with his ex-wife, although at this point it seemed to be more for her amusement than for any input she may have had on his theories.

On the eve of World War II, and just before Einstein moved to the United States, he went to Zurich to visit his son Eduard, who was schizophrenic and in a mental institution. Mila's relationship with her ex-husband was by then pleasant enough for her to offer him and Elsa her own apartment to live in, though the offer was declined. This was the last time Albert Einstein ever saw his first wife.

Mileva Maric Einstein died quietly in a hospital in August 1948 and was buried in Zurich.

Einstein Field Equations

Field equations describe through mathematics what happens over an area of space, or "field." Einstein created field equations that described the gravitational forces over the entirety of space. With one simple equation, he overturned Newton's theory of gravity, and created the foundation for all of cosmology.

The general theory of relativity can be expressed in a fairly short field equation: $G_{\mu v} = 8\pi T_{\mu v}$. It's not quite as pithy as $E = mc^2$, nor as easy to translate into nonscientific language, but it is still considered an elegant equation that with just two terms describes the very shape of the universe. It is called a field equation because it describes the nature of gravitation across a wide swath of space—thus describing a field, as opposed to a specific point. The equation sums up ten other field equations (technically they are "coupled hyperbolic-elliptical nonlinear partial differential equations") that together describe how space warps around a given mass—how space stretches and squeezes up and down, left and right, top and bottom.

The left side of the equation, the "G," describes the curve of space, and it is known as the Einstein tensor. The right side of the equation, the "T," is called a stress-energy tensor, and it describes how matter is distributed.

The equation does two things. First, it replaces the Newtonian idea of gravitation. In Einstein's description, objects are attracted to each other since space is curved, not by the force-at-a-distance concept of gravity proposed by Newton. (For those who are comparing equations, Newton's gravitation formula $F = GM_1 m_2/R_2$ may not seem any more simple than Einstein's.)

But Einstein's field equations also describe the geometry of the whole universe, representing how all the matter that exists shapes space. Of course, to determine that shape requires knowing just how much material is in the universe as well as having a great deal of time to plug that huge amount of information into the equations.

Einstein was aware that despite the simple concept behind his theory, no one would be able to solve the equations for the entire universe in the foreseeable future. Einstein was fairly startled however, when within just a few days of his publishing the equations in 1915, someone did solve his equation for a much smaller system—a star. The German physicist Karl Schwarzschild (1873–1916) presented a solution for the

Einstein equations as they applied to a perfectly symmetrical sphere, showing just how a gravitational field curved around it. To this day, however, there has been no definitive solution to the Einstein equations for all of the universe, though the incredible details astronomers have since gathered about distant galaxies as well as modern supercomputers are bringing us closer to a solution.

Einstein-Podolsky-Rosen Argument

Also referred to as the Einstein-Podolsky-Rosen paradox, or even simply EPR, this argument was one of Einstein's most subtle and intriguing in his attempt to prove that the theories of quantum mechanics were not complete.

Presenting their ideas in a 1935 paper in the journal *Physical Review*, Einstein, Boris Podolsky, and Nathan Rosen described a thought experiment that suggested that certain qualities of atoms, such as position or momentum, were physically real, measurable quantities. Quantum mechanics couldn't measure these qualities, however, and so Einstein argued that it didn't perfectly describe the atomic world.

In their argument, Einstein, Podolsky, and Rosen offered readers a thought experiment that is deeply couched in the math and concepts of quantum mechanics. They began with two particles—say, perhaps two hydrogen atoms bound together—that by virtue of being together have shared properties. They obviously have a shared position, but they also have a shared orientation: one of the atoms is upright, while the other one is upside down. (While no one has ever seen an atom with their own eyes, this is obviously a simplification of what's really happening—atoms aren't really right-side up or upside down. Scientists refer to them as having "spin," a fairly abstract concept that relates to their angular momentum and the direction the atom is spinning. Thinking of them merely as being up or down, however, is a perfectly acceptable way to walk through this thought experiment.)

According to the experiment, it doesn't matter *which* hydrogen atom is upright; all that matters is that one is up and the other down. There is no way the atoms could ever both be down, or both up—there must be one of each. But quantum physics offers up an additional counterintuitive description: neither atom is specifically up or down. Instead, they are each both partly up and partly down, until and unless someone measures them. At that point, if some experimenter checks the spin of one of the atoms and finds it to be "down"—then the other atom coalesces into a definite state, namely "up."

The important point for the EPR argument is this: the standard interpretation of quantum mechanics insists that without measuring, experimenting, or otherwise interfering with a particle, it does not have definitive characteristics. All one can say about the qualities of a given particle is that they are partially in one state and partially in another—a concept referred to as a "superposition" of states. In effect, the atoms exist in an indefinite state until someone tries to define them. It is only upon measurement that the particle collapses into a specific state.

Einstein, Podolsky, and Rosen set out to show that this basic quantum mechanical assumption was untrue. Particles, they believed, have definite qualities even without being pushed and prodded. To show this, they asked readers to imagine separating the two hydrogen atoms and take them miles and miles away from each other. No matter how far away they were—even if one was in New York City and one was in Tokyo—these two atoms would still remain "entangled," like twins separated at birth. They may be distant, but the two atoms would always share certain properties. One atom will remain up, while the other one will stay down. Of course, you would have no way of knowing which one was which—for that you'd have to measure one of the atoms.

So, imagine that a scientist in New York decides to examine one atom. He finds his atom to be up. "Ah ha!" he thinks. "I now know with absolute certainty that the other atom points down." Of course, moments before, the other atom had also been in an indefinite state— by measuring the atom in New York, the scientist forced the atom in Tokyo into a specific state. This isn't the main point of the EPR argument, but it is nevertheless a downright odd bit. Einstein felt that this alone was enough to show the problems with quantum mechanics. If quantum theory insisted that neither atom was up or down until measured, then how did the down atom, so many miles away, know the other one was being measured? The information would have to be relayed instantaneously—an impossibility given Einstein's own theories that nothing in the universe could travel faster than the speed of light. Einstein referred to this—obviously impossible, he thought— immediate transference of information as "spooky action at a distance."

Regardless of the enigma of how the second atom would know its twin had been measured, Einstein and his coauthors felt they had found an inherent contradiction within quantum physics. After all, the scientist in New York just definitively measured the atom in Tokyo without ever touching it. The hydrogen atom in Tokyo has a physically real quality of spin; it's in a definite down state, even though it has not been interfered with in any way. Thus, there is a sense in which qualities of an atom were real, even in the absence of an observer. Quantum mechanics, on the other hand, only had the math to describe fuzzier versions of an atom's properties. So, according to EPR, there is a physical measurable reality and quantum mechanics couldn't measure it. The conclusion was clear: quantum mechanics was not equipped to completely describe how particles interacted. The theory was incomplete.

"Einstein Attacks Quantum Theory"

On May 4, 1935, the New York Times got ahold of the story and published an article with the headline: "Einstein Attacks Quantum Theory." Einstein was sorely displeased, and on May 7, the Times printed a statement in which Einstein disparaged that wording. After all, Einstein never thought quantum mechanics was wrong, per se. He knew that quantum mechanics was highly successful at predicting how atoms should behave. Einstein never meant to attack the validity of quantum theory; he merely thought that it wasn't the final answer. It was a situation Einstein was familiar with. His theories of relativity were better than Newton's, but they still incorporated the previous Newtonian mechanics, and so Einstein thought a new science would someday incorporate quantum mechanics and improve upon it. Many scientists did, and still do, accept quantum physics as a fully realized theory, but Einstein didn't—and he wanted the rest of the community not to rest on their laurels but to search further.

Responses

The Einstein-Podolsky-Rosen argument was a fairly subtle one to begin with, and the physics community's rebuttal was equally so. The main founder and champion for the standard answer—known as the Copenhagen interpretation—of quantum mechanics was Niels Bohr. Bohr wrote that the EPR argument took quantum mechanics out of context and used it in an experiment it wasn't meant for. Quantum mechanics never, said Bohr, purported to do anything other than analyze a system that was being measured by some macroscopic tool. Quantum mechanics did not concern itself with the history of how particles became entangled, coalesced into up or down spin states, or were separated from each other. It was not meant to describe those scenarios, but only to describe what happened once the system was observed. Since the EPR argument was trying to disprove the Copenhagen interpretation based on applying quantum mechanics to a situation no one claimed it could describe, the entire thought experiment was irrelevant.

For most modern scientists this is conclusion enough; the EPR argument was successfully rebutted. But the history of the Einstein-Podolsky-Rosen argument did not end there. Einstein continued to elaborate on the initial thought experiment, and even today scientists are designing experiments to test it.

Einstein believed one explanation for how quantum mechanics might fit into a larger scientific theory was that there were "hidden variables." For example, if you flip a coin it appears to be a random process, and the only way to predict whether it will be heads or tails is to give broad probabilities: flip it enough times and you should get heads about 50 percent of the time and tails about 50 percent of the time. Quantum mechanics does something similar with the two hydrogen atoms: measure the atom in New York enough times and it should be up about 50 percent of the time and down about 50 percent of the time. But with a coin, we know there is more going on with the flip—we just can't or don't measure it. There's the exact pressure of the thumb on the coin, the air pressure, the precise value of gravity at that point on Earth, the weight of the coin, and a whole host of other variables. If you knew all of this information, you should be able to predict exactly which way the coin would land every single time. The coin toss seems random not because coin flipping is inherently random, but because there are just too many variables to easily take into consideration. Perhaps, suggested Einstein, there were additional factors—factors we didn't realize, hidden variables even—that go into deciding whether the atom in New York would be up or down. (This is not the only option Einstein considered in order to enhance quantum mechanics, but it was a fairly prominent one.)

In 1964, Irish physicist John Bell (1928–1990) tackled these hidden variables. He showed that even if you didn't know what the hidden variables were, there would be different results in the EPR experiment if such hidden variables did indeed exist. In other words, if you did the experiment many times, you could predict a different outcome if there were some mysterious hidden variables—and you would get that result even if you didn't know anything about those variables. Bell's work paved the way for experiments in the 1980s that showed no hidden variables were present. Of course, just getting rid of hidden variables is not proof that quantum mechanics is completely correct. But almost all modern physicists accept Bell's work as support for the Copenhagen interpretation. However, there are also scientists who have expanded on Bell's theory, and believe that it only works for certain kinds of hidden variables; perhaps performing actual EPR experiments didn't quash the idea of hidden variables after all.

Modern Experiments

Regardless of whether the EPR argument disproves quantum mechanics, the concept that two atoms could affect each other even though they may be miles apart is fascinating—so much so that physicists continue to be attracted to it and perform in real time and space what was once merely a thought experiment. Early attempts didn't separate the entangled atoms very far from each other, but in the mid-1990s physicists in Geneva conducted EPR experiments at a distance of a mile apart and achieved exactly what they expected from the Copenhagen interpretation: measuring the atom in one place, and thus forcing it into a certain state, automatically forced the other atom into the opposite state without otherwise interfering with it. Einstein's "spooky action at a distance" was all too real.

At a scientific level, such experiments are meant to show that, despite the oddities of quantum mechanics, it does indeed seem to work—even if one is unable to understand the mystery of how two such distant atoms can be in communication with each other. At a science fiction level, EPR experiments are often compared with the transporter of *Star Trek* fame. On the television program, the transporter was essentially a teleportation device that could beam someone from place to place. If one can change an atom miles away, goes the thinking, one might be able to create replicas—in essence mimicking an object or even a human body in a remote location, which is as good as transporting them. Of course, the mere fact that one atom over here can affect an atom way over there leaves quite a bit of technology to discover before one can build a transporter, but the EPR idea has never-theless turned out to be a catalyst for that kind of creative thought.

See **Bohr, Niels; Hidden Variables; Quantum Mechanics.**

Einstein Ring

Beautiful ellipses of light in the night sky, Einstein predicted the exis-tence of these glowing rings in 1936, but thought they would never actually be spotted by human eyes.

Early on, Einstein realized that the general theory of relativity meant light would bend as it passed by any large object like a star. This bend-ing quickly proved to be an important astronomy tool in the form of a gravitational lens: the British astronomer Sir Oliver Lodge realized in 1919 that as light from a distant source, say a galaxy, moves past a closer object, the light would bend around each side. The light would essentially be doubled as it reached Earth, thus creating the appear-ance of a much brighter galaxy than actually existed. The very gravity of the massive object in the way creates a lens that increases the far-ther object's brightness much as an optical lens or magnifying glass would. The first gravitational lens was discovered in 1979, and ever since they've been used to help map the heavens.

Even before then, however, Einstein showed there might exist a special category of gravitational lens—if the two objects were perfectly lined up, the distant galaxy would appear to our eyes as a perfect ring around the closer lensing object. Einstein thought the chances of two such bodies lining up so precisely was almost negligible, and so he assumed no one would ever see such a thing.

But in 1987 an Einstein ring was finally seen. Jacqueline Hewitt, an astronomer at MIT, discovered a bright oval in the sky using a tel-escope in New Mexico, known as the Very Large Array, or VLA. After various attempts to explain away the odd shape, she and her col-leagues had to agree they were looking at the long-elusive Einstein ring. Since then, only a handful have been spotted. One of the bright-est and most beautiful was captured on film in 1998 by the Hubble Space Telescope. What looks like a bright ring of fire surrounds the galaxy that lensed the image—it was so bizarre a sight that the researchers assumed it was an artificial defect before finally realizing they had captured the best image of an Einstein ring to date.

Einstein Tower

The Einstein Tower is an observatory in Potsdam, Germany, that was built from 1919 to 1923 at a time when Einstein had just become an international celebrity. The tower was originally supposed to house an astronomy lab for Einstein, but he left Germany during the rise of Nazism. In his absence, the tower—a fairly modern and avant-garde building—was easily turned into a symbol for those who would mock Einstein.

The Einstein Tower is a tall, narrow, white building with rounded windows, covered in asymmetric, surrealistic-looking melting eaves. A long wide base at the bottom turns the whole building into what looks much like a big boot. It is eye-catching and considered a classic example of Expressionist architecture—a movement that tried to use art as a way of expressing the feelings and politics of society at large. The architect, Erich Mendelsohn (1887–1953), knowing the building was to be used as an astronomy lab, built an especially vertical building to give it an aerodynamic feel—one might almost expect it to launch like a rocket ship. The tower is typical of a certain kind of architecture of the time, but nonetheless its striking modernity didn't sit well with many.

Plans for the building were to make it a state-of-the-art observatory, one that Einstein could use to test the general theory of relativity by observing how light rays bent in gravitational fields as they made their way toward Earth. Indeed, the tower was considered one of the premier observatories until World War II, though in the absence of Einstein, who left Germany in 1932 as the Nazis gained power.

At that time, Nazi propaganda insisted that Jews were incapable of producing solid science, that they never stuck to the facts, and that they presented their results in the popular press instead of through the proper scientific channels. Given the milieu, the outlandish tower was easily turned into a symbol of all that they believed had been wrong with Einstein and his theories. When Einstein renounced his German citizenship, a gleeful cartoon showed him leaving the country, taking the fantastic tower with him. The tower, of course, did not in fact go anywhere, and it is currently part of the Albert Einstein Institute in Potsdam, a center for gravitational studies.

Einsteinium

Einsteinium, named after Albert Einstein, is a man-made element that forms from plutonium or uranium. It's a silvery, radioactive metal dis-covered in the Pacific Ocean after the first hydrogen bomb was deto-nated on the Pacific island of Eniwetok. Its element symbol is Es.

Einsteinium is the seventh element larger than uranium, which in the early 1900s was thought to be the heaviest element possible and is indeed the heaviest element found in nature. In 1952, a team led by the Berkeley physicist Albert Ghiorso discovered the element when they searched the debris left over after the United States detonated a test thermonuclear bomb in the Pacific. In coral samples, they found an iso-tope that had been formed when uranium atoms fused and then decayed. Einstein died in 1955, and shortly thereafter this new element was named einsteinium. He might well have considered it a dubious honor; Einstein fought all his life against the proliferation of nuclear weapons, and an atom created by them seems an odd memorial.

Einsteinium has atomic weight 252 and atomic number 99. Its most stable isotope is einsteinium 252, which has a half-life of about 471.7 days. Since einsteinium doesn't occur in nature, it is incredibly rare. Tiny amounts of einsteinium are made as a by-product of pluto-nium nuclear reactors, and researchers have made larger amounts of einsteinium through processes that can take five or six years at a time. Because einsteinium is only man-made, it has no biological uses; because it is so rare, it has no technological ones. At the moment it is only ever used for research.

Electrodynamics

Electrodynamics describes the physics of rapidly changing electric and magnetic fields. It grew out of electromagnetic theory, a subject that was well studied in the nineteenth century and that fascinated Einstein—leading to his creation of the special theory of relativity.

In 1831, the English scientist Michael Faraday (1791–1867) first connected electricity and magnetism, saying that the heretofore distinct forces were two sides of the same coin. Faraday discovered that a moving magnetic field would create electricity, and vice versa. The concept of electromagnetism was born. Several decades later, the Scottish physicist James Clerk Maxwell (1831–1879) realized that light itself was an electromagnetic wave. Physicists promptly applied this new concept to all sorts of previously studied science laws with great success—two light beams that crossed paths created interference patterns that looked like two water waves interfering, for example, but there were occasional contradictions. The main one was that light seemed to travel at the exact same speed no matter who observed it. (A car doesn't do that—it looks like it's traveling at totally different speeds if you are standing on the sidewalk or in another car traveling next to it.) If this was true, then just what medium was light traveling through that didn't move with Earth, but was somehow stock still with respect to the entire universe? More confusing, a consistently steady speed of light implied that different observers might deduce entirely different laws of physics, and this was unacceptable. Something was wrong, either Maxwell's equations, or Newton's physics, and no one was sure which.

Einstein was fascinated by light even as a teenager, and unraveling the electrodynamic conundrum continued to haunt him as a young adult. Einstein's self-taught electrodynamics caused him problems growing up: his fascination with Faraday and Maxwell was one of the many points of contention between Einstein and his professors. And so it was not his classes, but discussions with young physicist friends on this, one of Einstein's favorite topics, that spurred him on to find a solution.

Finally, in 1905, Einstein solved the electrodynamics problem when he published his paper on the special theory of relativity titled "On the Electrodynamics of Moving Bodies." By accepting that light simply never changed speed, Einstein decided it must be space and time that differed for different observers. This leap of intuition—one so contrary to what we experience on a daily basis—neatly solved the issues then facing electrodynamics. Ultimately, what this meant for physics was that the traditional rules of Newton's world weren't accurate when one approached the speed of light—so it turned out to be Maxwell's equations that were correct, and classical physics that was wrong. The field of electrodynamics has continued to evolve with the advent of quantum mechanics, but it was Einstein's special theory of relativity that first launched electrodynamics into the modern world.

See **Light; Relativity, Special Theory of.**

Ether

To the nineteenth-century scientific community, ether was a medium at a perfect state of rest through which light waves traveled—much the way a wave of water can't exist without the medium of water to move through, and how sound waves can't travel without air. But Einstein's theory of special relativity, published in 1905, discarded the ether, establishing that light didn't need it at all.

At its most basic, ether is a mysterious substance that pervades the universe. First proposed by the ancient Greek scientist Aristotle, the concept of ether, or "aether" as it is sometimes spelled, has had dramatically different connotations over the centuries. To Aristotle, everything higher than Earth's atmosphere—the sun, the moon, the stars, all things divine—all were fabricated out of a mysterious substance that could never be seen on Earth, the ether.

In the 1800s, the word "ether" still connoted mystery. No one could see it or touch it, but now it was thought to fill not just the heavens, but the Earthly atmosphere as well. In the mid-1800s, James Clerk Maxwell (1831–1879) formulated his theory of electromagnetism that became the dominating theory of light for fifty years and described light as an electromagnetic wave traveling through the ether. Maxwell was aware of how often scientists and philosophers invoked the concept of ether to name what they couldn't otherwise sense. Maxwell wrote in the ninth edition of the *Encyclopedia Brittanica*, that "all space had been filled three or four times over with aethers."

Nevertheless, Maxwell and the other physicists of his day embraced the ether as the only way to explain what they understood about light. For one thing, light was undeniably a wave. When two beams of light were focused together on a screen, they created what was known as interference patterns, patterns of light and dark that could only come from two waves interacting. But everyone knew waves had to move *through* something. So physicists hypothesized that light traveled through a medium that was at rest with respect to everything.

Holes in the ether theory soon appeared, however. Most important, no one seemed able to detect the stuff. One carefully executed experiment, conducted in 1887, is known as the Michelson-Morley experiment. It was designed to measure the speed of Earth's movement through the ether—which should make a kind of "wind" across the land. The experiment attempted to measure the change in speed of the light when it was going with or against this ether wind, but no change was detected.

While the experiment failed to find the ether, this was just the first nail in the theory's coffin. Most scientists simply saw this as proof that the theory was flawed, not that the ether didn't exist. In time, Hendrik Lorentz created a new version of the ether theory to take the Michelson-Morley experiment results into consideration.

Einstein grew up and received his physics education at a time when the existence of the ether was just beginning to be questioned. At the age of sixteen, Einstein wrote what might be called his first paper—a study of how a magnetic field generated by a current affects the ether. He mailed the paper to his uncle describing it as "rather naive and imperfect, as might be expected from such a young fellow like myself." Yet, Einstein was, in fact, tackling one of the greatest physics problems of his day: how electromagnetism interacted with the ether. More important, it shows early signs of Einstein's interest in electromagnetism, matter, and energy—work that would eventually culminate in his groundbreaking relativity paper of 1905.

By 1905, Einstein had dismissed the notion of ether completely. He often claimed to have never heard of the Michelson-Morley experiment, though early letters of his show that he had read papers that referred to it, so this is probably not strictly true. Regardless, it is clear that, whether by picking it up from other scientists of the time or simply through his own mulishness, Einstein firmly believed there was no ether. This assumption is a crucial one for the development of his new theory of light. By eliminating the ether and postulating that light always travels at the same speed and that there is no absolute frame of rest anywhere in the universe, Einstein developed an entirely new theory of light: the special theory of relativity.

While many scientists quickly accepted relativity, this did not translate to immediate death of a search for the ether. There were still a few who kept trying. In 1921, when Einstein was on tour in the United States, a scientist named Dayton Clarence Miller (1866–

1941) built on the Michelson-Morley experiment and announced he had finally found the ether. Upon hearing the news, Einstein didn't bat an eyelash, dismissed this as an impossibility, and offered up one of his more well-known quotes: "Subtle is the Lord, but malicious He is not." Einstein later wrote in a letter to his friend Michele Besso that he did not for a moment take Miller's results seriously. As it was, subsequent trials of Miller's experiment did not confirm the existence of the ether.

Ether Reborn

Einstein didn't completely abandon the use of the term "ether," however. While he never again thought of ether as a medium necessary for light waves, he did use the word sometimes when discussing general relativity. In 1920, he gave a talk at the University of Leiden called "Ether and the Theory of Relativity," in which he reiterated that the ether Maxwell had discussed was dead, but that one had to accept there were physical properties of space itself, which in themselves constitute a kind of ether. He said, "To deny the ether is ultimately to assume that empty space has no physical qualities whatever. The fundamental facts of mechanics do not harmonize with this view." He went on to describe that space itself has a gravitational field associated with it and that while this was nothing like the ether required for the "mechanical undulatory theory of light" it was nevertheless an assertion that space itself was not a characterless void, but had describable attributes. He concluded his speech saying, "We may say that according to the general theory of relativity space is endowed with physical qualities; in this sense, therefore, there exists an ether."

As Maxwell had pointed out years before, it is clearly easy to modify the mysterious term "ether" to match whatever scientific theory makes sense. Einstein took a word that in his day conjured up images of "whatever is mysteriously filling up space" and used it to describe something—the gravitational nature of the universe—that was markedly different from what it had been used to describe twenty years earlier.

Today, however, the word ether is never associated with relativity by modern physicists. What Einstein was describing is now called the "gravitational field." Ether, on the other hand, is solely thought of as the substance dismissed by the Michelson-Morley experiment, and it is regularly referred to as one of the great mistaken, but for a time universally accepted, theories of science's history.

FBI

Like many of those with outspoken liberal views during the Cold War, Einstein was investigated by the FBI for Soviet espionage. Under the authority of J. Edgar Hoover, the FBI read Einstein's mail, taped his conversations, and interviewed his colleagues, but ultimately weren't able to make the case that he was a spy.

The FBI file on Einstein was first released to the world in 1983, when an English professor named Richard Schwartz obtained a copy through the Freedom of Information Act. The 1,427-page file seen by Schwartz (and available to anyone viewing the FBI Web site) is censored in many places. However, the files were brought to even more public attention when the journalist Fred Jerome sued the government for a more complete version, which he details in his comprehensive book *The Einstein File: J. Edgar Hoover's Secret War Against the World's Most Famous Scientist.* The file is nearly 2,000 pages long and makes for fascinating reading, varying from the reasonable (a collection of newspaper clippings describing Einstein's political views) to the schizophrenic (letters to the FBI from informants who claimed Einstein was developing death rays and sentient robots).

The file on Einstein was started when he was preparing to teach at the California Institute of Technology and began the process of getting an American work visa. Upon hearing the news, a group called the Woman Patriot Corporation wrote a letter, dated November 19, 1932, to the State Department requesting that Einstein not be granted access to the United States since he was, besides being a vocal pacifist and anarchist, "affiliated with Communist groups that advocate the overthrow by force or violence of the government of the United States." The letter is reasonably well written, including a legal brief citing the points of law by which the United States could deny an alien the right to immigration, and that Einstein was just such a suspicious alien who belonged, claimed the letter, to more Communist organizations than Stalin. The allegations were serious enough that Einstein was interrogated while in Germany before being granted his visa. Infuriated, Einstein immediately spoke to the media, and an Associated Press article described the event: "Professor Einstein's patience broke. His usual genial face stern and his normally melodious voice strident, he cried: 'What's this, an inquisition? Is this an attempt at chicanery? I don't propose to answer such silly questions. I didn't ask to go to America. Your countrymen invited me; yes, begged me. If I am to enter your country as a suspect, I don't want to go at all. If you don't want to give me a visa, please say so. Then I'll know where I stand.'"

Under the scrutiny of media attention, and perhaps the knowledge that as Einstein told a reporter "the whole world would laugh at America" if they didn't let him in, Einstein had a visa by noon the next day. But the women's letter was sent on to the FBI, and a file on the scientist was begun.

The file grew during World War II, when Einstein's skill as a physicist made him one of numerous scientists considered to work on the Manhattan Project to build an atomic bomb. The FBI pulled together a short biography for army intelligence that described Einstein's connections to organizations that, while not being Communist per se, were close enough to the left side of the political spectrum for Einstein to be denied security clearance to be sent to Los Alamos.

It was not until after the end of the war that Einstein's FBI file began to swell. Despite what seems to have been some disappointment at not being allowed to aid the U.S. war effort, Einstein was always glad he had not helped build the atomic bomb, and he spoke out early and often against the arms race between the United States and the USSR. Announcements such as the one he made in 1950 on a TV talk show hosted by Eleanor Roosevelt in which he decried the recent announcement by President Truman that the country was fast on its way to building a hydrogen bomb, were just the kind of thing to catch the eye of fiercely nationalistic J. Edgar Hoover. The FBI began to focus on Einstein in earnest, dogging his footsteps the last four years of his life, trying to prove that he and his secretary, Helen Dukas, were a Soviet spy team.

Hoover and his colleagues knew that Einstein's celebrity gave him a certain degree of immunity. While many well-known people were falsely accused of treason during the 1950s, the backlash would have been too large if the FBI attacked Einstein without concrete proof. The agents must have felt as if their hands were somewhat tied, because they couldn't interview anyone close to Einstein for fear of tipping him off that he was under investigation. As such the information collected in Einstein's FBI file is downright laughable at times, as no tip was considered too outrageous or too small. Any letter that made its way to the bureau seems to have been included, and so we hear tell of accusations that the scientist had his hand in all sorts of diabolical plots inspired by 1950s science fiction. Scribbled notes from agents in the file do show, however, that the FBI did not deem that the various death rays and fighting automatons the evil genius Einstein was said to be building were particularly plausible.

But the agents doggedly followed other leads—leads which with the clarity of hindsight were just as unbelievable. A particularly dramatic description of Einstein's life in Berlin describes the "Communist center" of his office there, in which two secretaries helped him translate coded messages from a Soviet espionage ring in the Far East, in order to send them on to the Kremlin. This myth persisted for a number of years until Hoover finally authorized someone to interview Dukas directly—under the pretense of asking her about others suspected of Communism—to find that she had been his one and only secretary for decades. Later, neighbors of Einstein's from Germany confirmed that he had not, in fact, even had an office.

Another "outstanding lead" was Einstein's mysterious, long-lost son Eduard, whom the FBI believed would hold the key to information regarding his father's deeds. The mentally unstable Eduard was at that point living out his days in a Swiss sanitarium.

Additional parts of the file spark interest as well. When, in 1934, a sheriff from Ventura, California, wrote to ask if Einstein was indeed a Communist and he should warn the parents of his town to not let their children "idolize him," Hoover wrote back disingenuously that "there is not federal legislation in effect at the present time under which so-called radical or Communistic activities are subject to investigation on the part of this Division, and the files of this Division, therefore, contain no information relative to the activities of Dr. Einstein . . . in connection with the Communist Party."

A January 1949 scrawled postcard sent to the bureau says: "If it is within FBI jurisdiction would it not be a good idea to keep a protective watch on Mr. Albert Einstein who is now in a Brooklyn, NYC, hospital, until he is on his feet? Their [sic] are certainly individuals who think they would benefit from his physical weakness." There is also a record of Einstein turning to the Polish Ambassador at a 1948 dinner party to say, "I suppose you must realize by now that the U.S. is no longer a free country, that undoubtedly our conversation is being recorded. The room is wired, and my house is closely watched." Since, the conversation made it into the files, one can only assume that Einstein was correct.

Ultimately, despite false rumors that Einstein was in league with the Russian spy at Los Alamos Klaus Fuchs (they never actually met) or concerns that he was rallying in favor of convicted spies Ethel and Julius Rosenberg, the FBI was never able to make a case that Einstein or Dukas was a spy. Toward the end of Einstein's life, the ferocious anti-Communist attacks of the 1940s and 1950s began to lose their popularity. Einstein's "un-American" activities ceased to arouse much interest for the Bureau even before the scientist's death. Einstein died on April 18, 1955, and four days later J. Edgar Hoover closed the file.

See **Communism; McCarthyism.**

Freud, Sigmund

As two of the leading minds of the last century, Freud and Einstein are often grouped together as the yin and yang of mental achievement. Einstein's theories created the modern age of physics; Freud's theories created the modern age of psychology. They collaborated only once— writing a treatise supporting a view of international politics that favored peace over war.

Albert Einstein and Sigmund Freud met face-to-face in pre-war Berlin. Freud was there to visit his family for Christmas in 1926, and Einstein and his wife, Elsa, visited the famed psychoanalyst. In a letter to a friend, Freud described their meeting as a pleasant chat, though he did add, "[Einstein] understands as much of psychology as I do of physics."

The two remained in cordial, if distant contact for many years. Einstein's openness to Freud's theories of the meaning of the subconscious and dreams is a bit remarkable in light of the fact that Einstein had a great fear of mental illness and he was emphatically disinterested in psychoanalysis, once saying: "I should like very much to remain in the darkness of not having been analyzed." But like Einstein, Freud questioned everything, even his own thoughts, which pleased Einstein. In addition, they had a connection in that both were known for being Jews who openly questioned religious notions.

The two had a passing acquaintance until 1932. That year, the League of Nations asked Einstein to choose someone with whom to reflect on a pressing problem or question. At the time, militarism in Germany was on the rise, and thus as his question Einstein chose, "Is there any way of delivering humankind from the menace of war?" For his discussion partner, Einstein chose Freud.

Freud was well known for his theory that there was absolute good and evil—having published very pessimistic views on the propensity of community psychology to err toward the latter. But Freud's seventeen-page response to Einstein's one-sentence query was surprisingly optimistic. Freud put forward the idea that mankind was split between a drive for life and a lust for death. He wrote that, at times, our aggression could push us toward war, but the drive for love would push it away. Einstein responded that laws could offset the human drive toward violence, and he strongly supported an international body that would undercut nationalism and settle conflicts.

The dialogue between the two grew into the book *Why War?*. The League of Nations' International Institute of Intellectual Cooperation published it simultaneously in English, French, and German in 1932. And yet, the hope of the book, to encourage peace throughout the world, was not to be. Only one year later, Hitler gained further power in Germany and copies of this discussion, along with all other works by Freud and Einstein, were publicly burned by the Nazis in Berlin.

In addition to their direct collaboration, Freud and Einstein are linked in the collective consciousness, since they were both profound and quirky thinkers at a pivotal time in world history, as well as both being famous European Jews who escaped the Nazis.

See **Pacifism.**

Friedmann, Alexander
1888–1925

The Russian meteorologist Alexander Friedmann was one of the first scientists to apply Einstein's relativity equations to a model of the universe. Friedmann created a model that showed an expanding universe—a model that has since turned out to be correct. But Einstein rejected Friedmann's model, claiming the math must be wrong.

Alexander Friedmann witnessed the early seeds of revolution in cosmology while living in a time of revolution in Russia. He was born in St. Petersburg on June 16, 1888, and died in the same city at the young age of thirty-seven, but by then, his hometown was called Leningrad. Friedman was trained to study the weather, and in later years, he occasionally joked that bad mathematicians become physicists, and bad physicists become meteorologists—but Friedmann was never a bad physicist and always kept his hand in modern science, teaching mathematics and physics at what was briefly called Petrograd University (St. Petersburg having been renamed Petrograd) and the Petrograd Polytechnic Institute. Always keeping a watchful eye on new developments in physics, Friedmann also taught himself general relativity by reading Einstein's papers, even though other Russian scientists mostly ignored the topic.

Using general relativity, Friedmann proposed a new model of the universe. Believing in the perfect beauty and simplicity of Einstein's math, Friedmann refused to adjust the relativity equations, as Einstein himself did, to incorporate an arbitrary "cosmological constant" used to hold the universe at a stable size. Instead, Friedmann's universe had an even distribution of matter—imagine something equally dense everywhere like a body of water. This universe could change size either by expanding, or possibly expanding and then contracting before expanding again repeatedly over time. A universe that is expanding implies a universe that used to be smaller. Take this to its logical conclusion, suggested Friedmann, and the universe must have begun as a tiny speck, growing ever larger through the millennia. The idea that the entire universe began at a single point—and moment in time—eventually grew into the modern Big Bang theory, and Friedmann was one of the first to conceive of it.

Of course, Friedmann didn't believe the universe existed in a state of even density—it's not a lake or an ocean with matter distributed evenly throughout. So he knew his model was a simplistic one for the universe, and not even the only one that corresponded to Einstein's relativity equations. (For example, another physicist named Willem de Sitter (1872–1934) created an equally unrealistic model around the same time that described a universe devoid of all matter.) To what degree Friedmann truly embraced the idea that the universe was born at some specific time in history is unclear—but he did know that his model was mathematically and scientifically interesting, one more tool to help interpret our world. Friedmann published his model of the universe in 1922 in a paper called "On the Curvature of Space" in *Zeitschrift für Physik* (The journal of physics).

Einstein responded within months, writing a single paragraph in the same journal, stating that Friedmann's work was "suspicious" and that this model did not, in fact, jibe with his relativity equations. Friedmann wrote a polite letter to Einstein showing the mathematical foundation for his paper, but it was only after a colleague nudged

Einstein to give the letter thorough attention that Einstein realized Friedmann's math was, in fact, impeccable. It was Einstein who had made a mistake. Einstein was man enough to publish a statement that he'd been wrong as far as the underlying math went—but nevertheless he still rejected the validity of Friedmann's model on more ephemeral grounds. Einstein simply wasn't comfortable with the idea of a universe that changed over time. And he wasn't alone; most contemporary scientists felt just as strongly that our universe was eternal, that it could only have been static and could only have existed for eons in exactly the same shape and size that it exists today.

It was 1929, when Edwin Hubble (1889–1953) showed the universe to indeed be expanding, that Einstein accepted the possibility that Friedmann's model, and other ones like it, were reasonable interpretations of relativity. It was not until after Einstein died that the Big Bang theory itself became fully accepted. Friedmann died in 1925, most likely of typhoid fever, and he didn't live to see his theories appreciated.

See **Cosmology; Cosmological Constant; de Sitter, Willhelm; Lemaître, Georges.**

Germany

Throughout Einstein's life his home country oscillated between being proud that Einstein was German and rejecting him outright as a Jewish fraud. Einstein himself was torn between pride in his German heritage and disgust at the country's militaristic ideology. In the end, after the atrocities of the Holocaust came to light, Einstein wrote his friend Arnold Sommerfeld on December 14, 1946: "After the Germans massacred my Jewish brothers in Europe, I will have nothing further to do with Germans."

Einstein was born in Germany in the small village of Ulm, along the Danube River. He recalled later a great love of the German folk tales his father told him when he was a child. Einstein seemed to live quite happily in Germany. The family moved from Ulm to Munich, where he spent his grade school years. But as he entered high school, Einstein began to rail against his teachers' methods and, when the family moved to Italy for business and left Einstein behind to finish his senior year, Einstein quit school and joined his startled parents.

The move made Einstein a voluntary exile because he escaped German military service. According to German law, if a boy left the country before the age of seventeen, he was absolved from the military without being categorized as a deserter. The move would have repercussions throughout Einstein's life, as he would later lose, regain, and renounce his German citizenship before his lifetime was over. He finished secondary schooling and university in Switzerland and was therefore released from German citizenship. For a number of years he was stateless, but eventually became a Swiss citizen in 1901. Ensconced in Switzerland, away from academic life, Einstein wrote the five physics papers that would secure his place in history, gaining the notice of officials at the new Kaiser Wilhelm Institutes in Berlin. Established in 1910 by the Kaiser Wilhelm Society, the ambitious institutes sought to become the pillar of scientific study throughout all of Europe—and they did become such for a brief time before the rise of Nazi political power. (After the horrors of World War II, the institutes were reborn in 1948 as the Max Planck Society.)

In 1911, the German chemist Fritz Haber (1868–1934) became the director of the Kaiser Wilhelm Institute for Physical Chemistry and Electrochemistry in Berlin. He decided he wanted the famous young physicist to be the feather in the cap of the new institute, so in the summer of 1913 he sent Walther Nernst (1864–1941) and Max Planck (1858–1947) to Zurich to lure Einstein. Part of their offer was a professorship without any teaching obligations at the maximum salary allowed—12,000 deutsche marks—as well as election into the elite Prussian Academy of Sciences. At thirty-two years old, Einstein would become its youngest member.

In addition to the juicy job offer, Einstein had his own reasons for wanting to move back to Germany. He was two years into an intense affair with Elsa Einstein, his cousin who lived in Berlin. In a letter to her at the time, Einstein wrote, "One of the main things that I want to do is to see you often."

Life in Berlin

The Kaiser Institute was located in Dahlem, a suburb of Berlin. In the spring of 1914, Einstein, his wife, Mileva, and their two young sons moved into an apartment in a large comfortable house that Mileva had chosen the previous winter. But within weeks of his family's arrival, Einstein refused to live in the same building with them. Mileva, twelve-year-old Hans, and four-year-old Eduard soon left Einstein and returned to Zurich.

The same year, World War I began, and Einstein took part in his first political act, in response to an earlier document signed by German political and intellectual leaders, referred to as "The Manifesto of the 93 German Intellectuals." The manifesto denied German atrocities and asserted the country's innocence in causing the war. Einstein was shaken that so many of his colleagues signed the paper. He believed World War I to be insanity, and so he responded by signing the "Manifesto to Europeans," an antiwar political plea launched by a Berlin physician. The second Manifesto, however, was never published in wartime Germany.

Despite the trials of World War I, Einstein focused on his work, and developed what would become one of his grandest achievements: the general theory of relativity. Einstein had shaken the foundations of physics with his 1905 papers. Now, with the publication of the general theory, finalized in 1916, he began to set the stones of modern physics. In October 1917, the Kaiser Institutes created an Institute of Theoretical Physics. It was a time of fantastic activity in the field. More and more physicists began to accept Einstein's theories of relativity and his stature in the scientific world continued to grow.

And yet, even in the halls of science, politics interfered. One of Einstein's colleagues, Philipp Lenard (1862–1947), also a German professor, lobbied extensively against Einstein in the scientific and popular press. Lenard's accusations not only attacked Einstein's science, they were also anti-Semitic. Lenard's diatribes against the failings of "Jewish science" mirrored the attitude of everyday Germans who wanted someone to blame for the failing German economy. In addition, Einstein's opposition to World War I and German policies worried the authorities enough that by January 1918 the head of the Berlin police was ordered to consult with the military before giving certain pacifists, including Einstein, permission to travel abroad.

Despite this, Einstein continued a lecture tour to scientific conferences and universities. But as Einstein's capital in the scientific world rose, the German deutsche mark spiraled downward. At the time, Einstein was supporting two families—his soon-to-be second wife and her two daughters, and his first wife and family, now living in Switzerland. Einstein's salary from the Prussian Academy of Sciences was essentially worthless, so Einstein returned to the skills he acquired at the Swiss Patent Office nearly ten years before and became a consultant on patents for many large industrial companies in Germany, even at times appearing in court on infringement cases.

Throughout it all, Germany's reaction to their homegrown scientist was mixed. Einstein's fame was heralded with pride by many Germans, but his adamant denunciation of their national pride and unbridled military also made him a target. In February 1920 Einstein's university lecture was disrupted by his students, and the press described the interruption as having anti-Semitic undertones. In August of that year, newspapers screamed with banner headlines about public meetings to denounce Einstein's theories.

Germany Claims the Prize

In 1921, Einstein was awarded the Nobel Prize while he was on a lecture tour of Japan. The custom in such instances was that a representative from the scientist's home country would make the acceptance. Just what this meant for Einstein, however, was unclear. He traveled under a Swiss passport, but he had regained German citizenship the moment he'd been inducted into the Prussian Academy of Sciences. After bureaucratic wrangling, the German ambassador accepted the Nobel Prize on behalf of Einstein, happily claiming the Jewish scientist as a pinnacle in German achievement. For at least a while, the German government cheered Einstein's triumphs and heralded him as a great emissary.

Hitler Rises; Einstein Flees

But the uglier side of Germany, which had been brewing for years, was beginning to boil over. As German politics leaned ever more toward fascism, Einstein spent more time on pacifist causes. He also traveled extensively, speaking out not only about physics, but also in support of disarming nations; on the evils of the military; and on his fears for his homeland. But militant thought in Germany seemed irreversible; in 1930 the National Socialist party, the Nazis, made a stunning advance, increasing their number of seats in the Reichstag from 12 to 107.

Beginning that year, Einstein began to spend a significant amount of time at the California Institute of Technology in Pasadena. And between 1930 and 1932, safely in

[The Germans] have always had the tendency to treat psychopaths like knights. But they have never been able to accomplish it so successfully as at the present time.

—Einstein's notes, July 28, 1939

the United States, Einstein made his most radical pacifist statements. During these trips, Einstein also decided he would no longer be able to stay in Germany and quietly began to make preparations to leave.

When Hitler came to power on January 30, 1933, Einstein was on a trip to Pasadena. He instantly spoke out vehemently against the Nazis. (Ironically, the purpose of Einstein's trip had originally been to strengthen U.S.-German relations.) With the scientist away, the Nazis raided Einstein's summer cottage in Caputh, Germany, on the pretext of searching for weapons hidden there by the Communist Party. The only remotely dangerous thing the Nazis found, however, was a bread knife. Nevertheless, the Nazis confiscated Einstein's sailboat. Einstein criticized the raid in the newspapers, calling it "one example of the arbitrary acts of violence now taking place throughout Germany."

Einstein never returned to the home of his birth, going instead to Belgium as the last of his preparations to leave Europe were completed. Immediately upon arriving in Antwerp, Einstein went to the German legation and publicly renounced his citizenship, as well as his member-ship in Germany's two scientific societies, the Prussian Academy of Sciences and the Bavarian Academy. Nonetheless, on March 23, 1933, the German government called on the Prussian Academy to start for-mal disciplinary proceedings against Einstein—they expelled him from the academy. Later that year, one of Germany's most famous citizens moved to the United States. In Germany, Einstein's books were burned, his property confiscated, and his bank accounts frozen; luckily, for the previous three years Einstein had been depositing his foreign earnings in banks in the Netherlands and in New York.

Gadfly from Afar

Although he was now ensconced in his new Princeton home, Einstein retained his concern for the people of Germany, and his anger over the Nazi government increased. After decades of being an ardent pacifist, he had to change his mind in light of what he saw happening in Germany; there were indeed situations so extreme they demanded fighting back. As a world-famous Jew, Einstein was called on time and again to plead the case in the United States for those left behind. And personally, Einstein worked to move many Jewish scientists and others out of the country, helping to get young students into Princeton.

Even after the war was over, Einstein's anger raged. As reconstruc-tion began in Germany, some wanted Einstein to lend his support to policies that would better the lives of everyday Germans. Einstein brusquely responded, "The Germans butchered millions of civilians according to a well prepared plan, in order to move into their place. If they had butchered you too, this would not have happened without some crocodile tears. They would do it again if only they were able to." Einstein felt that "not a trace of a sense of guilt or remorse is to be found among the Germans."

Einstein's resentment extended to German scientists who stayed behind as well. To Otto Hahn's request that Einstein become a foreign member of the new German scientific organization, the Max Planck Society, Einstein responded with a crushing statement in a letter dated January 28, 1949: "The crimes of the Germans are really the most hideous that the history of the so-called civilized nations has to show. The attitude of the German intellectuals—viewed as a class—was no better than that of the mob. There is not even remorse or an honest desire to make good whatever, after the gigantic murdering, is left to make good."

Einstein did not even want the Germans to read his work. When his old publishing house, Vieweg, wished to republish his slim, lay-audience book on the special and general theory of relativity, they were informed by Einstein, in a March 25, 1947, letter, "After the mass murder committed by the Germans against my Jewish brethren I do not wish any publications of mine to appear in Germany."

See **Anti-semitism; Hitler, Adolf; Nazism; Switzerland; United States.**

God

Einstein's concept of God is hard to pin down due to conflicting testaments, especially his own, on the subject. He mentioned often that he did not believe in a "personal God" and yet cited "God" in numerous essays and letters, showing a belief in some concept of the divine.

In 1927 a banker in Colorado wrote Einstein, asking if he believed in God. Einstein replied, "I cannot conceive of a personal God who would directly influence the actions of individuals, or would directly sit in judgment on creatures of his own creation." On numerous other occasions Einstein said he didn't believe in the existence of a traditional Judaeo-Christian God. An all-knowing father figure was unequivocally not part of Einstein's world view.

One of the reasons Einstein cited for his denial of this embodiment of God was his complete and total belief in a world that followed causal laws. Einstein's scientific view of the universe insisted it was a place where one occurrence always led to a predictable outcome. Current events naturally led to future events, cause and effect always held true. Such a place had no need for an omnipotent presence to intervene. It also left no room for a soul—bodies, thought Einstein, were complete in and of themselves and worked according to the laws of science. There was no need to invoke some additional ghost into the machine.

This last idea is one that Einstein shared with his favorite philosopher, Baruch Spinoza (1632–1677). Einstein's views were strongly influenced by this Dutch Jew, and in 1929 he famously announced he believed in Spinoza's God. A Jewish newspaper reported a telegram exchange between the physicist and Rabbi Herbert Goldstein. The rabbi sent "Do you believe in God? Stop. Prepaid reply fifty words." Rising to the challenge, Einstein wrote back: "I believe in Spinoza's God who reveals himself in the orderly harmony of what exists, not in a God who concerns himself with fates and actions of human beings."

It was the awe-inspiring "order" of the universe, then, in which Einstein recognized the divine. In *Einstein and Religion* by Max Jammer, however, the author draws a distinction between how Einstein perceived God, and how Spinoza did. Both believed that knowledge of Nature was the only way to experience God, but for Spinoza this was due to pantheism—that is, because Nature itself was God. For Einstein, appreciating the underlying order and beauty of Nature was how one appreciated the divine, something that was greater than the mere sum of Nature's parts. A review of Einstein's writings does seem to indicate that while he didn't hold a conventional vision of God, he was not merely a pantheist, and definitely not an atheist. For one thing, he used the term "God" too often.

When Einstein was arguing against quantum mechanics' rejection of causality, he said, "God doesn't play dice with the world." When he didn't believe the results of an experiment that—wrongly as it turned out—showed the existence of the ether Einstein had long since disproven, he said, "God is subtle, but He is not malicious." Einstein exclaimed upon hearing the violinist Yehudi Menuhin play, "Now I know there is a God in heaven!" And perhaps most eloquent of all:

"I want to know how God created the world. I am not interested in this or that phenomenon, in the spectrum of this or that element. I want to know His thoughts, the rest are details."

It has been argued that Einstein used the word as merely a figure of speech—the word God represented the complete and total sum of laws about how the universe worked. But his consistent use of the term belies this. Einstein was a product of his times, and one could certainly argue that it might have been too outrageous for him to jettison the idea of God completely so he used a euphemism—but this doesn't jibe with what we know of Einstein's personality. He was never afraid to buck tradition, and he was only too happy to announce that he wasn't religious. He was careful with his word choice, and by referring to God he seems to have meant something slightly more mysterious than simply the totality of science.

> *Einstein was prone to talk about God so often that I was led to suspect he was a closet theologian.*
>
> —Friedrich Dürrenmatt in *Albert Einstein: Ein Vortrag* (Albert Einstein: A lecture)

In 1929, Einstein sent a letter to the author of a newly released book, *There Is No God,* saying he wasn't sure whether or not one should contest others' belief in a personal God. "I myself would never engage in such a task," Einstein wrote. "For such a belief seems to me preferable to the lack of any transcendental outlook of life, and I wonder whether one can ever successfully render to the majority of mankind a more sublime means in order to satisfy its metaphysical needs." In other words, Einstein thought that belief in the divine so important to humans he would rather they believe in even a personal god than be an atheist, with no "transcendental outlook." It is hard to get any more definitive than that. Einstein may have had a complex understanding of the term, but he did believe in God.

See **Judaism; Religion.**

Gravitation

While Isaac Newton first fleshed out our concepts of what gravity is— that two bodies attract each other and that gravity keeps the planets spinning about Earth—it was Einstein who created our modern under-

standing. With general relativity, he provided a new way to understand why two bodies fall toward each other.

One of the catalysts for Einstein's special theory of relativity was his belief that the laws of physics should be the same for everyone regardless of whether the observer was moving or standing still—certain aspects of Newton's mechanics and the current understanding of light didn't allow for that. With his theory, Einstein solved the problem when it came to two people who were traveling at constant speeds with respect to each other. But what if one person was accelerating? How could one reconcile the very different ways that those two people would perceive light and gravity—and time and space—around them?

Einstein was famous for his thought experiments—self-imposed brain-ticklers that would stretch his mind to form new ideas. One such experiment turned out to be the catalyst he needed as he tinkered with this idea of accelerating reference frames. He wondered what it would feel like if one were in a free-fall—for example, down a particularly long elevator shaft. If there was no outside sensory perception, you couldn't see, hear, or feel; then, reasoned Einstein, you wouldn't realize you were falling at all. You wouldn't feel gravity. (This is of course, the same feeling of weightlessness that astronauts have while circling Earth in the space shuttle. In actuality, the space shuttle is in constant free-fall, being pulled toward Earth by its gravity, but without the visual sense of hurtling toward the ground, there is no feeling of falling at all.)

If a person accelerating due to gravity could not feel gravity, and if, as Einstein believed, the same laws of physics should hold true no matter what reference frame you are in, then Einstein realized that the concept of gravity as a force was fictitious. If one didn't feel gravity when one was accelerating, then it also couldn't exist when one was still. And so with that, Einstein set about creating an all new theory of how gravitation works.

Instead of this mysterious action at a distance where two bodies were inexplicably attracted to each other—the lack of an explanation for this attraction bothered Newton as well as every scientist after him—Einstein offered a new reason for gravitation. Mass itself warped the space around it, as firmly and as definitely as a bowling ball sitting on a water bed. Objects nearby slipped down toward the mass, in the way marbles on the water bed would fall toward the bowling ball. To an outside observer, especially if the water bed were somehow clear, and one couldn't see its changed shape, this would look just as if the bowling ball had pulled the marbles in, as if it was sending out some mysterious gravity. Space itself curved unseen like this, said Einstein, thus causing gravitation in the universe.

See **Newton, Isaac; Reference Frames; Relativity, General Theory of.**

Gravitational Waves

In 1916, within months of publishing the final version of his general theory of relativity, Albert Einstein postulated that the theory implied moving masses like giant stars caused ripples in the very fabric of space. These ripples are called gravitational waves, and, as an ocean wave travels through water, or a sound wave travels through air, gravitational waves travel through space-time, causing measurable distortions in the universe.

One of the consequences of general relativity, discovered Einstein, is that gravitational fields are akin to electromagnetic fields. Light waves are made of oscillating electromagnetic fields, so Einstein realized that gravitational fields too should cause waves that move at the speed of light. But the effect they would have on the universe would be so small that Einstein assumed they'd never be detected. Indeed, they were such a fidgety feature of relativity that most scientists relegated them to a corner for hypotheticals that might or might not ever be studied. Some thought these waves were merely mathematical artifacts that would one day be shown to not exist at all—Sir Arthur Eddington, the man who first proved the general theory of relativity by studying the way light bent around a solar eclipse, was highly skeptical, saying: "Gravitational waves propagate at the speed of thought."

Some forty years later, in the 1960s, gravitational waves were accepted and believed to exist in a physical, actual way. It was shown that if a large object like a planet or a star emitted gravitational waves, it would simultaneously lose mass in a way that should be detectable. In 1974, astronomers observed a binary star system in which two gigantic neutron stars orbited each other. One of the stars was slowing down at the rate of 75 microseconds a year, which corresponded to how much it should slow down if it was losing mass due to gravitational waves. The first evidence of a true gravitational wave had been found.

It will be much harder to detect gravitational waves directly on Earth, since they lose strength as they travel, just as sound and water waves do. And they change the very nature of space-time as they move, causing space itself to lengthen and contract, making these waves a fairly difficult thing to measure. In 2002, scientists completed the first large-scale experiment to measure if space on Earth ever lengthens or contracts. Called the Laser Interferometry Gravitational Observatory (LIGO), it is an intricate setup of lasers and mirrors over two miles long that can measure the most minute change in length. (There are actually two such setups—one in Louisiana and one in Washington state.) If a gravitational wave rolls by, it will change the distance between the farthest ends of LIGO by a mere one-hundred-millionth the diameter of a hydrogen atom. That is, if the entire LIGO experiment were as long as the distance between Earth and the nearest star system, the change in length due to a gravitational wave would be the width of a human hair. So far, LIGO hasn't detected such a wave, but it is sensitive enough to handle the task if the wave comes from reasonably nearby. The strongest waves LIGO could hope to detect would be from an exploding supernova in our own galaxy, but that's a rare event—the last one occurred in 1604.

Wherever a gravitational wave comes from, if LIGO ever senses one rolling through space-time, it will be another important experimental proof of Einstein's general relativity.

Grossmann, Marcel
(1878–1936)

Marcel Grossmann was Einstein's college classmate and lifelong friend, despite their personality differences. At school Grossmann was as steady and respectful as Einstein was unpredictable and rebellious. An accomplished scientist in his own right, Grossmann worked with Einstein on Einstein's theories of gravitation—publishing together in 1913.

The main collaboration between Einstein and Marcel Grossmann is known as the Einstein-Grossmann paper, a forerunner to Einstein's general theory of relativity, published in 1913. Grossmann's contribution was in calculus and other mathematical details to support Einstein's arguments—he was the first of a long line of collaborators who had a better grasp of mathematics than Einstein did. The paper has not gone down in history as a great breakthrough. While it is an important step along the way toward the final theory, the Einstein-Grossmann paper is dotted with sloppy reasoning.

But this was just one example in a lifetime of Grossmann's aid to Einstein. Grossmann let Einstein use his notes so extensively throughout their college days that Einstein dedicated his doctoral thesis to him. Upon graduation, Einstein floundered, casting about for teaching positions and even asking Grossmann for advice on whether he should obscure his Jewish looks when seeking a high school teaching position.

In the end, Grossmann bailed out his friend—convincing his father to recommend Einstein to Friedrich Haller, the director of the Swiss Patent Office. After a year of floundering, this helped Einstein finally land his first job. Only a year went by before Grossmann joined his friend at the patent office, but after a brief stint there, Grossmann was hired as a professor at the ETH. In the meantime, Einstein took a series of jobs that didn't quite suit him, culminating with an ill-fated move to teach in Prague. Einstein hated the city, so when Grossmann offered him a professorship at the ETH where Grossmann was now dean of physics, Einstein jumped at the chance. But Einstein's wandering for the perfect position continued, and, despite Grossmann, he stayed there only a year before moving on to another job in Berlin.

Einstein's move didn't greatly affect their friendship or their collaboration. Their theories were published in 1913, and Grossmann continued to be Einstein's sounding board for many of his scientific ideas. It is also through the two men's letters that we know so much of what Einstein was working on at any given time, for Einstein often wrote his friend updates discussing, for example, kinetic gas theory or the movements of matter relative to the ether or the concept of a universal molecular force—and that was all just in letters sent in 1901.

Sadly, however, their friendship was cut short. Grossmann became ill with multiple sclerosis in the 1920s. The man who was Einstein's rock—beginning in college when Einstein would skip his mandatory math classes to attend more interesting ones and yet pass due to Grossmann's help, to Grossmann's looking after Einstein's son Eduard when he was first hospitalized for schizophrenia—died in 1936.

Einstein wrote Grossmann's wife his condolences: "I remember our student days. He, the irreproachable student, I myself, unorderly and a dreamer. He, on good terms with the teachers and understanding everything, I a pariah, discontent and little loved. But we were good friends and our conversations over iced coffee in the Metropole every few weeks are among my happiest memories."

Despite his friend's early death, Einstein cherished him until the end of his life. In 1955, just before he passed away, Einstein wrote an autobiographical sketch—something he was loath to do—but wrote in the dedication that "the need to express at least once in my life my gratitude to Marcel Grossmann gave me the courage to write this."

Hair

Einstein the icon could not have been possible without his wild mane of gray hair. Thanks to that unruly hair coupled with his astounding scientific theories, and his lasting worldwide fame—our modern image of "scientist" is one of an absentminded genius, too intelligent to be concerned with our petty world—and too busy to be concerned with something so mundane as a hairbrush.

Historians have attributed Einstein's wild hair simply to rebellion: he disdained the rigorous formalities expected of a German professor. But Einstein had kinky hair and perhaps it was just hard to groom. Throughout his life, Einstein struggled with his hair, at times even complaining that he inherited his hair and his temper, both difficult to control, from his mother, Pauline. But as he grew older, he clearly relished his unconventional appearance, commenting often on how children would describe him as a lion.

In his later years in Princeton, Einstein happily joined in with mocking his hair. He took part in a skit by the Princeton Triangle Club, in which the scene was the interior of a barber shop with the barbers lined up grooming customers in chairs. There was a big glass window at the back of the stage, and the whole of Einstein's perform-ance was to walk by the window. According to Denis Brian in the biography *Einstein: A Life*, the silent gag brought down the house.

But Einstein didn't always par-ticipate. In 1934, Einstein's wild shock of hair earned him a letter from an inventor who announced the development of a "remarkable

Dear Mr. Einstein, I am a little girl of six. I saw your picture in the paper. I think you ought to have your hair cut, so you can look better. Cordially yours, Ann.
—Letter to Einstein, 1951

hair restorer." "It is guaranteed to cure baldness, dandruff and itchy scalp. As you are known the world over to possess a truly wonderful head of hair, I am going to name my product 'Albert Einstein Hair Restorer,' and also, I plan to print your picture on the label of the bottle. I am quite sure you will not refuse this honor, so would you please write me an endorsement? If you desire, I will mail you a complimentary bottle." Einstein may have been willing to laugh at his appearance, but while he was alive he never used his image to endorse a product, so he refused the "honor."

See **Clothes.**

Heisenberg, Werner Karl
(1901–1976)

The German physicist Werner Heisenberg was one of the early contributors to quantum mechanics, helping to devise its equations and contributing to the commonly accepted understanding of them, known as the Copenhagen interpretation. Einstein was one of Heisenberg's early heroes, and the two scientists came together numerous times to discuss the implications of quantum theory, but they often didn't see eye to eye, disagreeing on everything from science to politics.

Werner Heisenberg first discovered Einstein's work while in college at the University of Munich when he took a course on relativity with Arnold Sommerfeld (1868–1951). Heisenberg reveled in Einstein's insistence that we should only theorize about that which we perceive—all of relativity stemmed from the insistence that while different people observe different occurrences, all of those observations are valid. This concept lodged itself in Heisenberg's brain, and would become one of the fundamental beliefs that shaped all of his subsequent science.

Heisenberg wanted to write his thesis on the subject of relativity, but he was dissuaded by his classmate, Wolfgang Pauli (1900–1958), who would grow up to win the Nobel Prize for his work in quantum mechanics. At the time Pauli was writing what was to become the first great essay on relativity theory, but it was a field of science he believed to have been already fairly well established. The real future, Pauli told Heisenberg, was in atomic physics.

Heisenberg nonetheless continued to be intrigued by Einstein. In the summer of 1922, the young German set off for Leipzig for a lecture by his hero. It would have been the first time Heisenberg encountered the man whom he so respected, but it was not destined to happen. The timing of the lecture coincided with the beginning of Germany's anti-Semitic attacks against Einstein—upon arriving, Heisenberg had thrust upon him a leaflet, which, wrote Heisenberg later in his book *The Part and the Whole*, denounced Einstein as "alien to the German spirit, and blown up by the Jewish press." Heisenberg, a Christian, had been part of Germany's national youth movement for most of his life, but he was entirely surprised and upset by this nationalistic attack on an entire scientific field. As it was, Einstein had sensed the political climate and decided to lie low for awhile; he bowed out from giving the lecture, and the speaker was Max von Laue (1879–1960) instead.

Heisenberg and Einstein did finally meet in 1924, during a visit Einstein made to the University of Göttingen. At that point, the theory of quantum mechanics was just being developed, and Einstein didn't like the way those theories were going: as scientists tried to offer new explanations for how atoms gave off radiation they developed theories that only offered probabilistic answers. Their theories could predict a range of possibilities for how an atom would act, but again and again, scientists were forced to believe there was no definite outcome for any given occurrence. When it came to particles, claimed these physicists, there simply wasn't a perfect correlation between cause and effect. Heisenberg was caught up in the excitement of creating this new field of science. Einstein, on the other hand, couldn't believe the madcap direction physics was taking. So the meeting between Heisenberg and Einstein was an interesting one—the youth encountered his hero, only to discover they had very opposite ideas. It was the start of the growing separation between Einstein and most of his contemporaries, but Heisenberg still hoped to convince his elder of the correctness of the new science.

It was in September 1925 that Heisenberg made his first stunning contribution to physics. He published a paper that formulated the math to create the probabilistic predictions others were studying. This was essentially the first version of quantum mechanics. Heisenberg's math is called "matrix algebra," and it accomplished the same thing as the kind of math another physicist, Erwin Schroedinger (1887–1961), developed a year later. There was a bitter rivalry between the two men over which type of math should be used. Today both types of math do get used, but most scientists prefer the simpler Schroedinger's wave mechanics.

Later in life, Heisenberg would say that he developed his theories while relying heavily on what he saw as Einstein's philosophy of only analyzing observables. But Heisenberg's matrix paper did nothing to entice Einstein over to the other side. Almost immediately, Einstein shot off a letter to Heisenberg raising numerous objections, and Heisenberg responded in November with counterarguments. In this letter it seems that Heisenberg still believed their two viewpoints could someday be reconciled.

A Negative View of Positivism

The gulf between the two men was wider than Heisenberg believed. In April 1926, the two physicists met face-to-face for the second time after Einstein attended a lecture Heisenberg delivered at the University of Berlin. Heisenberg later told the story of how when Einstein offered an objection to Heisenberg's matrix algebra, Heisenberg tried to use Einstein's philosophies against him—pointing out that he had done just what Einstein did with relativity, using only what one could directly perceive to formulate his theories. After all, this philosophy, known as positivism, had always been dear to Heisenberg's heart. Einstein, however, was taken aback, saying, "But you don't seriously believe that only observable magnitudes must go into a physical theory?" Startled, Heisenberg said: "I thought that it was exactly you who had made this thought the foundation of your relativity theory." Einstein replied, "Perhaps I used this sort of philosophy; but it is nevertheless nonsense. Only the theory decides what one can observe."

Einstein's views had clearly changed from twenty years earlier. He now believed that one had to use more than just observations to come up with a valid theory. When it came to developing the emerging field of quantum mechanics, Heisenberg had to face the fact that the man he saw as a pioneer of modern physics did not support him.

In 1927, Heisenberg developed the theory for which he is most famous, the Uncertainty Principle. Building on the inherent fuzziness of the behavior of particles, Heisenberg postulated that certain atomic properties could never be known with certainty. If, for example, one knew the exact position of an atom, one could not also know its exact speed. At first, Heisenberg explained this by saying one simply couldn't measure the position without disturbing the speed; to measure position was to change its speed, and vice versa. One could never know both qualities at the same time. But shortly thereafter, Heisenberg and most of the physics community accepted a deeper truth about the Uncertainty Principle: it wasn't that one couldn't measure both qualities simultaneously, but that both qualities simply could not be precise at the same time. If the atom had a definite speed it must be smeared out in space, without a definite position. If it had a definite position, then it could not have a definite speed. Einstein, as was to be expected, disliked Heisenberg's new theory as much as he'd disliked the previous ones.

This is not to say there was disrespect between the two scientists. Einstein quickly realized how accurately quantum mechanics, including Heisenberg's math, predicted the inner workings of atoms. He thought there was a great deal of value in the new science—he was merely convinced the theories weren't complete. Indeed, Einstein nominated Heisenberg for the Nobel Prize in 1928, 1931, and 1932; in the 1931 nomination, he wrote of quantum physics: "This theory contains without doubt a piece of the ultimate truth." Heisenberg won the Nobel in 1932.

World War II and the Atomic Bomb

Einstein and Heisenberg were also linked for reasons other than science. They both experienced Nazi persecution, and both were forced to make difficult decisions during World War II. In the mid-1930s, all modern physics became taboo in Germany, mocked as a "Jewish science." To practice it was to court ostracization, and Heisenberg found that as a founder of quantum mechanics he was barred from jobs at various German universities. He was also labeled a "white Jew"— though he was Christian—and he was paired with Einstein in attacks from the German media and anti-Semitic German physicists like Philipp Lenard and Johannes Stark. A Nazi newspaper wrote in July 1937: "Heisenberg is only one example of many others. . . . They are all representatives of Judaism in German spiritual life who must all be eliminated just as the Jews themselves." Although Heisenberg rejected Nazi philosophies, he was devoted to his homeland, and despite the persecution and numerous invitations from American scientists to come to the United States, he made the decision to stay in Germany.

While relativity was publicly disparaged by the Nazis, no one questioned the validity of Einstein's $E = mc^2$—the equation that would make it possible to build a nuclear bomb. In 1939, Einstein was living in the United States, and knowing how destructive such a bomb could be, he wrote a letter to President Franklin Roosevelt warning him of the danger. Heisenberg, however, was still in Germany, and as a physicist with usable skills he suddenly found himself in favor with the Nazi administration, and was asked to work on building a bomb. As it happens, Heisenberg spent most of the war working on nuclear reactors for energy, not weapons. Later in life, Heisenberg claimed this was due to his own manipulations: he had done his part for peace by obfuscation—downplaying to the Nazis the practicality of building an atom bomb and leading them astray by telling them it probably couldn't be done. Heisenberg says he told his superiors that he believed the war would be long over before anyone could manage to build a bomb. Since there is no outside collaboration on this, we have only Heisenberg's version of the story. There are historians who take Heisenberg at his word, though most simply believe Heisenberg just made a mistake. His strength was in theoretical physics and not experimentation—perhaps Heisenberg truly believed that building an atom bomb was next to impossible. Regardless of his motivations at the time, it's clear that after the war, Heisenberg worked to limit the use of nuclear weapons and to repair relations between Germany and the rest of the world.

The last time Heisenberg and Einstein met was in 1954 in Princeton, but their scientific differences were the same as they ever were. Heisenberg tried one last time to sway Einstein with testaments to the correctness of quantum theory, but Einstein swept it all away by saying, "I don't like your kind of physics. I think you are all right with the experiments . . . but I don't like it." Einstein died in 1955, never reconciled to the quantum mechanics that Heisenberg embraced.

After Einstein died, Heisenberg wrote an article in which he attacked Einstein for his letter to Roosevelt, saying that a pacifist should never have initiated the effort to build a weapon that would ultimately result in the death of thousands. But blaming Einstein for somehow beginning the entire Manhattan Project seems grossly unjust, as well as untrue. Heisenberg's article probably was more inspired by the issues he had with Einstein, suggesting there may have been more problems between the two than Heisenberg otherwise admitted.

See **Quantum Mechanics; Uncertainty Principle.**

Hidden Variables

Einstein proposed the existence of hidden variables to explain what he—almost alone amongst his contemporaries—perceived to be problematic features of quantum mechanics. Quantum mechanics insists that there is an inherent randomness to the universe; Einstein, on the other hand, thought this "randomness" would be explained away the moment we better understood what was going on.

Most scientists agree on a description of quantum mechanics known as the Copenhagen interpretation, which says that at a very fundamental level, atoms act randomly. Quantum mechanics can be used to predict the chances that an atom might be in this place or that one, at this speed or that speed, at this energy level or that one, but it can't predict any of these qualities exactly. Einstein was an important pioneer in the development of quantum mechanics and he knew that it predicted these chances with incredible accuracy, but other scientists believed the accuracy of quantum mechanics meant reality itself was random. Einstein, on the other hand, believed reality operated with definite laws of cause and effect, actions that could be predicted—if you had all the information possible—precisely and perfectly. To his death, Einstein insisted that we simply didn't understand nature well enough, there must be additional factors, some hidden variables at work that we didn't yet understand. (Einstein's biographer, Abraham Pais, points out that Einstein does not ever seem to have used the term "hidden variable" per se, but the concept was certainly his.)

As an example of hidden variables, imagine rolling a six-sided die. We perceive this to be a random process, one in which we can come up with probabilities—a six should come up approximately one-sixth of the time—but we can't predict the roll each individual time. If, however, one delves a little further, one realizes that the roll of the die is only "random" because there are so many variables at work. If one knew the exact spin your hand put on the die, the force with which you threw it, the strength of the bounce on the table, the air pressure of the room, and a whole host of other factors, one would be able to predict exactly which number would come up.

It was variables like this that Einstein believed might rule our world; we just had yet to identify them. "God," Einstein liked to say, "does not play dice." A divine or superhuman being that could know all aspects of what was going on would be able to determine exactly which side of the die would come up every time, or exactly how a particle was going to move. Nothing random about it.

The concept of hidden variables has become closely linked over time to a thought experiment called the Einstein-Podolsky-Rosen argument, in which the three authors attempted to disprove quantum mechanics by showing that one could, in fact, measure definite qualities of a particle. Later, the mathematician John Bell revisited the EPR thought experiment. Careful mathematical analysis showed that if one could do the EPR experiment in actuality, one would get different results if there were or were not hidden variables. In the 1980s scientists carried out the EPR experiment in real time and determined that, according to Bell's work, there truly aren't any hidden variables.

But the story does not end there. Even more recent theoretical work in 2001 the by physicists Karl Hess and Walter Philipp of the University of Illinois at Urbana-Champaign shows that not all hidden variables are ruled out by Bell's theories. A pair of hidden variables that change over time, and are related to each other, could slip into an EPR experiment undetected—so the existence of hidden variables has not yet been ruled out completely.

Nonetheless, most modern physicists are comfortable with the idea that Einstein refused to accept: particles truly do act in a random manner, and even if one had total and complete knowledge of all the facets of a particle, one couldn't predict exactly where it was going or how it would move. Einstein's hidden variables do not seem to exist.

See **Einstein-Podolsky-Rosen Argument; Quantum Mechanics.**

Hilbert, David
(1862–1914)

David Hilbert is one of the all-time great mathematicians whose work had an impact on numerous fields, from abstract algebra to number theory to quantum mechanics to general relativity. For decades, Hilbert was associated with Einstein because the two men apparently arrived at the equations for general relativity within days of each other. The near-synchronicity of the two men's work has made for, at best, great tales of the "race" for the general relativity equations and, at worst, questions of whether Einstein saw a version of Hilbert's paper ahead

*of time and borrowed from it. Recent research however, has exoner-
ated Einstein completely, and turned the tables so that Hilbert is now
the suspect of possible plagiarism.*

Hilbert and Einstein met for the first time in the summer of 1915
when Einstein gave a series of six lectures at Göttingen, where Hilbert
was a professor. Einstein stayed with the Hilbert family, and the two
men discussed Einstein's struggles with the theory of gravity. Einstein
had published several papers since 1911 in an attempt to broaden his
special theory of relativity to incorporate gravity as well, and while he
hadn't presented a complete theory yet, these papers were the precursors to what would become the general theory of relativity. After several days in Einstein's company, Hilbert was eager to put his math
skills to use on these new ideas of gravitation. (At that time, the
physics community in Göttingen was heavily theoretically and mathematically minded when it came to modern physics, and Einstein later
noted that they did more to advance the math of relativity than his
own colleagues at the University of Berlin. Einstein may have had
mixed emotions about this, which perhaps came into play in his later
dealings with Hilbert.)

Over the next few months Einstein entered a feverish phase of
work. He realized he had been on the wrong track and he had now hit
upon the correct way to formulate his gravitation theory. During this
time he dropped all correspondence with anyone—except Hilbert. It
is clear from these letters that the two shared information about their
work: Einstein announced when he had discovered his earlier proofs
had been wrong; Hilbert shared that he was working on connecting
gravity and light theory.

But somewhere during this exchange, Einstein began to worry that
Hilbert was overly involved. In November, Hilbert offered Einstein his
latest set of equations, and Einstein—who had just, as it happened,
finally come up with the general relativity equations—wrote back
immediately, clearly trying to establish priority: "The system you furnish agrees—as far as I can see—exactly with what I found in the last
few weeks and have presented to the Academy." A few days later he
wrote another postcard to Hilbert stating again that he had developed
his equations independently: "Today I am presenting to the Academy
a paper in which I derive quantitatively out of general relativity, without any guiding hypothesis, the perihelion motion of Mercury discovered by LeVerrier. No gravitation theory has achieved this until now."

Einstein here was not only stating his priority, but—as casually as possible—pointing out the incredible achievement that he was quite definitely claiming as his own. (He didn't mention that he'd worked on the perihelion problem for several years previously, and so the achievement was not in fact one he'd just dashed off in several days.) Hilbert could do nothing but write a congratulatory note.

Nevertheless it's clear that Einstein still worried about Hilbert. As soon as Einstein published his paper on November 25, he wrote to his friend Arnold Sommerfeld: "The theory is beautiful beyond comparison. However, only one colleague has really understood it, and he is seeking to 'partake' in it . . . in a clever way. In my personal experience I have hardly come to know the wretchedness of mankind better than as a result of this theory and everything connected to it."

While Einstein's preoccupation with the issue of priority goes far to suggest Einstein did indeed develop the general relativity equations by himself, it also implies that Hilbert, too, found them on his own. Consequently, the conventional story of the discovery of relativity has always included this extra twist—the close call Einstein had, where but for the grace of several days, Hilbert might well have published first. Some historians have taken the question of the race for relativity even further. Einstein's general relativity paper was published on November 25, 1915, while Hilbert's paper—printed in March of the next year—showed a submission date of November 20. It has been suggested that Einstein saw Hilbert's proof before he published his own work, and could easily have made use of Hilbert's work in his paper.

In 1997, however, all questions about who came up with what first were put to rest. John Stachel of Boston University published a paper in *Science* citing new evidence from archives of Einstein's and Hilbert's papers. For one thing, the submission date on Hilbert's paper turns out to be incorrect—it wasn't submitted to the publishers until December 6, 1915, two weeks after Einstein's paper was published. More important, neither Hilbert's original submission nor, it turns out, the proofs Hilbert had earlier sent Einstein prompting such worry over his priority, included the correct general relativity equations. Einstein seems to have overreacted to Hilbert's work, and perhaps even misunderstood the mathematician's equations, seeing it through the filter of his own struggles. It is clear that Einstein took nothing in his general relativity paper from Hilbert.

Indeed, it appears instead as if Hilbert altered his paper to accommodate Einstein's newly published equations. Hilbert's paper, it should be noted, also did not attempt to do what Einstein's had done—namely develop a new theory of gravity. Instead Hilbert was trying to tie together both gravity and previous research on the electromagnetic spectrum. His paper was given the ambitious title of "The Foundation of Physics," so it made sense that it should be edited to include the latest word on gravity; he seems to have edited his original submission, incorporating Einstein's new gravitation work for the published version of the paper. This is understandable; the only issue is the backdating of the submission date of the paper, which led everyone to believe Hilbert developed those equations on his own. Whether that backdating was a mistake or a conscious act will probably never be known. And, regardless of how much he contributed to general relativity, it remains clear that Hilbert was a brilliant mathematician in his own right as he demonstrated in numerous other fields. (Indeed, an integral mathematical tool for quantum mechanics is called "Hilbert space.")

Despite the brief contention between Hilbert and Einstein, this episode did not lead to long-term animosity. On December 20, 1915, Einstein wrote a letter to Hilbert saying, "There has been a certain ill feeling between us, the cause of which I do not wish to analyze. I have struggled against the feeling of bitterness attached to it, and this with complete success. I think of you again with unmixed congeniality and ask that you try to do the same with me. Objectively it is a shame when two real fellows who have managed to extricate themselves somewhat from this shabby world do not give one another pleasure." While it's not known what Hilbert wrote back, the two men remained cordial ever after.

Hitler, Adolf

Einstein was an outspoken opponent of Adolf Hitler, and although they never met, it was one of the most frequent questions asked of Einstein. His stock answer to the question was, "No, but I have seen his photographs and they are sufficient."

Like many of his fellow Germans, Einstein was at first dismissive of Hitler's power. In 1931, at the end of his second visit to the United States, Einstein was asked his opinion of the young politician. Einstein said, "I do not enjoy Mr. Hitler's acquaintance. Hitler is living on the empty stomach of Germany. As soon as economic conditions in Germany improve he will cease to be important."

But the Nazi Party had won a significant number of political seats in the 1930 election, and Hitler's influence wasn't going to abate any time soon. Einstein had done his part to combat this; although he was traveling extensively, Einstein took time to campaign in those elections. But it was for naught— the Nazis went from 12 seats in the Reichstag to 107. With the Nazi regime gaining more and more power, the now-famous Einstein began to speak out against Hitler and broadcast his pacifist beliefs.

> *Without some intelligence, not even a dictator flanked by bayonets can maintain his rule indefinitely. Hitler and his minions lack even that minimum degree of intellectual ability required by a dictatorship under modern conditions.*
>
> —Einstein, September 9, 1933

Einstein also began to make preparations to leave his homeland, and luckily was out of the country when on January 30 Germany's president buckled under right-wing pressure and appointed Hitler as the country's chancellor in 1933. In March of that year, the German government approved an "empowering law," essentially installing Hitler's dictatorship. Once Hitler was installed, Einstein never visited his homeland again.

See **Germany; Nazism; Pacifism.**

Inventions

Unlike many other theoretical physicists, Einstein relished dealing with creating applications for his science. Over the years he worked on everything from voltage measuring tools to hearing aids.

In 1906, Einstein published a paper on how to study Brownian Motion under a fluctuating electric voltage. He began to build a *Maschinchen*, a "little machine" to test his ideas. At the time, the best available meters for electricity could only detect a few thousandths of a volt, but Einstein needed to observe less than one-thousandth of a volt.

Einstein's friend and member of his Olympic Academy, Conrad Habicht (1876–1958) had a brother, Paul (1884–1948), who had started a small instrument-making business. Working with Paul, Einstein built the machine. Writing his friend Max von Laue (1879–1960),

Einstein said, "You wouldn't be able to resist smiling . . . if you could see my home-botched glory." Einstein didn't patent the invention; he tried, but was unsuccessful since no manufacturers were interested in producing it.

However the two Habicht brothers went on to tinker with the machine and after a few years managed to obtain a patent and manufacture it. Unfortunately, it wasn't very accurate and eventually was obsolete. While Einstein wasn't on the patent, the brothers thanked him with a notation that the experiments were done "jointly with A. Einstein at the Zurich University laboratory." Many years later, when Paul died, Einstein wrote his brother a letter of condolence, "That was fun, even though nothing useful came of it."

Nothing came of Einstein's attempts to develop a new aircraft wing either. In the summer of 1915 Einstein published a short paper, "Elementary Theory of Waves in Water and of Flying," and he proposed a hunchbacked wing profile. But no one followed up on the work.

Next Einstein tried developing a new compass. This was much more successful and ultimately was used by the German Navy. The building of the compass had its beginnings when a wealthy young man named Hermann Anchütz-Kaempfe wanted to explore the North Pole by submarine. This was tricky because a submarine couldn't surface to get its bearings, and the metal hull was havoc on a magnetic compass. So Anchütz developed a rapidly rotating top that could be an alternative. Einstein was the independent expert appointed by the district court to investigate Anchütz's patent claim on his "gyroscope." The patent was accepted, and the two men stayed in touch.

After World War I, the pair collaborated intensively on the development of a fundamentally improved version of the gyroscope device and patented it. By 1930, virtually every navy in the world had a gyrocompass. Einstein had a contract to receive 3 percent of the sales and 3 percent of the revenue from licenses. Ironically, for a device that was used by the German Navy, Einstein deposited the money he received into a bank in Amsterdam, and used the money to help Jewish colleagues escape the Nazis.

In 1927, Einstein tried out another invention. He and his colleague Leo Szilard (1889–1964), designed a refrigerator pump that wasn't mechanical but electromagnetic. Liquid metal in a tube moved back and forth when affected by an alternating electromagnetic field. The pump was elegant and, unlike other pumps, completely silent. The two men patented their device, and followed up with seven more over the next two years. But the refrigerator fizzled because conventional models improved, so there was no need for one that used potentially toxic metals. Many years later the nuclear reactor industry had a brief flirtation with the pumps, but it didn't develop into heavy use.

Other Einstein inventions included an automatic exposure camera developed in 1936 with his friend Gustav Bucky. In addition, Einstein became the coauthor of experimental papers dealing with a hearing aid, and the permeability of membranes for colloids.

Israel

Einstein championed the Zionist cause for a Jewish state as early as 1911. When Israel was finally established, he called it "the fulfillment of our dreams."

Einstein first considered the advantages of a Jewish state during his brief time in Prague, where he fell in with a host of intellectual Jews, including Franz Kafka. As a group, they convinced Einstein that a Palestinian nation was a necessary safety net for the Jewish people in the face of continued anti-Semitism. The seeds of Einstein's support for Israel began to take root.

By 1921, Einstein had fully embraced the cause. His first trip to the United States was on a fundraising mission for the creation of the Hebrew University in Jerusalem. At the time, most universities had limits on how many Jewish students they would admit, and Einstein wanted a respected university that would be open to all. With Einstein's backing, the funding for the Hebrew University flowed, and in 1923 Einstein delivered the inaugural address at the new school. Despite his deep love of the Jewish people, Einstein wasn't particularly religious, and fretted over the lecture—for it had to be in Hebrew.

During his visit, many tried to convince Einstein to settle in Israel, but Einstein was still welcomed, if not warmly, in his native Germany. This changed over the next decade, and when Einstein finally left Berlin it was to move to the United States, not Palestine, leading many to question Einstein's commitment to Zionism and to the Hebrew University.

Chaim Weizmann, the Zionist with whom Einstein had made his very first trip to United States, felt betrayed that Einstein did not take a job at the university in Palestine. Earlier Einstein had a falling out with some administrators at the university, but Weizmann promised to, and did, make changes. And yet Einstein refused to move to the nascent state. One of the reasons Einstein gave for not accepting Weizmann's offer was the Jews' treatment of the Arab people.

In April 1938, Einstein said his mixed emotions at the creation of a Jewish state were grounded in his dislike of any sort of extreme nationalism. While he saw value in a safe haven for Jews, he didn't want it to fall into a militaristic stance, defining itself as a country apart from its neighbors. During a speech given in 1938, titled "Our Debt to Zionism," Einstein said, "Apart from practical considerations, my awareness of the essential nature of Judaism resists the idea of a Jewish state with borders, an army and a measure of temporal power no matter how modest."

However, when the State of Israel was founded in May 1948, Einstein was among the many who cheered. It is not possible to understate Einstein's despair at the treatment of his fellow Jews at the hands of the Nazis, and he absolutely supported a place where Jews could have full civil rights. Einstein released a statement, calling Israel the "fulfillment of an ancient dream . . . to provide conditions in which the spiritual and cultural life of a Hebrew society could find free expression."

The foundation of the State of Israel, however, did little to stem the violence between Jewish settlers and Arab Palestinians. And as always, Einstein was not shy in his criticism of what he saw as strong-arm nationalistic solutions. When Menachem Begin visited the United States in the winter of 1948, Einstein joined others in signing an open letter printed in the *New York Times* on December 4 that compared the tactics used by Begin's Irgun Zvai Leumi party as resembling those of the Nazis.

But it is clear that his criticism stemmed from his strong commitment to seeing Israel evolve into a peaceful nation. And Israel was committed to Einstein, too. The country offered him the presidency in 1952 when President Chaim Weizmann died. (Though it is reported that those in charge also hesitated: What on earth would they do if he actually accepted?) Einstein heard of the offer from a phone call by the *New York Times*, and was officially informed by a telegram. Einstein's secretary, Helen Dukas, reported that Einstein was distraught over how to decline the offer, pacing the floors of his little Princeton home muttering, "This is very awkward, very awkward." He did not want to embarrass the country but he was going to refuse. He called the Israeli

If I were to be president [of Israel], sometimes I would have to say to the Israeli people things they would not like to hear.

—Einstein to his stepdaughter, Margot

ambassador in the United States and told him he couldn't possibly take the position saying, "I am deeply moved by the offer from the State of Israel, and at once saddened and ashamed that I cannot accept it. All my life I have dealt with objective matters, hence I lack both the natural aptitude and the experience to deal properly with people and to exercise official functions."

Japan

Einstein has always been a wildly popular figure in Japan. When he toured the country in the 1920s he spoke to packed houses—and even today a professor at Japan's Kinki University holds one of the largest collections of Einstein memorabilia in the world.

Einstein first visited Japan in November 1922, when he and his wife, Elsa, began a lecture tour of the Orient sponsored by the Japanese magazine *Kaizo*. It was a grand time for such a tour: Einstein's name had in the previous few years become world-famous, and many wanted to hear what he had to say. The six-month trip also coincided with political unrest and the rise of anti-Semitism in Germany; it was a good time for Einstein to leave Europe behind for a while. He was forewarned that he would likely receive the Nobel Prize in physics that year, but given the developments back home, Einstein decided to continue with the trip even though he would have to miss the Stockholm ceremony.

Despite the unrest in Europe, Einstein was warmly welcomed in the Far East, and the admiration was mutual. Einstein heard he'd won the world's top prize in physics while on a steamliner on his way to Japan, but he seemed to have no regrets about continuing his voyage. In a letter to his friend and colleague Niels Bohr (1885–1962), Einstein wrote, "The trip is splendid. I am charmed by Japan and the Japanese and am sure that you would be too."

In all, Einstein and Elsa visited Singapore, Hong Kong, Shanghai, and Japan, but the Japanese were the most enamored of the wild-haired physicist: not only was he the most famous scientist of his day, but the Japanese characters for "relativity principle" are similar to those of "love" and "sex"—adding to his allure.

One condition of his tour was to write a popular article about his impressions of the trip for *Kaizo*. In his writings, Einstein lauded the Japanese traditions of family ties. And while he applauded their ability to admire the intellectual achievements of the West, Einstein cautioned that the Japanese "must not forget to preserve those great values, superior to those in the West, namely the artistic shaping of life, simplicity and unpretentiousness in personal needs and the purity and calm of the Japanese soul."

Morikatsu Inagaki was Einstein's host and translator for much of the trip, and the two men were of a like mind politically. Inagaki was a member of the Japanese executive committee for the peace treaty after World War I. The pair kept in communication throughout their lives and in 1954, long after World War II had ended, Inagaki invited Einstein to return to Japan to attend the Congress of the World Federalists in Hiroshima. Einstein was forced to decline the invitation due to his poor health, but as an intense pacifist he commented, "it is reassuring that the Japanese find themselves in the favorable situation of having lost the war; success, particularly in this field, is a very poor teacher."

Einstein had a hand in Japan's losing that war. He had encouraged the president of the United States to develop an atomic bomb, and it was his famed equation, $E = mc^2$, that made the idea of such a devastating weapon possible. In 1952, a Japanese magazine editor asked Einstein about his role. Einstein reiterated his belief that the advancement of science could never be right or wrong, but it was up to humans to decide whether to use science for good or evil. However, Einstein never publicly condemned America's use of the bomb against Japan.

Today in Japan, Einstein's name doesn't seem to be overly connected with Hiroshima and Nagasaki. Indeed, Japan has somewhat of a cultish fascination with Einstein's image. In 1944 a copy of his paper on the special theory of relativity handwritten by the scientist himself was auctioned off in Japan for $6 million, and one of the most complete collections of Einstein memorabilia in the world is owned by a math professor named Kenji Sugimoto.

Jokes about Einstein

No one in the public eye can avoid being mocked. Einstein is one of the most famous people of all time, and so jokes and humorous anecdotes at his expense abound.

A favorite joke is about how Einstein's driver used to sit at the back of the hall during Einstein's lectures. One day he said he'd probably be able to give the lecture himself. Einstein took him up on the idea: they switched clothes, and the driver gave a flawless lecture with Einstein watching from the back of the room. At the end, an audience member asked a detailed question about the subject and the lecturer said, "'Pshaw, the answer to that question is so simple, I bet that even my driver, sitting up at the back could answer it."

Along with poking fun at the scientist himself, many jokes attempted to explain his theories. In 1924, a Caltech professor wrote a parody of Lewis Carroll's "The Walrus and the Carpenter" titled "The Einstein and the Eddington." It was read at a faculty club dinner honoring Sir Arthur Eddington and had verses such as, "The time has come, said Eddington, To talk of many things; Of cubes and clocks and meter-sticks. And why a pendulum swings, And how far space is out of plumb, And whether time has wings."

In another, less esoteric, rendition of Einstein's science the British anthropologist Ashley Montagu once told Einstein a joke he'd just heard of a Jewish tailor trying to explain to another tailor who Einstein was: "He's the guy who invented relativity! You don't know what relativity is? Schlemeil! This is relativity. Supposing an old lady sits in your lap for a minute, a minute seems like an hour. But if a beautiful girl sits in your lap for an hour, an hour seems like a minute." And the other tailor was quiet for a moment and then said incredulously: "What? From this he makes a living?" Einstein laughed and said it was one of the best explanations of relativity he'd ever heard.

Some of the best jokes about Einstein are by Einstein himself. He clearly had a good time poking fun at himself, his science, and his public image, once saying, "The contrast between the popular estimate of my powers and achievements and the reality is simply grotesque." Einstein was quick to paint a humorous picture of himself: he once dismissed his ability to mull over a scientific problem until finding an answer as not a sign of smarts but instead, "All I have is the stubbornness of a mule. No. That's not quite all. I also have a nose."

What he also had was a quick wit. During a lecture he once said that the best advice for success was summed up in the formula: $A = X + Y + Z$. A is success, X work, and Y play. "But what is Z?" piped up someone in the audience. "Z is keeping your mouth shut," was Einstein's retort.

And one last Einstein joke to finish off:

Question: Why did the chicken cross the road?
Einstein's answer: It didn't. The road moved underneath it.

Judaism

Born to assimilated Jewish parents, Einstein grew up in a family that didn't practice Jewish traditions: he never learned Hebrew, he never had a bar mitzvah, and he certainly didn't attend synagogue. He remained irreligious all his life, but as he got older he regained a sense of Jewish identity. As Nazi anti-Semitism in his native Germany grew, Einstein found himself supporting the heritage he'd discarded.

In his *Autobiographical Notes*, Einstein described religious lessons he received as a child of eleven and twelve, given to him by a relative. For the first time in his life, he learned about the Jewish faith and he embraced it to an extreme. He wanted to keep kosher, and he studied the Bible with a fervor that must have distressed his nonpracticing parents. This soon changed, when young Einstein discovered his first science book. He was instantly taken with this alternate way of interpreting the world, and science quickly replaced religion as his foremost interest. Science offered a way of interpreting nature that made sense to him, and he dismissed the Bible tales he'd learned as mere fabricated stories. His period of observant Judaism ended as quickly as it had begun—and was never to be revived.

Einstein soon began to think of himself as being of no religion whatsoever, and he even wrote that he was *konfessionslos*, "without religion," on his passport when he obtained Swiss citizenship in 1901. But to be so described was not acceptable to most European nations at the time. When Einstein took a job for a year at the University of Prague in what was then the Austro-Hungarian empire, he was required to define himself; without a religious affiliation he could not be a professor. He wrote himself down as a Jew, and in 1911 he wrote to his friend Hendrik Zangger that "dressed in a most picturesque uniform, I took the solemn oath of office in front of the viceroy of Bohemia yesterday, putting to use my Jewish 'faith,' which I put on again for this purpose. It was a comical scene."

While Einstein may have thought that his claim to Judaism was a mere formality, the natives of Prague placed him in a fairly rigid box. Jews were to spend time with Jews; Christians kept to themselves. Finding himself amidst a community of observant Jews, the "without religion" Einstein—who was married to a gentile—had a hard time finding company. This lack of close friends certainly was one factor that led to his leaving the post within two years.

But Einstein had learned an important lesson: he discovered that his Jewish heritage would define him in European eyes no matter how he perceived himself. In response, Einstein embraced his Judaism proudly, defining himself as a Jew once more, and speaking out on Jewish issues. In 1914, Einstein was invited to speak in Russia, but he rejected the offer stating that he would not travel in a country where his fellow Jews "were so brutally persecuted."

Einstein lived in Berlin from 1914 to 1933, employed as a professor at the Kaiser Wilhelm Institute. During that time what had been a thoroughly pervasive but still background anti-Semitism swelled into a vehement national hatred against the Jews. Like so many, Einstein experienced personal attacks due to his religion, which only served to make him all the more proud of his birthright. Einstein said later in life that being defined by non-Jews did more to make him a Jew than the Jewish community did.

He began to campaign for Zionist causes much to the chagrin of many of his assimilated Jewish friends who worried that his outspokenness would backfire on the community. German Jews were aware that anti-Semitic rhetoric was on the rise, but they hoped that like other such flare-ups in European history this would die back down. Their optimism was, of course, dramatically misguided, as Hitler ultimately ordered the deaths of some six million Jews in his attempt to exterminate the entire race. Einstein was lucky; he had the luxury of being a Swiss citizen with a Swiss passport, which allowed him to travel extensively, and he was able to immigrate to the United States when Hitler rose to power. Others were not so fortunate, and Einstein worked to help Jews move to the United States.

It was, in fact, in the United States where Einstein seemed to finally find a good fit with his own Jewish background, working with a number of various Jewish organizations. He clearly enjoyed the company of American Jews, finding them quite different than people in Europe. In an article titled "About Zionism," published in 1930, Einstein said, "It was in America that I first discovered the Jewish people. I have seen any number of Jews, but the Jewish people I had never met either in Berlin or elsewhere in Germany. This Jewish people, found in America, came from Russia, Poland, and Eastern Europe genetically. These men and women still retain a healthy national feeling; it has not yet been destroyed by the process of atomization and dispersion."

Despite his increased connection to Judaism, Einstein did not become observant. After his youth, he never stepped foot inside a synagogue, and on his deathbed Einstein asked to be cremated, which is forbidden under Jewish law. Clearly, the scientist associated himself with the people but did not choose to embrace the religious faith associated with Judaism. On the other hand, his connection to Judaism was genuine. He always said that had he been born in rural Eastern Europe he most assuredly would have been a rabbi—the intellectual striving and problem solving of the Jewish traditions would have satisfied him just as physics did.

See **Anti-Semitism; God; Israel; Religion.**

Kaluza-Klein Theory

Kaluza-Klein theory was the first unified field theory. It attempted to connect Maxwell's electromagnetism theory with Einstein's theories of relativity by assuming that the universe is made up of five dimensions: one of time and four of space.

In 1919 an unknown Russian mathematician, Theodor Kaluza (1885–1954), mailed a paper to Einstein in which he built on the concept of space-time by adding another dimension. Space-time within Einstein's general relativity has four dimensions: the three dimensions of space and another of time. While it's hard for humans to envision the world around us as if it is really four-dimensional, it's perfectly easy for a mathematician to make this assumption. Einstein's theory of general relativity could easily be adapted to more dimensions, and suddenly—thanks to Kaluza—it appeared as if relativity and electromagnetism could be part of an overarching theory that works in five dimensions.

When Einstein received Kaluza's paper, he responded, "The idea of achieving [a unified theory] by means of a five-dimensional cylinder world never dawned on me. . . . At first glance I like your idea enormously." In 1921, Kaluza published the paper, and in 1926 the mathematician Oskar Klein (1894–1977) used the new quantum theories to offer an explanation for just why we couldn't experience that fifth dimension. Klein said that the extra dimension was just 10^{-33} centimeters long. That's more than a trillion trillion times smaller than the width of an atom—so small that in real life, we never experience it. It's as if you stood on an extremely short platform; if the platform were taller it would be a perfect cube, but as it is, it's just micrometers off the floor. For all intents and purposes it's as if you were standing on a two-dimensional square, not a three-dimensional raised platform. Just as the three-dimensional object has a height so small that you experience it as two-dimensional, so in our day-to-day world that fifth dimension is unnoticeable.

Unifying light and gravity was one of Einstein's main goals throughout the second half of his life, and while the Kaluza-Klein theory didn't completely succeed—partially because many scientists thought adding a fifth dimension amounted to so much hocus-pocus—it was an important first step in trying to do so. Using this theory as a jumping-off point, Einstein published several papers between 1927 and 1932 that used five dimensions. But soon, Kaluza-Klein theory dropped by the wayside. A new theory had caught the imagination of most young physicists: quantum mechanics. This new science explained electromagnetism so well that the Kaluza-Klein theory seemed superfluous—Einstein himself was one of the few who continued to seek a unified theory.

But adding extra dimensions was a technique that was destined to last. While no one resurrected Kaluza-Klein theory for sixty years, it has made its way back into modern science with the advent of M-theory (also known as superstring theory)—this idea took those original five dimensions and added six more. This modern version of Kaluza-Klein theory attempts to unite not just gravitation and electromagnetism, but the atomic strong and weak forces as well. It's a well-studied theory that seems logically consistent—but as of yet is untested.

See **Unified Theory.**

League of Nations

Einstein cheered the foundation of the League of Nations, which rose out of the ashes of World War I with the stated goal of making war impossible. He believed the world now had an arbiter to overcome what he saw as the divisive pressures of nationalism. But, as the League failed to contain Germany's military advances and instead dissolved into power struggles between members, Einstein cut his ties to it.

At the height of its popularity and power, the League of Nations invited Einstein and other intellectuals to join a "Committee on Intellectual Cooperation." Fellow physicist Marie Curie (1867–1934) was instrumental in convincing Einstein to join the group, which aimed to mobilize the intelligentsia to work for peace. Believing "that science is and always will be international," Einstein signed up, but he quickly became disillusioned not only with the League, but also, it seems, with human nature. Only one month after joining the committee, Einstein's friend and fellow Jew, Walther Rathenau, was assassinated, and Einstein resigned saying that with the growing anti-Semitic feeling in Germany, he was not comfortable representing his homeland on the committee.

In addition to his concern about his own country, Einstein was disappointed with the League's inaction on many conflicts within Europe, and quit. But a year later, convinced that the League was the only outlet for the type of world government he believed in, Einstein rejoined the committee, saying he still believed in its mission. However, whether he took its rule as seriously as before is questionable. Committee members were invited to give a lecture to the students of Geneva University; when it was Einstein's turn he charmed them by playing his violin instead.

Einstein attended meetings regularly for nearly ten years, but in 1930, as it became clear that conflicts within Europe were not being resolved, Einstein again withdrew. He wrote that the committee lacked "the determination needed to make real progress towards better international relations." That year was the tenth anniversary of the League, and Einstein commented, "I am rarely enthusiastic about what the League has accomplished, or not accomplished, but I am always thankful that it exists." The League disbanded eight years later when faced by threats to international peace around the world, including the Spanish Civil War, Japan's war against China, and Hitler's rise to power.

Lemaître, Georges
(1894–1966)

A Belgian astronomer and Jesuit priest, Georges Lemaître was the first to suggest that the entire universe began as a single "primeval atom" at some point in history—the first version of what has become the modern Big Bang theory. Einstein initially disparaged Lemaître's model—as Einstein did with all such expanding universe models—but in the end had to admit that Lemaître may have been correct.

Georges Lemaître was ordained as a priest in 1923, and then went on to study physics at the Massachusetts Institute of Technology. It was there that Lemaître first began thinking about the history of the universe. He was not, in fact, conversant in Einstein's relativity equations—he didn't create a model of the universe's history on ideas about the shape of space as Willem de Sitter (1872–1934) and Alexander Friedmann (1888–1925) had done before him. Instead, Lemaître relied on the laws of entropy, the laws that state that every system is moving from a state of order to a state of disorder. Another way to think of entropy is that in every system usable energy is lost over time, until all that energy eventually disappears. If this was true of every system, reasoned Lemaître, it was true of the universe as well. The universe, therefore, must have started in a state of maximum energy, losing energy over time until it would eventually die. The logical conclusion of thermodynamics, said Lemaître, was a model of the universe that was expanding over time—one that began much smaller than it is today, so small that the whole universe was originally squished into one tiny atom. Our entire universe sprang from this amazingly dense first particle and this universe would continue to expand, losing energy and gradually coasting to a halt. Lemaître published the theory on what he referred to as the "primeval atom" in 1927, upon returning to Belgium to teach astrophysics at the University of Louvain.

At the time, most scientists assumed the universe had always existed exactly as is. To believe in a changing universe, that is, to believe in a moment of creation, seemed to draw too much on religion and mysticism. Indeed, despite his Catholic training, Lemaître also felt that science and faith should not be confused with one another; different methodologies came to play in each, and he never used one discipline to confirm or deny the other. Nonetheless Lemaître's comfort with the genesis story in the Judaeo-Christian bible and his inherent belief in a Creator probably affected his easy acceptance of a theory that suggested the universe had "started" at some point. Unlike many of Lemaître's contemporaries, he believed his primeval atom theory was a genuine physical reality, not simply a mathematical model of interest, as de Sitter and Friedmann would have said of their models.

By the time Lemaître first published his theories, Einstein had already made his opinions of an expanding universe quite clear. He had published criticism of expanding models produced by de Sitter and Friedmann, and his response to Lemaître was no different. Einstein was forced to agree the math seemed to work, but he complained Lemaître's physics was "abominable." Without giving his prejudices much thought, Einstein simply dismissed the idea of an expanding universe out of hand.

Unlike de Sitter and Friedmann, however, Lemaître did not create his model solely for intellectual purposes. He believed it corresponded to reality. Building on contemporary physics, Lemaître hypothesized that the first primeval atom was made of radioactive elements that started a chain reaction. The energy from the reaction forced a dramatic, immediate expansion of the universe; in the process, it also created life. Lemaître acknowledged that his version of the start of the universe would undoubtedly be modified over time as atomic and nuclear physics were better understood. It wasn't until the 1960s that the modern version of the Big Bang theory was accepted, and as Lemaître predicted, the theory on what existed in those first moments and why they began expanding was very different from his original ideas. Lemaître was the first scientist, however, to truly embrace the concept that the universe had a beginning.

Einstein too, came around to Lemaître's views. The 1929 announcement by Edwin Hubble that observations did indeed point to an expanding universe finally convinced Einstein to jettison his preconceived notion of a static universe. Some ten years later, Einstein gave Lemaître due praise. At a talk in which Lemaître described the expanding universe, Einstein reportedly complimented the lecturer, saying: "This is the most beautiful and satisfactory explanation of creation to which I have ever listened."

See **Cosmology; de Sitter, Wilhelm; Friedmann, Alexander.**

Lenard, Philipp
(1862–1947)

Philipp Eduard Anton von Lenard won the 1905 Nobel Prize in Physics for his work with cathode rays, but he is less remembered today for his science than for his politics. He joined the Nazi Party in 1924 and became a rabid spokesman against Einstein.

Lenard began his career studying cathode rays—a beam of electricity traveling through a vacuum tube—and the very character of the electron beams themselves. The electron itself was only discovered in 1897, and so much of Lenard's research was to try to understand the nature of electricity. In 1899 Lenard proved that cathode rays are created when light strikes metal surfaces—and he saw that the presence of electric and magnetic fields affected the rays.

How light and metal could create electrons, or why they slowed down or changed direction in the face of different fields was unclear. The mechanisms weren't understood until 1905, when Einstein published his paper on the photoelectric effect—the concept that light quanta caused individual electrons to pop out of metal. Thus, Lenard's early work would forever be associated with Einstein's name.

At first, this brought the two scientists together. Lenard and Einstein wrote letters to each other following up on their research and showing great admiration for each other. A letter from Einstein to Lenard called him a "great master" and a "genius." Lenard, in turn, crusaded to appoint Einstein a professor at Heidelberg and once described him as a "deep and far-reaching thinker." But their relationship took a turn for the worse within a short five years.

Lenard's increasing dislike—perhaps, hatred—of Einstein seems to have stemmed from a combination of issues. For one thing, Lenard grew disdainful of Einstein's theory of relativity. He clung to the theory of ether—the idea that there was a physical substance that filled up the vacuum of space. Einstein believed the ether theory had long since been disproven. Indeed Einstein's theory of relativity relied on the fact that there was no ether. Moreover, Einstein wasn't reticent in his opinion: in 1910, Lenard gave a lecture defending the ether, and Einstein described the talk as infantile. In 1917, Lenard stated that he accepted the special theory of relativity but accepted only part of the general theory. (Lenard would soon also change his mind about the special theory.) The scientists battled it out in a series of publications—Lenard attacking general relativity, Einstein defending it. These publications became increasingly personal, due, most likely, to two causes: simple jealousy—Einstein had made a name by dramatically improving on work Lenard had originally done—and anti-Semitism.

Lenard did not officially join the Nazi Party until 1924, but early on he espoused many of their anti-Semitic beliefs. He began to speak out against Jewish scientists in general, and Einstein and Max Born in particular. He made such statements as: "the Jew conspicuously lacks understanding for the truth, in contrast to the Aryan research scientist with his careful and serious will to truth." Lenard founded a group known as the Anti-Relativity League, and they gave lectures on the "Jewish fraud" that was the theory of relativity.

At one such lecture, on August 24, 1919, Einstein himself attended and was seen chuckling to himself from his chair, despite the angry epithets being thrown at him. Notwithstanding his apparent nonchalance, Einstein responded to the group in a public letter printed in the German newspaper the *Berliner Tageblatt*. History has decided that the letter was not his most eloquent work, as in it Einstein appears defensive—and vulgar—not only explaining his theory but also accusing Lenard of being a second-rate theoretical physicist and "superficial" to boot.

For all Lenard's vehemence, however, he did not succeed in affecting public opinion beyond those already inclined to anti-Semitism in Germany—with one exception: he managed to stall Einstein's Nobel Prize for nearly ten years. Lenard lambasted the committee with his opinions that Einstein's theory of relativity had never been proven, and wasn't particularly important one way or the other, successfully creating enough confusion that awarding the prize to Einstein was delayed for over a decade. It was not until 1921, when Lenard's influence had waned, that Einstein was awarded the Nobel Prize in physics—and even so, he was awarded it for his work on the photoelectric effect instead of relativity.

See **Anti-Semitism; Nobel Prize in Physics; Photoelectric Effect.**

Lorentz, Hendrik
(1853–1928)

Weeks before his death, Einstein said that the Dutch physicist Hendrik Lorentz was one of the few scientists he truly admired, and he thought of him as a precursor to his own science. Indeed, many of their contemporaries saw Lorentz as an almost equal creator of Einstein's special theory, suggesting that the two scientists should share in a Nobel Prize for their work. In hindsight, Einstein's work was a real break from Lorentz's, but nonetheless, the two were intricately entwined and good friends. Einstein saw Lorentz almost as a father figure.

Lorentz grew up in the Netherlands, and he became intrigued by Maxwell's electromagnetic theory while at university. He wrote his doctorate on the reflection and refraction of light, and he continued to study light once he became a full professor of mathematical physics at Leiden University in 1878. His initial focus was on the ether—the undetectable medium through which light waves were thought to travel. Lorentz was initially a firm believer in the existence of the ether, and so he merely dismissed early experiments by Albert Michelson (1852–1931) that couldn't find the substance. But by the end of the nineteenth century, when continued work by Michelson and his associate Edward Morley (1838–1923) still showed negative results, Lorentz began to worry. His papers turned toward an attempt to modify the theory of light to account for the Michelson-Morley work.

The Michelson-Morley experiment sought to measure the rate at which Earth was traveling through the ether. It sought to measure the changed velocity of light as it moved either upstream or downstream through that ether—as if the light was a boat motoring on a river that could move much more quickly with the river's current than against it. Since the experiment found there was no change in velocity whatsoever, Lorentz tried to explain this by showing that the movement of Earth was irrelevant to the measurements.

Lorentz is a marvel of intelligence and exquisite tact. A living work of art!

—Einstein, in a letter to Heinrich Zangger in November 1911

He hypothesized that at the incredibly fast speeds light traveled, space and time contracted, thus compensating for the movement through the ether, making the length and time of the light's trip—and therefore its velocity—identical. The equations for how space and time changed are today known as the "Lorentz transformations."

Time for Relativity

Einstein was an early devotee of Lorentz's writing, and this is where Einstein learned that there was something of a crisis occurring within light science. Einstein always attributed much of his early fascination with electromagnetism to reading Lorentz; however, Einstein was able to take Lorentz's work a step further. In his *Theory of Electrons,* published in 1915, Lorentz stated: "The chief cause of my failure [to discover relativity] was my clinging to the idea that only the variable t can be considered as the true time, and that my local time . . . must be regarded as no more than an auxiliary mathematical quantity." In other words, Lorentz included in his equations two concepts of time—one for an outside observer, and one for the reference frame in which the light was traveling—but he assumed this was just a mathematical construct, not that time itself was indeed different for both reference frames. Einstein, however, was able to make the leap that the math didn't work just in principle but was an accurate portrayal of what was happening in reality. Time and space were actually different for different observers. This insight opened up the door for Einstein's conceptual leap to the special theory of relativity—a leap Lorentz didn't make.

Indeed, there is some question of whether Lorentz ever completely accepted Einstein's new theory. As innovative a thinker as Lorentz was—even before the electron was discovered he had hypothesized in the 1890s that light was formed when an electric charge in the atom oscillated, and he won the 1902 Nobel Prize for the mathematical formulation of the electron—he was firmly mired in classical physics thought. He felt comfortable with the world of Newtonian mechanics, Maxwell's electromagnetism, and the ways in which cause neatly led to effect in macroscopic, observable ways. Decades after Lorentz's death, Max Born wrote that he believed Lorentz "probably never became a relativist at all, and only paid lip service to Einstein at times, to avoid arguments."

Lorentz also voiced reservations about Einstein's light quanta theories. As steeped as he was in electromagnetic wave theories about light, he was unwilling to accept that light could possibly be made of particles. Lorentz certainly agreed that the new atomic theories that claimed energy came in packets of quanta as Planck had suggested seemed to work very well, but he would not accept that light actually propagated in these cohesive, discrete clumps of energy. This middle ground epitomized Lorentz's position in the history of physics, as he sat squarely between the old classical physics and the new science being created. He saw the need for change and he understood that the new dynamics made a certain amount of sense, but he could not believe that the oddities that came with the new quantum mechanics were completely correct. (Einstein, too, would ultimately veer away from the path the rest of his contemporaries were following, but he still embraced more of the new science than Lorentz did.)

The Moderate Moderator

Balanced as he was between the old science and the new, Lorentz was a perfect moderator for the first Solvay Conference held in 1911. Devoted to atomic physics, the conference brought together the greatest physicists of the day to discuss the conflicts between Newtonian and modern theories. Lorentz kept the peace beautifully between different factions, because he could see the value of both viewpoints. In his opening address he said; "In this stage of affairs there appeared to us like a wonderful ray of light the beautiful hypothesis of energy elements which was first expounded by Planck and then extended by Einstein. . . . It has opened for us unexpected vistas, even those, who consider it with a certain suspicion, must admit its importance and fruitfulness."

Regardless of their scientific sentiments, Lorentz and Einstein held each other in extreme admiration. Einstein repeated often that Lorentz was the most well-rounded person he'd met in his entire life and he wrote to his friend Johann Laub in 1909 that "I admire [Lorentz] as I admire no other, I would say I love him."

Einstein respected Lorentz so much that he was nearly talked into replacing Lorentz when he retired from Leiden in 1911. Einstein had already accepted a position at Zurich—a position he preferred—but it seems as if he would have let his feelings for Lorentz take precedence if the latter had insisted. Upon turning down the Leiden offer, he wrote to Lorentz after the Solvay Conference: "I write this letter to you with a heavy heart, as one who had done a kind of injustice to his father. . . . If I had known you wanted me . . . then I would have gone."

In 1916, that "father" came through for Einstein by encouraging him with the general theory of relativity. Einstein had published early versions of the theory in 1915, and Lorentz was one of several scientists trying to follow Einstein's train of thought. As Einstein's own understanding improved, and Lorentz began to see just what Einstein was attempting to accomplish, he gave the younger man his praise and said the time had come for Einstein to write the theory up in as simple a way as possible for the benefit of the entire physics community. This seems to have been one of the important factors in Einstein finally publishing in 1916 both an *Annalen der Physik* article as well as a separate fifty-page booklet on his theory that summed up the general theory of relativity in the most succinct form yet published.

Hendrik Lorentz died in 1928 and Einstein, representing the Prussian Academy of Sciences, took the trip to Holland for the funeral. He spoke to the mourners gathered around, saying: "I stand at the grave of the greatest and noblest man of our times. His genius led the way from Maxwell's work to the achievements of contemporary physics. . . . His work and his example will live on as an inspiration."

Mach, Ernst
(1838–1916)

Ernst Mach is best known today for lending his name to the speed of sound—something is said to travel at Mach 2 if it travels twice the speed of sound, Mach 3 if three times, and so on—but to Einstein, Mach was the man who laid the groundwork for relativity and a beloved hero who spent a great deal of time thinking about how one should practice science.

Einstein read Mach as a student and was already taken with him by 1902, when he lived in Zurich and met regularly with his friends Conrad Habicht and Maurice Solovine. Einstein had the group read both books Mach had published at that point: *The Development of Mechanics* and *The Analysis of the Sensations*.

Mach was an exemplar of a kind of academic who became increasingly rare in the twentieth century—a scientist whose interests covered a vast range of subjects, including optics, mechanics, wave dynamics, sensory experiences, cognition theory, and philosophy. It was the philosophy that initially caught Einstein's attention. Mach was an outspoken and extreme positivist, a philosophical style that states one can only draw conclusions about that which one can directly sense. Scientific theories, according to Mach, can go no further than to be a summary of observable facts. To draw inferences that were not directly attributable to something you could see, touch, or otherwise sense, was to enter the world of fantasy. All scientists would agree, of course, that theories are ultimately based on what one can sense, but Mach took this view further than others. For example, for years he refused to believe in the existence of atoms since they are too small to be perceived directly with one's own eyes.

Mach's studies of mechanics and inertia also affected Einstein. Because Mach believed in only touchable quantities, he stated emphatically that "time" had no real meaning. He wrote that it was an abstract idea, produced by humans and subject to the vagaries of the human mind. This rejection of "absolute time" seems to have freed the thinking of young Einstein; when Einstein's special theory of relativity was published in 1905, it directly relied on the concept that there is no absolute time or space. Indeed, all of the special theory of relativity is derived from human perception—since people in different reference frames experience different things, Einstein stated that reality itself was in fact different in those reference frames. It was a positivist attitude Mach approved of.

Indeed, Mach had had somewhat similar ideas himself when younger. Einstein always believed that Mach was on the path to discovering relativity in some of his early work, and that the only reason he didn't was because the timing wasn't quite right. Einstein began to think about the problem at a time when the scientific community was focused on the fact that light moved at a constant speed, while Mach had done his work a couple of decades earlier. The constancy of light was an important catalyst for developing relativity, and one to which Mach had not been granted access.

Einstein also turned to Mach's work some ten years later when he was writing the general theory of relativity. Mach had made a proposition, which Einstein dubbed Mach's principle, that the reason any traveling object stays at rest or continues to move is directly attributable to its relationship with all the other objects in the universe. This was a modification of the law of inertia first promoted by Isaac Newton in the 1600s: an object at rest tends to stay at rest, and an object in motion tends to stay in motion. Mach wanted to determine just why Newton's law was so, and his answer was that the distribution of mass throughout the universe was responsible. One can see how, if the idea that mass affects inertia was wedged into Einstein's brain, it might have helped him create his theory of general relativity, which states that mass essentially creates gravity.

Einstein always gave Mach's ideas credit as being the catalysts to his theory of relativity. But Mach chose to distance himself from Einstein's work. By the time the general theory of relativity was published in 1915, Einstein had gone too far in the direction of what Mach referred to as "metaphysical" concepts. The general theory of relativity explains gravity by postulating curves in the very shape of space; for Mach the theory was far too abstract to be acceptable. Einstein, however, never quite acknowledged that his hero had rejected relativity, blaming Mach's attitude on his old age.

Even so, Einstein, too, pulled away from his strict adherence to Mach's work. For one thing, it became increasingly clear that Mach's principle does not, in fact, have much to do with general relativity; the former has to do with inertia, the latter with gravity. Indeed, despite Einstein's initial reticence to accept the idea, relativity actually allows for a universe that has no mass whatsoever. By his last decade, Einstein had completely ceased to associate Mach's principle with his own work. He wrote in a 1954 letter that "one should no longer speak of Mach's principle at all."

Einstein also ceased—fairly emphatically—to follow Mach's positivism. While relying solely on the senses helped him to create his first theory of relativity, Einstein dropped this rigid attitude as he grew older. As his colleagues developed quantum mechanics, most of the community accepted a theory that also relied only on direct measurement of the atomic world. But the theory held innate complexities that Einstein thought still needed to be resolved—direct measure-

> *Mach was as good at mechanics as he was wretched at philosophy.*
>
> —Einstein, in a 1922 paper for the *Bulletin of the Society of French Philosophy*

ment wasn't enough. (Mach also rejected quantum mechanics, because even if it was relying solely on measurements to draw conclusions, these measurements were of a particularly abstract kind; who, after all, had ever actually laid eyes on an electron? Without sensory experience, Mach wasn't interested in this new branch of science.)

Despite their scientific differences, Einstein always believed Mach to be one of the important influences in his life. In 1916, Einstein wrote an obituary for Mach that praised the man who had spent as much time studying how science should be done as science itself. Without such self-examination, said Einstein, "Concepts that have proven useful in ordering things easily achieve such an authority over us that we forget their earthly origins and accept them as unalterable givens. . . . The path of scientific advance is often made impassable for a long time through such errors."

Just weeks before Einstein died he gave an interview in which he stated that Mach was one of only five scientists—including Isaac Newton, Hendrik Lorentz, Max Planck, and James Clerk Maxwell—whom he believed were his true precursors.

See **Positivism.**

Mathematics

Einstein didn't fail math—that's a myth. But it's true that he wasn't a particularly creative mathematician. His genius was in physics, and he saw math as merely a means to an end, which meant that on more than one occasion he had to rely on others to help him over some mathematical hurdles.

Einstein taught himself math and physics at a fairly young age. In 1949, he wrote in his *Autobiographical Notes* that he discovered the wonders of a "holy" book on geometry at the age of twelve. He attributed this early experience of studying geometric proofs with teaching him the joys of using thinking to solve a problem. Relying on outside books for his mathematic knowledge, Einstein was always far enough ahead of the rest of the class to achieve high marks. Nonetheless, math itself didn't thrill him. Later in the autobiography he wrote: "My interest in the knowledge of nature was . . . unqualifiedly stronger; and it was not clear to me as a student that the approach to a more profound knowledge of the basic principles of physics is tied up with the most intricate mathematical methods. This dawned upon me only gradually after years of independent scientific work."

This seems a particularly apt description of the math in Einstein's theories of relativity; at first he was unconcerned with the math and only later learned how important it could be. After he published his special theory of relativity in 1905, his math professor from graduate school, Hermann Minkowski (1864–1909) expressed surprise, since he couldn't imagine how the young man who'd skipped so many classes had the skills

Dear Barbara, . . . Do not worry about your difficulties in mathematics; I can assure you that mine are still greater.

—Einstein's reply to a letter from a twelve-year-old girl, January 7, 1943

to produce such a groundbreaking theory. Upon closer examination, Minkowski discovered the math was indeed less elegant than he believed it should be. At the time, there was an elite group of German and Swiss mathematicians who believed physics was really too tough for physicists—it should be left to those better equipped to handle it. So Minkowski set out to save the day.

Because Einstein's special theory of relativity involved changing time and space, Minkowski created a new set of tools to describe space-time itself. Einstein's first reaction was negative, because he thought that it made his simple theory infinitely more complicated, but he soon changed his tune. Minkowski's math provided special relativity with both a foundation and a vocabulary, which opened the door for others to better work with the new theory. And as Einstein turned his attention toward extending his relativity theory to describing gravitation, Minkowski's math proved quite useful.

Another mathematician helped Einstein as well. Einstein published a version of the general theory of relativity in 1911 but knew there was work yet to be done. He turned to his friend Marcel Grossmann (1878–1936), announcing he would go crazy if Grossmann didn't help. Grossmann suggested that an obscure branch of geometry called Reimann geometry might be applicable, though according to Abraham Pais's biography of Einstein, *Subtle Is the Lord*, Grossmann also told Einstein it was a "terrible mess which physicists should not be involved with." Regardless, Einstein jumped in, and Reimann geometry turned out to be the missing piece needed to develop his general theory of relativity equations, the final version of which was published in 1916.

The course of science and mathematics often goes hand in hand. In the seventeenth century, Isaac Newton (1642–1727) devised calculus in order to advance his mechanics theories, and Einstein too found that a complete mathematical system didn't exist for his new ideas. Building on Reimann, he was able to cobble together what he needed for general relativity. But it wasn't his destiny to truly expand on the ideas. Mathematicians jumped in, advancing the field of this esoteric bit of geometry, which ultimately helped the advance of science as well.

That Einstein needed to rely on others for mathematical help in this way may well have been to his benefit. As David Hilbert (1862–1943), a professor of math at Göttingen University said, "Every boy in the streets of our Göttingen understands more about four-dimensional geometry than Einstein. Yet, despite that, Einstein did the work and not the mathematicians. Do you know why Einstein said the most original and profound things about space and time that have been said in our generation? Because he had learned nothing about all the mathematics and philosophy of space and time."

McCarthyism

While Einstein was never brought before the House Committee on Un-American Activities, his outspoken views and strongly leftist politics certainly attracted attention during the era when Senator Joseph McCarthy (1908–1957) began his campaign against Communism.

Einstein advocated nuclear disarmament and making peace with the Soviet Union at a time when the Cold War was in full swing. Coupled with his defense of those accused of Communist activities—though he claimed that he himself was not a Communist—Einstein's views earned him suspicion. Many with such leanings were called by McCarthy to have their loyalty to the United States determined in front of a House congressional committee; but Einstein's celebrity kept him from such an occurrence. Without a little more proof of treason-ous activity, calling Einstein in front of the House of Representatives would have resulted in a serious backlash.

Every intellectual who is called before one of the committees ought to refuse to testify; i.e. he must be prepared for jail and economic ruin, in short, for the sacrifice of his personal welfare in the interest of the cultural welfare of his country.

—Einstein, in a letter to William Frauenglass concerning the McCarthy hearings, May 16, 1953

Einstein soon turned his unguarded tongue to the McCarthy hearings themselves. As someone who had lived in Berlin during the rise of the Nazi Party, Einstein saw the world through a very particular prism.

He was quick to judge any curtailing of human rights as similarly fascist, and spoke out against it. When the English teacher William Frauenglass was called to testify before the Senate in 1953, Einstein advised him not to speak, writing a letter that was published in the *New York Times:* "The problem with which the intellectuals of this country are confronted is very serious. Reactionary politicians have managed to instill suspicion of all intellectual efforts into the public by dangling before their eyes a danger from without." Einstein advocated what he described as Ghandi's way of noncooperation as the only possible solution. This naturally brought on McCarthy's wrath, who was quoted in the *New York Times* as saying: "Anyone who gives advice like Einstein's to Frauenglass is himself an enemy of America."

In 1954, someone closer to Einstein was called to Washington—J. Robert Oppenheimer. Oppenheimer was the most well-known scientist to face the Un-American Committee, and Einstein knew him since they both worked together at Princeton. As soon as Oppenheimer was called to testify, journalists sought out Einstein's opinion—and at first his reaction was simply to laugh. All Oppenheimer needed to do was tell Congress they were being ridiculous, thought Einstein. Of course, this was too simple a solution given the climate of the day, and Einstein was one of several who spoke in defense of Oppenheimer during the hearing. Regardless, while Oppenheimer was not found to be a spy, his judgment was called into question and his security clearance revoked.

Einstein never received such a punishment, since he had never been given security clearance to begin with due to the fact that the U.S. government knew he had some association with known Communist organizations long before the war. In fact, it was his outspokenness that may well have kept him from being called to trial. He wore his political feelings on his sleeve and published them in newspapers; he was not given to secret acts that might undermine the United States and so, ultimately, McCarthy had no grounds to call him to a hearing.

See **Communism; FBI; Oppenheimer, J. Robert.**

Michelson-Morley Experiment

Conducted in 1879, the Michelson-Morley experiment is considered the definitive work that finally eliminated the nineteenth-century belief that light waves traveled through a medium called ether. The standard science story told to first-year physics students is that once the Michelson-Morley experiment disproved ether, everyone knew there was a crisis, and Einstein boldly stepped in to solve this problem with his special theory of relativity in 1905—but this is a highly simplified version of what really happened.

Albert Abraham Michelson (1852–1931) began to work on the search for ether when he was a young student in Berlin on leave from the U.S. Navy. Later, when he became a physics professor at the Case School of Applied Science in Cleveland, he teamed up with Edward Williams Morley (1838–1923), an American chemist at nearby Western Reserve University. Morley was known as a great experimenter, and Michelson liked the challenge of creating a meticulous experiment to measure the speed of Earth through the ether that was supposedly in space. The measurements needed to be so precise that many said it couldn't be done. (Late in his life, Michelson told Einstein that he had devoted so much energy to getting the necessary precision simply because it was "fun.")

James Clerk Maxwell (1831–1879) was the first to describe light as an electromagnetic wave. At the time, physicists understood waves fairly well. Sound waves, for example, are created from a vibrating object that alternately compresses and decompresses the surrounding air. Pockets of dense and less dense air then travel to one's ear and are interpreted by the brain. Water waves are waves with crests and troughs instead of dense and less dense packets, but they, like sound waves, need a medium to travel through. Maxwell believed that light must have a medium as well—and this was a mysterious substance called "ether." Ether would be at rest with respect to some absolute space in the universe, and the Earth, naturally, would travel through it. Maxwell proposed that there would, therefore, be an ether wind of some kind—blowing into one's face if one looked in the direction Earth was moving, at one's back if one turned around. And light, one would expect, would travel at different speeds depending on which direction it was moving through this ether, much as a person finds it easier to walk with the wind at his back. The concept that light could move at different speeds lay at the heart of the Michelson-Morley experiment, and it is exactly that notion that Einstein would eventually dispel.

The experiment cited as the official Michelson-Morley experiment happened in 1887 and was based on a fairly innovative design with a new technique Michelson developed: interferometry. Interferometry depends on the fact that when two waves interfere they form very specific patterns—much the way two water waves do when they intersect. An interferometry experiment begins by splitting a single beam of light and then focusing those two new beams on a screen to analyze the pattern made. These patterns change depending on how far each beam has traveled, and so analyzing the final image gives information about the speed and path of the light. Michelson had already used interferometry both to measure the most accurate speed of light yet found and to determine the official length of a meter for the U.S. National Bureau of Standards.

For their ether experiment, Michelson and Morley set up two light beams to travel at right angles to each other—one beam traveled in the same direction as the ether and one traveled across it. Imagine two people swimming in a river with one swimming up the river and then back, while the other swims to a point directly across the river and back. Both swimmers must fight against the current, but they do so in different ways, and consequently the time it takes them to swim the exact same distance will be different—the time for the swimmer crossing the river will be longer. If Earth is traveling through the ether, the ether creates a current, just like a river current, and a light beam traveling against it and back should take a shorter time than a beam traveling across it and back, even if they travel the same distance.

The experiment was beautifully designed, but no matter how many times Michelson and Morley tried it, both beams took the same amount of time for their travels. The pair did the experiment over and over, always receiving the same answer. Their reputation in the scientific community was impressive enough that the most famous physicists of their day all took the Michelson-Morley results at face value. Clearly, there was a problem with the ether theory.

The concept of ether was not, however, completely discarded at that point. The consensus was only that the current hypothesis was not complete. Michelson tried the experiment numerous other times throughout his life—even taking his equipment up to the top of a hill, in case the ether dragged along with Earth and so one might only feel the ether wind higher in the atmosphere.

While there were physicists who knew of Michelson and Morley's work, and knew that their results must be incorporated into a new theory of light, it is unclear whether Einstein—the man who finally came up with that theory—had heard of it. His paper on special relativity certainly doesn't reference it, but then that paper really didn't reference anything since it was so new that Einstein could legitimately claim it wasn't based on anyone else's previous work. Later in life Einstein contradicted himself on the subject of whether he'd heard of the Michelson-Morley experiment. Numerous times he said that he did not know of it, and he does not mention it in his *Autobiographical Notes,* which describes how he developed his theories. Late in life, however—at a time when his memory was not infallible—he said he'd first heard of the Michelson-Morley experiment from studying Lorentz in 1895, and some of his early letters discuss having read a paper that referenced it.

Regardless of whether Einstein knew of the Michelson-Morley experiment per se, Einstein certainly developed the theory of special relativity believing firmly that the ether did not exist. This conviction did not occur in a vacuum. Reading other great scientists of his day, many of whom did know of the interferometry experiment, would most certainly have influenced Einstein's assumptions, and if others knew of the consequences of the Michelson-Morley experiment, this would have trickled through to Einstein.

After Einstein published the special theory of relativity, he learned of Michelson and Morley's work and interacted a few times over the years with Michelson. In 1931, Michelson attended a dinner honoring Einstein in California. In Einstein's speech he said, "You, my honored Dr. Michelson, began with this work when I was only a little young-ster, hardly three feet high. It was you who led the physicists into new paths, and through your marvelous experimental work paved the way for the development of the theory of relativity." The comment hon-ored Michelson nicely while skirting the issue of whether Einstein had actually drawn on his work.

After Michelson died, in honor of Einstein's seventieth birthday, the famous American physicist Robert Millikan, who was one of Michelson's protégés, wrote an article in which he drew a direct link between the theory of relativity and Michelson's earlier search for the ether. Millikan wrote: "The special theory of relativity may be looked upon as starting essentially in a generalization from Michelson's exper-iment." He then went on to write how after Michelson and Morley showed there was no ether, "light physicists wandered in the wilder-ness" seeking a new theory of light. Millikan wrote, "Then Einstein called out to us all, 'Let us merely accept this as an established exper-imental fact and from there proceed to work out its inevitable conse-quences,' and he went at that task himself with an energy and a capacity which very few people on Earth possess. Thus was born the special theory of relativity." Like Athena full-blown out of the head of Zeus, Millikan described Einstein's theory as having sprung from Michelson's work. Real science—real history—doesn't usually work quite so simply, but this idea that the Michelson-Morley experiment led directly and neatly to the theory of special relativity has been part of Einstein lore ever since.

Millikan, Robert
(1868–1953)

Robert Millikan was one of the most famous scientists of his day. He won the Nobel Prize for physics in 1923 for measuring the charge on the electron and for experimental work confirming Einstein's theory that light was made of particles. Ironically, Millikan had set out to disprove the theory, and insisted for years that his work only confirmed that Einstein's theories were valuable mathematical tools, not that they proved the existence of photons.

The second American to win a Nobel Prize in physics, Millikan characterized what was to become the conventional image, if not the actual stereotype, of the American scientist of the 1920s and 1930s: a gregarious, confident man who focused on precise and innovative experiments rather than theory—which was still the purview of the Europeans. In 1896, Millikan was hired by the University of Chicago and was still there in 1905 when Einstein published a paper claiming that the only way to make sense of how light imparts energy to electrons is if light is made of discrete particles just as an electrical current is. Einstein found that the energy of a light particle is equal to its frequency, multiplied by a constant, h, that has come to be called Planck's constant. Millikan already had a respected reputation as the man who measured the charge on an electron, thus showing that electrons indeed were physical entities with consistent properties, and that electricity was an atomic phenomenon. But just because he accepted that electrons were discrete quantities didn't mean he believed light operated the same way. He knew too well the experiments that showed two light beams interacting with each other just as they would if they were both waves. For fifty years scientists had accepted that light was made of waves, and Millikan agreed. So he set out to prove Einstein wrong.

Millikan's experiment measured the energy of electrons that were knocked off a plate by an incoming beam of light. However, much to his surprise, the experiments seemed to confirm Einstein's idea that light consisted of particles and was not a wave. Moreover, not only did Millikan's experiment prove Einstein's theory right, he also managed to determine the most precise value for Planck's constant yet found. Decades later, as Millikan described his work, a bit of his frustration came through clearly: "I spent ten years of my life testing the 1905 equation of Einstein's and contrary to all my expectations, I was compelled in 1915 to assert its unambiguous verification in spite of its unreasonableness."

Nonetheless, Millikan did not yet admit that this experiment proved light came in quanta; he would only say that Einstein's math corresponded to his experiments. In his paper on the photoelectric effect, Millikan wrote, "Einstein's photoelectric equation . . . appears in every case to predict exactly the observed results. . . . Yet the semi-corpuscular theory by which Einstein arrived at his equation seems at present wholly untenable." Millikan also described Einstein's theory on discrete light particles as a "bold, not to say reckless, hypothesis." Millikan knew that without Einstein's equations the phenomenon of photoelectricity was still unexplainable by the classical understanding of light, and so he knew something had to change, but the arbitrary introduction of photons was not, he thought, the answer. In addition, Millikan worked with Michelson—who believed all his life in the existence of an ether through which light waves traveled—and so the two men were doubly reluctant to give up the idea of light waves.

While the scientific community kept an eye on these developments, in 1919 Millikan and Einstein were both mentioned together in the popular press. That November, experimental tests confirmed Einstein's general theory of relativity, granting him instant fame and a flurry of New York Times articles that described a somewhat supercilious Einstein who claimed only twelve people in the world understood his theory. After days of this, there was, unsurprisingly, a bit of a backlash, and a Times editorial on November 13 stated, "People who have felt a bit resentful at being told that they couldn't possibly understand the new theory, even if it were explained to them ever so kindly and carefully, will feel a sort of satisfaction on noting that the soundness of the Einstein deduction has been questioned by R. A. Millikan."

And yet, while Millikan continued to deny the existence of photons, his "confirmation" of them was a factor in helping Einstein receive the Nobel Prize in 1922. In 1923, Millikan's work with the photoelectric effect was cited along with his work on electrons, when Millikan himself won the Nobel. In his Nobel speech, however, Millikan again mentioned that "the conception of localized light-quanta out of which Einstein got his equation must still be regarded as far from being established."

There was never, however, any personal animosity between the two men, and they greatly respected each other. In 1921, Millikan took a job at the California Institute of Technology, and he set out to make it a top-of-the-line research institution. Millikan offered Einstein a job at Caltech in 1923, but the German physicist refused. Einstein did, however, accept an invitation to visit the United States, and Millikan hosted dinners and lectures for him. Eventually—it is unclear completely why, though increasing anti-Semitism in Germany may have had something to do with it—in 1931, Einstein accepted a job teaching part-time at Caltech. At Caltech, Einstein gave a few lectures on cosmological problems, and, to the displeasure of his host who wished for issue-free lectures that would help with fundraising for the university, he also spoke out on pacifism and racial discrimination.

In 1950, at age 82, Millikan wrote his autobiography. By then, all of the scientific community had fully accepted the existence of Einstein's discrete particles—now called photons—and Millikan did too. In the book, Millikan doesn't mention that he stalled for decades before accepting Einstein's theories. History is often told in neat little step-by-step stories that don't account for the complexity of what really happened; the history of science is no different. Many tales of the photoelectric effect describe Millikan as experimentally confirming Einstein, without mentioning that this had not been his intention. Even so, it's rare that the participants write a book that puts the same kind of sheen on history. One isn't sure whether this was how Millikan truly remembered what happened, or whether vanity got the best of him and he didn't want to reminisce about what had clearly been a mistake.

The Harvard science historian Gerald Holton points out that it is when we imagine Millikan as *not* originally accepting the photon that he comes off more admirably—after all, he maintained scientific objectivity. Although his heart said the theories were wrong, Millikan didn't let his bias ruin his experiment, and he went ahead and published results that contradicted his own beliefs. Holton cites this same point in defense of what has recently been criticism of Millikan for publishing only some of his results—those that supported his hypotheses. Indeed, if Millikan published only what he preferred to believe, then he never would have written about his proof of the photoelectric effect at all.

Miracle Year

Einstein's miracle year was 1905 when, at the age of twenty-six, the unknown scientist published five papers on wholly disparate physics topics. During that year, he developed the special theory of relativity, the paper that introduced the equation $E = mc^2$, a paper based on Brownian motion of atoms, a paper on the photoelectric effect (for which he would win the Nobel Prize), and his Ph.D. dissertation on molecular dimensions. Publishing them all together in one year is often heralded as one of the most impressive feats in scientific history.

Einstein often credited his job at the Swiss Patent Office with allowing him the freedom to create the prodigious output of his miracle year. Had he been a full-time professor—the kind of prestigious job he wanted—he would have had to focus on teaching and might not have had enough time to devote to his theories. As it was, his "lowly" job didn't affect his credibility, though it seems impressive that the ideas of a patent officer, especially such outlandish new ideas, were allowed such a prominent place in a public journal. It is highly unlikely that this would happen today. But the *Annalen der Physik* had a policy that anyone who had ever been published on their pages would automatically have any subsequent articles published. Having printed Einstein's minor, conventional papers before, they went on to include his 1905 work.

Later in life, Einstein considered only one of his papers, the one on the photoelectric effect, "revolutionary." In fact, none of Einstein's five papers were the very first of their kind, and none of them were the last word, either. Even Einstein's special theory of relativity built, to some degree, upon the ideas of other scientists, and Einstein himself considered the theory incomplete. (Later, Einstein fully rounded out the theory by creating the general theory of relativity.) Nevertheless, Einstein's five papers were each major contributions to their fields.

Einstein certainly was aware of the importance of his papers. Earlier that year, he wrote to his friend and fellow physicist Conrad

Habicht: "I promise you four papers. . . . the [first] paper deals with radiation and the energetic properties of light and is very revolutionary, as you will see. . . . The second paper is a determination of the true sizes of atoms from the diffusion and viscosity of dilute solution of neutral substances. The third proves that, . . . bodies . . . must already perform an observable random movement . . . which they call 'Brownian molecular motion.' The fourth paper is only a rough draft at this point, and ... employs a modification of the theory of space and time."

The First Paper: The True Nature of Light

The first of Einstein's papers that year—the one he considered "revolutionary"—was published on March 17, 1905, and was titled "On a Heuristic Point of View Concerning the Production and Transformation of Light." It is now referred to as his paper on the "photoelectric effect." Einstein was awarded the 1921 Nobel Prize for this paper.

In it, Einstein tackles the problem that confounded contemporary physicists: the current theories of light did not seem to be complete. For two hundred years, scientists assumed that light was made up of particles, as Newton had claimed. In 1864, however, James Clerk Maxwell (1831–1879) described light as an electromagnetic wave. While it took a quarter century for this theory to be accepted, Maxwell's idea dramatically improved the understanding of how light worked. This wave theory seemed completely confirmed because by 1901, new technology allowed people to communicate by sending radio waves (a kind of light wave) around the globe. Although this showed light to be a wave and not a bunch of particles, there was still a problem. When energy from a light wave was transmitted to electrons— say, by aiming light at a metal plate and measuring how many electrons bounced off—the results didn't match what the wave theory predicted. Brighter light waves should have knocked off the same amount of electrons, but transferred more energy to them. Instead, bright light knocked off more electrons and each carried the same amount of energy as they had with dimmer light.

In this, his first paper of the miracle year, Einstein brought back the idea that light might be made of discrete particles. He drew on contemporary work that was being done by Max Planck, in which Planck suggested energy might come in packets—or "quanta"—of energy. In other words, radiation could not be thought of as something continuous, like water going through a hose, but instead was made up of small bits. Like fine sand being forced through the hose instead of water, it appears continuous from a distance. However, when you look at it from up close, it isn't.

By applying this idea to light, Einstein showed that brighter light—light that's made up of more photons, but photons of the exact same energy level as in dimmer light—would naturally knock off more electrons, and not change their energy level. Dividing light up into particles solved the photoelectric problem. With this paper, Einstein introduced the quantum theory of light, a theory that would go on to play an important role in the development of quantum mechanics.

The Second Paper: Atoms are Real

One month later, Einstein published his second paper, which was based on his dissertation. It was called "A New Determination of Molecular Dimensions." In this paper, Einstein made use of current hydrodynamic theory to determine the size of molecules suspended in a viscous liquid. In 1827, a botanist named Robert Brown discovered that particles in a liquid vibrated randomly of their own accord. This became known as Brownian motion, and it is caused by the way heat, even room temperature heat, makes water molecules move. Using Brownian motion, Einstein determined the exact size and number of atoms in any given solution.

Not only was Einstein's method a sound one, but it helped resolve what was still a controversy at the time: whether molecules and atoms were, in fact, real, physical entities. While this paper never captured the popular imagination, in many ways, it is the one that has had the most effect on modern society. While not everyone can explain what the special theory of relativity means, most people know that atoms exist.

The Third Paper: More Brownian Motion

A mere eleven days after his second paper, *Annalen der Physik* published Einstein's third. Printed on May 11, the title was "On the Motion of Small Particles Suspended in Liquids at Rest Required by the Molecular-Kinetic Theory of Heat." In this paper, Einstein described the ways in which particles move in a liquid and why they do this, showing that the motions were so big they could be seen with a microscope.

Einstein did not claim to be describing Brownian motion per se. He began the article by saying that he might well be discussing so-called Brownian molecular "motion," but he didn't know for sure. Nevertheless, the paper has gone down in history as being a description of just that phenomenon.

The Fourth Paper: Introducing Special Relativity

Like all of the other papers that came from Einstein's miraculous year, the name of his fourth paper bears no association to how we refer to it today—the paper was called "On the Electrodynamics of Moving Bodies." This was the paper in which Einstein introduced what we currently call the special theory of relativity. Like the first paper of the miracle year, it also tackled some of the problems that were associated with light at this time. The fact that light was thought to move at different speeds in relation to different frames of reference (the speed of light coming from the flashlight of a person standing on a moving train was thought to be greater than the speed of light coming from the flashlight of a person standing still, for example) led to a paradox: the laws of physics would be different for those two people. Einstein theorized that the speed of light was identical, no matter what. Light would move at a very specific speed—186,000 miles per second—regardless of the reference frame. What changed instead, he claimed, were time and space.

It is interesting to note that in this paper, Einstein treats light as being the lovely continuous wave of Maxwell's theories. It seems Einstein had no problem writing two papers that relied on two different ideas about light in the same year. While the photoelectric effect paper insisted that light was made of discrete particles, this paper claimed that light was a wave. Einstein would spend much of his life trying to devise an understanding of light that would unite these two concepts, but nevertheless, he understood that interpreting light in both ways was valid. Today, most modern scientists simply accept this dual nature of light as one of its bizarre properties.

The Fifth Paper: $E = mc^2$

What may well be the most famous equation of all time, $E = mc^2$, came from the shortest paper Einstein published that year. His fifth paper, titled "Does the inertia of a body depend upon its energy content?", was essentially a postscript to his fourth, the relativity paper. By insisting once again that the laws of physics must be the same for all reference frames, Einstein realized that the only way to explain the changing speeds of an object that was emitting light was to understand that adjusting the amount of the object's energy was equivalent to changing that object's mass. Einstein wrote that energy and mass were descriptions of the same thing. Of course, we perceive them differently, but nevertheless, they are essentially identical. In addition, the amount of energy in any given object is related to its mass times the square of the speed of light (c)—in other words: $E = mc^2$. In this paper, the equation was not written specifically in that format. It was only over the next few years that it would be massaged into the form that we know so well.

What Everyone Else Thought

Even though every one of these papers was a fairly dramatic departure from currently understood physics, other scientists accepted them all fairly quickly. When the fact that the papers were written by a twenty-six-year-old who couldn't get a job in physics is taken into consideration, the acceptance of Einstein's work is quite amazing. When Einstein's sister, Maja, wrote a biography of her brother, she claimed that he was disappointed there wasn't an immediate reaction to his relativity paper. It's possible, however, that Maja's view of this was colored by hindsight, since Einstein didn't seem to have considered this particular paper to be more important than any of the others, nor was a positive response to any of his work particularly long in coming. The 1905 Nobel Prize winner, Philipp Lenard, on whose work Einstein's drew for his photoelectric paper, contacted Einstein shortly after its publication, admiring his work. By November, a paper in another scientific journal referenced Einstein's photoelectric effect paper, and Max Planck began teaching Einstein's relativity to his students almost immediately. Years later, Einstein credited Planck's teaching of relativity as the event that brought it to the attention of the scientific community, and why it was accepted so quickly.

See **Brownian Motion; $E = mc^2$; Photoelectric Effect; Relativity, Special Theory of.**

Monroe, Marilyn

In popular culture, Marilyn Monroe's name is often thrown together with Albert Einstein's. They're a classic combination: Monroe epitomized beauty the way Einstein epitomized brains. Add that they each became icons for their own professions—Marilyn is the most famous starlet in history; Einstein the most famous scientist—and the association between the two becomes natural.

Various works of art have been created that put Einstein and Monroe together and a popular play that was later turned into a movie (*Insignificance*) showed a chance meeting between Monroe and Einstein that culminated with the pink-dressed actress running around Einstein's hotel room smashing toy cars together in an effort to explain relativity. (The scene ends with Monroe admitting she has memorized the explanation but doesn't actually understand it . . . an unfortunate image of the "ditzy Marilyn," an image she herself pro-moted even though she was, in fact, quite bright.)

In real life, the pair never met, but they were contemporaries who certainly knew of each other's successes. Monroe is reputed to have said that Einstein was her idea of a "sexy man." In a story that is likely apoc-ryphal but nevertheless gets related over and over (even making it into a speech by President Reagan for the American Retail Federation in 1986), Monroe is said to have wished she could have had a child with Einstein; with her looks and his brain, it would have been perfect. The mocking response, of course, has always been, "but what if it had his looks and her brain?" (This response is even occasionally attributed to Einstein himself, though he is unlikely to have said anything so cruel.)

Mysticism

Einstein's fame—and pithy quotable comments—has made him the darling of numerous movements, various groups with various agendas all using the Einstein name to advance their cause. No such connec-tion is quite so subtle and complex as the New Age attempt to embrace Einstein as a mystic. Because his relationship with religion and faith was never a conventional one, it is fairly easy to portray him in different lights by taking his statements out of context. While Einstein did, in fact, associate himself with the mystical in a variety of key state-ments, it is a stretch to label him a spokesman for mysticism.

In 1930, Einstein wrote a lovely description of the mysterious in an article for the magazine *Forum and Century:* "The most beautiful experience we can have is the mysterious. It is the fundamental emotion which stands at the cradle of true art and true science. Whoever does not know it and can no longer wonder, no longer marvel, is as good as dead, and his eyes are dimmed. It was the experience of mystery—even if mixed with fear—that engendered religion. A knowledge of the existence of something we cannot penetrate, our perceptions of the profoundest reason, and the most radiant beauty, which only in their most primitive forms are accessible to our minds—it is this knowledge and this emotion that constitute true religiosity." This statement captures the feeling of wonder Einstein had in the beauties of the universe, whether one experiences it as a glimpse of the Grand Canyon, a Bach concerto, or the perfect simplicity of a physics equation. It is no wonder that leaders of the New Age movement take a quote like this and parade Einstein as one who understands their version of mysticism, one who connected himself to the central oneness of the universe.

And yet, Einstein would have rejected just about anything else associated with the modern concept of mysticism. He continued the above quote by saying: "In this sense, and in this sense only, I am a deeply religious man." Clearly, Einstein stood in awe and wonder of the universe, and one could argue that the experience of that awe is at the heart of what makes mysticism. However, he adamantly rejected any organized religion. He would have been incredulous at those who took his awe of the universe and turned it into anything more than simply expressing joy at the experience.

Also, important for most definitions of the word "mystic," Einstein rejected the idea that one's own consciousness could determine outside reality. He believed the universe existed in some kind of real way, independent of human observation or tinkering, and he certainly didn't believe that the human mind could bend or affect the outside world. One's point of view mattered in how the laws of physics manifested themselves (the theories of relativity stated that time and space were different for different observers) but these were still different in specific, quantifiable ways. It was not the power of one's brain that made time and space different, but a simple fact of science.

In no place was this more clear than in Einstein's attitude about quantum mechanics, the modern view of the universe that claims nature is random at a fundamental level. Quantum mechanics says that the movement of atoms and electrons and light can never be predicted with certainty. Modern mystics often embrace this to mean that the cut-and-dried world of cause and effect is meaningless. There is room for miracles, room for human conscious control of nature, room for the divine in every action, because particles simply aren't constricted to specific laws of physics. Whether or not quantum mechanics does, in fact, mean that this type of thing is open for debate, most scientists who accept quantum mechanics would say that it isn't meant to be used as proof of the mystical. Nevertheless, Einstein emphatically rejected all of these ideas out of hand. The universe, he insisted, followed the traditional laws of cause and effect as humans had believed for centuries; quantum mechanics simply wasn't thorough enough to predict them. Einstein questioned quantum mechanics precisely because it opened the door to such loose descriptions of the universe, descriptions that smacked too much of the mystical for a man who believed that everything was governed by strict physics laws.

The last word on the subject may be Einstein's himself. While he used the word "mysterious" to describe his wonder at the universe, the book *Albert Einstein, the Human Side*, written by his secretary, Helen Dukas, and the science historian Banesh Hoffman, quotes Einstein in the mid-1950s as denying mysticism per se: "What I see in Nature is a magnificent structure that we can comprehend only very imperfectly, and that must fill a thinking person with a feeling of humility. This is a genuinely religious feeling that has nothing to do with mysticism."

See **God; Realism; Religion.**

Myths and Misconceptions

As the world's most famous scientist—and the one responsible for creating our archetype of quirky geniuses—it's not surprising there are many myths about the man, describing his odd behavior. Like so many funny stories, however, many of the popular Einstein legends are too good to be true.

First and foremost, let us dispel one of the most popular, most beloved rumors about Einstein. He did not fail math. He got top grades in math and science all of his life. He also didn't fail out of school, though he did leave his secondary school abruptly when his family moved to Italy during his final year. However, he earned his diploma elsewhere and then went on to and graduated from college (albeit with only fair grades, and he was known to skip a lot of classes.)

To be honest, however, for a high-end theoretical physicist, Einstein's math was subpar. His earlier papers, while elegant, brief, and brilliant, often contain simple errors. But it must be remembered that Einstein was not balancing a checkbook, he was balancing the forces of gravity and the speed of light. The level of mathematics he was doing is far beyond two plus two. So, it's more correct to say that Einstein wasn't a mathematician and that he needed help from mathematicians quite often to make sure his theories panned out in the end.

Another highly exaggerated story about Einstein with some basis in reality concerns his clothing. Many say that Einstein wore the same thing every day and had a closet full of the exact same suits, shirts, ties, and shoes. This isn't true, especially when Einstein's second wife, Elsa, was alive. Elsa took a firm hand when it came to her husband's appearance, and pictures of the two of them touring everywhere from Japan to the American Southwest show Einstein in beautiful silk vests and dapper neckwear, as well as in a kimono and an American Indian headdress. After Elsa passed away and Einstein spent his last twenty years as a professor emeritus at Princeton, his clothing did become more erratic. He openly disliked wearing a suit and, already legendary for often going sockless, took to wearing only sandals. Perhaps the most common pictures of Einstein from that time show him happily shuffling around his Princeton study wearing a big gray sweatshirt. Luckily for Einstein, his life coincided with the invention of the cotton sweatshirt—a garment he loved.

Another popular urban legend about Einstein that has no basis in reality is that he sat next to Marilyn Monroe once at a dinner and she told him she wanted to have a child with him because with her looks and his brain, it would have been perfect. Einstein is said to have responded: "Ah, but what if it had my looks and your brain?" This story is clearly untrue because the two never met, and because the same story is often told of George Bernard Shaw and Isadora Duncan.

All manner of fable is being attached to my personality, and there is no end to the number of ingeniously devised tales.

—Einstein, in a letter to Queen Elizabeth of Belgium, March 28, 1954

However, the aforementioned myth leads to a few others. It is true that Einstein had a series of extramarital affairs. These were kept quiet for years, thanks to discrete partners and the rigorous attempts his estate took to keep his letters confidential. Einstein also had a lost child—a daughter with the woman who would become his first wife. We only know of the child's existence through the young lovers' letters. She seems to either have been adopted or died young—no one knows for sure. Many fanciful characters throughout the years have suggested they were the child, or, thanks to Einstein's sometimes wandering eye, that they were either another child or pregnant with Einstein's scion. At times, these biographical musings have even extended to the claim that Einstein's longtime secretary, Helen Dukas, is truly the missing daughter. However, this is unlikely, mostly due to our knowledge of Dukas's mother, father, and sisters. The question of paternity is a comment often made of famous men, and many of Einstein's private letters have still not been released to the public. It's possible, although not likely, that there is other Einstein progeny out there.

A few other odd ideas about Einstein can be discounted quickly. Despite the rumors among all the lefties out there, he was right-handed. He also was a heavy sleeper, often going for ten hours a night—none of this burning the midnight oil and getting by on just a few hours a night that he is often credited with. To dispel a particularly amusing myth, Einstein did not ever appear on *Gunsmoke*. The show premiered on TV six months after Einstein died.

One last entertaining, but apocryphal, story is of Einstein's visit to Las Vegas while he was working at Princeton. He was escorted around the casinos by a heavy hitter, "Nick the Greek" Dandolos, who knew that most of his friends wouldn't know much about physics. So Nick introduced him as "Little Al from Princeton—he controls a lot of the action around Jersey."

Other stories about the man have to do with his science per se. One that's espoused by an odd pairing of feminists and racists is that Einstein didn't develop his theories of relativity. Feminists point to the fact that Einstein's first wife, Mileva, was a college-trained physicist who took part in the long bull sessions Einstein had with other colleagues prior to his 1905 miracle year. But however influential Mileva's ideas were to the theory of relativity, it is clear that the ultimate work was Einstein's own. It was an insight that was hashed out by Einstein through rigorous discussions with others, but one original to him nonetheless. One other fact used in an attempt to prove that Mileva wrote Einstein's theory of relativity is that, in Einstein's divorce proceedings, he agreed to give her all monetary proceeds if he won a Nobel Prize. However, at the time, Einstein, like all Germans, was facing a financial crisis and his salary at the University of Berlin was nearly worthless. Money became a contentious issue between Einstein and Mileva early on in their divorce proceedings, so promising her funds that may or may not arrive probably seemed like a good bet.

Racists have also charged that Einstein stole his theory of special relativity, but those claims are so clearly couched in anti-Semitic attacks that they are easily discounted. In addition, Einstein went on to expound on relativity almost ten years after his original paper, developing the even more groundbreaking general theory of relativity. It's clear that this work is entirely original; Einstein's success in physics was indeed no myth.

See **Fame.**

Nazism

Under the leadership of Adolf Hitler, the Nazis extolled a philosophy of national pride and military rigor—two ideologies that Einstein, an extreme pacifist, believed were at the root of all evil. The Nazi Party in Germany stood for everything Einstein was against. And the Nazis made Einstein rethink his pacifist beliefs. Even before the atrocities of the Holocaust were exposed, Einstein often commented that the only way to stop Nazism was through equal—and justified—force.

The Nazi Party, short for the National Socialist German Worker's Party or Nationalsozialist in German, was founded in 1919. For a number of years, it was perceived to be just another political party. Early on, Einstein, like most Germans, dismissed Adolf Hitler and the Nazis as extremists who were unlikely to gain a following. Like other European Jews, Einstein faced anti-Jewish sentiment his entire life and the new brand of anti-Semitism from the Nazis didn't seem any different. It was not until 1922, when Einstein's colleague, the Jewish foreign minister Walther Rathenau, was assassinated that Einstein began to take the situation more seriously. Indeed, Einstein had reason to worry. He was more than just the average Jew and he had to contend specifically with anti-Einstein sentiment as well. Over the previous few years, he had been catapulted into the limelight as a famous scientist and he used his fame as a platform to speak out against what he saw as the evils of the world: militarism and nationalism. For many Germans, whose national pride was still reeling from the loss of World War I, any type of criticism, especially criticism from a pacifist Jew, was not looked upon favorably.

The Nazi Party, with Hitler at its head, used the pride of the German people to gain strength. As so many Germans felt downtrodden after World War I, Hitler's rhetoric that they were in fact a superior, chosen people landed on eager ears. The superior people had to eradicate the inferior, claimed Hitler, and he organized hostility against German Jews. At the time, inflation in Germany had reached near catastrophic levels. Einstein himself was forced to take on side work consulting on patents for various German businesses, as his professor's salary was nearly worthless. And still, many believed that times were merely difficult and that middle-of-the-road politics would eventually prevail.

Leaving Germany Behind

In the years between 1930 and 1933, Einstein spent most of his time traveling around the world giving physics lectures, attending scientific conferences, and raising funds for the Hebrew University in Israel. His knowledge of the increasingly oppressive politics of the Nazi Party were filtered through letters from his assistants, family, and friends, but it was enough to get him worried. The climate was getting worse and Einstein quietly began to consider that perhaps the time had come to leave Germany. In 1932, the newly formed Institute for Advanced Study in Princeton, New Jersey offered Einstein a six-month teaching position. Einstein told the Prussian Academy of Science and his friends that he would be back in April. But, he was not as unaware of the political climate as he pretended. As he and Elsa locked up their beloved villa in Caputh for the winter, he told her, "take a very good look at it." He said, "You will never see it again."

Einstein's prediction came true. On January 30, 1933, the German president, under fantastic pressure by a coalition of Nazi and right-wing politicians, appointed Hitler as the German Chancellor. At the time, Einstein was in California for a scheduled lecture. He decided right then not to return to their home in Berlin, and he and Elsa never again laid eyes on Germany.

While officially Einstein acted as if he would be coming back, confirming university salary notices and the like, his letters show that he had no intention of returning. On February 27, Einstein wrote his friend Margarete Lebach in Berlin, "In view of Hitler I don't dare step on German soil." The very next day, the Reichstag was in flames and the first wave of brutal Nazi restrictions against politicians, intellectuals, and journalists began.

Einstein announced his decision not to return to Germany in a public statement made in Manhattan in March. "As long as I have any choice in the matter, I shall live only in a country where civil liberty, tolerance, and equality of all citizens before the law prevail. . . . These conditions do not exist in Germany at the present time."

The announcement enraged newspaper columnists in Berlin. One publisher wrote, "Einstein has been hardly a day in New York before he has twice thrown his 'powerful personality' against Germany." The article concludes that Einstein was "a man who was never a German in our eyes and who declares himself to be a Jew and nothing but a Jew." Such sentiments were only to get worse. On April first, the Nazi government held a "boycott of Jews." At the university and the state library, Jewish students, assistants, and professors were banned from entering their offices and classrooms. Also, their IDs were confiscated. The German professor Max von Laue, who throughout World War II often spoke out against intellectual persecution, attempted on April 6 to stop the Prussian Academy from issuing a statement accusing Einstein of atrocity propaganda. He was not successful. The statement was issued, and not one voice dissented. It was even signed by Fritz Haber, who twenty years earlier, had been forceful in getting Einstein appointed to the society.

Einstein's stepdaughter, Ilse and her husband, Rudolf Kayser, were still in Berlin. Ilse tried to save the rest of Einstein's papers, library, and furniture from being seized by the Nazis, but by the end of May, another Nazi raid ransacked the apartment. Finally, anything that remained was brought out of Germany by the French ambassador.

On May 10, 1933, tens of thousands of Germans overflowed the large public square between Berlin University and the State Opera House. There they held a massive book burning of books of every intellectual stripe, including many of Einstein's. Over sixty other bonfires blazed throughout Germany. The next day, Max Planck bravely spoke in Einstein's favor at a crowded meeting of the Prussian Academy, comparing Einstein with Kepler and Newton. Later in May,

Planck spoke with Hitler, hoping to convince him that the deportation of Jews would kill German science. But his attempts were futile, and several of Einstein's former assistants were among the many Jews forced out of their jobs.

Einstein briefly settled in le Coq sur Mer on the Belgian coast. There, his friend Antonina Vallentin came to convince him that he was a target for Nazi assassination. She showed Einstein and Elsa a German magazine with Einstein's photo on the front and the caption "not yet hanged." Elsa was upset, and although Einstein dismissed the idea, he did not argue when the Belgian government decided to appoint guards to watch over the household-in-exile. Soon after, Einstein's position with Princeton's Institute for Advanced Study became official. In October, he moved his household to the United States for good.

In Germany, the attacks continued not just against Einstein, but against modern physics itself. Hitler promoted art and culture over science, which he saw as overly-intellectual and anti-German. Some still had the courage to support Einstein's ideas, if not the man himself. Werner Heisenberg, an Aryan German, defended theoretical physics by pointing out that Max Planck also worked in the field. But the Nazis were determined to show that Einstein's theories were wrong, or, at the very least, that Einstein stole them from a non-Jewish scientist. During World War II, Hitler produced a paper entitled "100 Scientists Against Einstein." In response, Einstein simply said, "If I were wrong, one would have been enough."

Nazism vs. Pacifism

Once in the United States, Einstein continued to do what he could to thwart the Nazi agenda. In 1939, he broadcast an appeal to help Jewish refugees. He also spent a significant amount of time and money helping friends, relatives, and strangers escape from Nazi-occupied territory. When writing relatives and friends, Einstein used the pseudonym, "Elsa Alberti" so the recipients of his letters could escape harassment by Nazi officials.

Even though Einstein held onto a strong pacifist ideology, he also advocated fighting against the Nazis. In an influential scholarly work, the 1949 essay, "Einstein's Social Philosophy," published in the book *Albert Einstein, Philosopher-Scientist*, Ohio State University philosopher Virgil G. Hinshaw Jr. writes that Einstein believed, "one should resort to violence whenever militant fascism arises; that is, whenever militant fascism, as did Nazism, seeks to wipe out humanity's best."

As the atrocities of the Nazi concentration camps began to come to light in the 1940s, Einstein's rage and grief were palpable. Like many Jews, Einstein lost family members during the war. His cousin Lina Einstein died in Auschwitz. Another cousin, Robert Einstein, committed suicide after hearing that the Fascists in Italy had killed his wife and sons.

In May 1946, Einstein spoke to Russian writer Ilya Ehrenburg about a recently published collection of diaries, letters, and statements by eyewitnesses concerning Nazi crimes against the Jewish people in the occupied territories. Einstein said, "I have often said that the potentialities of knowledge are unlimited, as is the knowable. Now I think that vileness and cruelty also have no limits."

See also **Anti-Semitism; Germany; Hitler, Adolf; Pacifism.**

Newton, Isaac
(1643–1727)

In the seventeenth century, Isaac Newton essentially created the modern world of physics, developing theories about gravity, light, inertia, mass, and even the math needed to understand these concepts. Newton's mechanics were hailed as the definitive description of the universe—until Einstein completely reworked those theories.

Einstein began the revolution in modern physics that overturned the old paradigm of Newtonian physics, and thus each created the foundation of a new way of thinking. Indeed, there are many parallels between the two scientists. Each had what has been called a "miracle year" in their mid-twenties. Newton's year was in what he called the "plague year" of 1666. That year, he created differential and integral calculus, discovered the law of universal gravitation, and determined how gravity caused the planets to move in ellipses. Einstein's miracle year was 1905, during which he published the special theory of relativity, the solution to the photoelectric effect (for which he won the Nobel Prize), an explanation for Brownian motion, and the equation $E = mc^2$. As it happens, Newton didn't publish much of his early work for decades, but by the time he did, it was heralded instantly as being correct. The two men are also linked by the fact that they both became hugely famous during their lifetimes. Isaac Newton was as much an iconographic figure in his time as Einstein was in his—just substitute a formal British wig for Einstein's unruly mane of hair.

Over the centuries, Newton's fame as the founder of modern physics embedded him in society's consciousness as the genius who essentially created science as we know it. There were several problems, however, most notably when it came to understanding light and optics. Newton had hypothesized that light was made out of "corpuscles"— particles like small balls. In the nineteenth century, physicists like James Clerk Maxwell (1831–1879) determined that light was actually a wave. But the problems for Newtonian mechanics were just beginning; Maxwell's theory called other facets of Newtonian mechanics into question. By the time Einstein was in graduate school it was clear to the most perceptive physicists that there was something of a crisis; either Newton was wrong or Maxwell. Einstein's special theory of relativity, published in 1905, was the deciding blow— Maxwell was the winner and Newtonian mechanics, with its dependence on absolute space and absolute time, was incorrect.

> *Let no one suppose, however, that the mighty work of Newton can really be superseded by this or any other theory. His great and lucid ideas will retain their unique significance for all time as the foundation of our whole modern conceptual structure in the sphere of natural philosophy.*
> —Einstein, "What Is the Theory of Relativity?" the *London Times*, November 28, 1919

But Einstein was not to stop there. While he certainly did not start out with a plan to dismantle Newton, he was the one destined to change the accepted concept of a hard and fast mechanical world. Einstein tackled gravity, seeing that the way it was then understood did not relate to his new theory of relativity. In 1911, he published the general theory of relativity, which did away with another of Newton's great theories: the law of universal gravity. Newton had postulated that all objects in the universe were attracted to each other by a force proportional to their masses. But he knew that he could offer no suggestion as to why this is so. He said of his lack of a theory, *"Non fingo hypotheses"* ("I do not frame any hypotheses"). With general relativity, Einstein offered a solution to why gravity worked: two objects were attracted to each other because a large mass warped the space around it so that any other mass nearby "slid" into it. At its simplest, Einstein's equations could be shown to be equivalent to Newton's; Newton wasn't wrong per se, but Einstein's equations were more complete.

Despite overturning so much Newtonian science, Einstein always held Newton in the highest esteem. In a 1940 article for *Science* titled, "The Fundamentals of Theoretical Physics," Einstein said that Newton was the first person to "lay a uniform theoretical foundation" to the world of science. Einstein went on: "This Newtonian basis proved eminently fruitful and was regarded as final up to the end of the nineteenth century. It not only gave results for the movements of the heavenly bodies, down to the most minute details, but also furnished a theory of the mechanics of discrete and continuous masses, a simple explanation of the principle of the conservation of energy and a complete and brilliant theory of heat." Newton had produced a comprehensive, systematic set of rules to unite all then-understood phenomena in the world. He found mechanics such a successful way to explain nature that he applied it to all he saw—as did everyone else for over two hundred years, until Einstein changed the world view yet again.

See **Gravitation; Light.**

Nobel Prize in Physics

Einstein won the Nobel Prize for physics in 1922. Like almost all aspects of his life, how and why he received the award is mired in world politics, scientific harangues, and above all, Einstein's ambiguous feelings about the honor itself.

To begin with, the dates are all wrong. Einstein received the Nobel Prize in physics in 1922—for the 1921 prize. Explanations for the year-long delay vary and some years, the Nobel Committee declines to grant a prize at all, but it seems one of the reasons the 1921 prize took an extra year was because of a controversy within the committee over whether to give it to Einstein at all.

Equally interesting is that Einstein didn't receive the prize for his world-famous equation $E = mc^2$, or his theory of relativity, but instead for his less well-known discovery of the law of the photoelectric effect.

Nominations, Nominations, Nominations

The procedure for awarding the Nobel Prize starts with a request by the Royal Swedish Academy of Sciences for nominations. Those suggestions are then handed over to a five-member Nobel committee. Those five men—at that time, they were all men—would study the proposals and supporting material and decide their recommendations by majority vote. But the Academy's Klass, or section, on physics is allowed to completely disregard the committee's suggestions and vote on someone else. Finally, the entire Academy votes on the prize. Throughout this process, the voting is done in secret and none of the votes are recorded. However, records are kept on who is nominated, so we know that Einstein was nominated for the Nobel Prize in physics almost every year between 1910 and 1922.

Murmurs throughout the physics community that Einstein was a Nobel Prize contender began almost immediately after his "miracle year" in 1905, when he published five papers that changed the foundations of physics. However, as momentum built to honor Einstein—a vocal minority opposed him. Some physicists were concerned that, ultimately, Einstein's revolutionary ideas on relativity could turn out to be incorrect. Others were swayed by the same anti-Semitic feelings that shadowed Einstein his entire life. The Hungarian physicist and former physics Nobel Prize winner Philipp Lenard was at the forefront of both charges against Einstein. This led to often contradictory arguments saying both that relativity was wrong and that it was so brilliant that a Jewish man like Einstein couldn't have conceived it. Lenard's arguments played a great part in convincing the academy to keep its distance.

Wilhelm Ostwald (1853–1932), the 1909 Nobel laureate in chemistry, was the first to nominate Einstein for a Nobel Prize. Ostwald pressed for Einstein's nomination (always for his work on relativity) again in 1912 and 1913. As it happens, Ostwald had turned down a request for an assistantship from the young Einstein in the spring of 1901. Now, however, he was obviously enamored with Einstein's theories. He was the only scientist to nominate Einstein in 1910, and in his nomination of Einstein for the 1912 award, Ostwald compared Einstein's work to that of Copernicus and Darwin. Three other physicists joined Ostwald's nomination of Einstein that year, although they declined to sign on to Ostwald's comparison.

Einstein was also nominated for the 1913 and the 1914 awards, again for his work on special relativity. By then, some doubt was beginning to creep in about his relativity work, as Einstein was wrapped up in his tussle over general relativity and confusing everyone, including himself. Although Einstein wasn't nominated in 1915, he was nominated in 1916 in the category of molecular physics for his work on Brownian motion.

Finally, by 1917, enough physicists were convinced that Einstein's work deserved a prize that he was beginning to be nominated for a variety of reasons: his new theory of gravitation, the general theory of relativity, his explanation of the movement of the planet Mercury, his work on quantum theory and relativity, and his overall work in theoretical physics. Einstein was nominated again in 1918 and 1919.

The Academy Hedges Its Bets

Many physicists of the day were adamant that Einstein should be honored for his work on relativity. In fact, in 1919 one even suggested that "it would appear peculiar to the learned world if Einstein were to receive the Prize for statistical physics . . . and not for his other major papers." But it must be remembered that, in 1919, there was no experimental evidence to prove Einstein's theoretical work unequivocally correct. It wasn't until the winter of 1919 that Sir Arthur Eddington's experiments would provide definite evidence.

So 1920 was the breakthrough year. At this point, such eminent scientists as Niels Bohr, Max Planck, and Eddington insisted that Einstein receive the prize for relativity. But the idea was still so revolutionary—tossing out as it did hundreds of years of Newtonian physics—that there were still some physicists who remained unconvinced. So, the Nobel Prize committee asked for a special report on Einstein's work to settle the issue once and for all.

Committee member Allvar Gullstrand was to prepare an account on Einstein's theory of relativity, and the secretary of the Swedish Academy of Sciences, Christopher Arrhenius, was to do one on the photoelectric effect. It's unknown why the committee picked Gullstrand, a professor of ophthalmology, to write about relativity. To be sure, Gullstrand was quite bright; he was the world's leading figure in the study of the eye. However, Gullstrand didn't seem completely convinced of Eddington's experiment, writing to the committee about general relativity, "it remains unknown until further notice whether the Einstein theory can be brought into agreement [with other experimental evidence]."

For his part, Arrhenius's report on Einstein's photoelectric effect noted that in 1918, Max Planck had already won for his work on quantum theory and if another prize was to be given in this field, it really should go to the experimentalists. Also, by the committee's request, Arrhenius added a statement on the consequences of Einstein's theory of general relativity, and Arrhenius, like Gullstrand, noted that there was still some experimental evidence against Einstein's theories, and stated that many scientists were also questioning the results of Eddington's 1919 eclipse expedition.

And so, while it is hard to give an exact reason, as the Nobel Prize committee does so much behind closed doors, possibly thanks to this conflict, there was no Nobel Prize in physics awarded at all in 1920.

Finally, a Decision . . .

The delay in awarding Einstein was beginning to rile many. In 1922, the list of physicists nominating Einstein was the longest yet. Academy member Marcel Birllouin wrote: "Imagine for a moment what the general opinion will be fifty years from now if Einstein's name does not appear on the list of Nobel laureates."

The committee asked Gullstrand for another analysis of relativity, but he changed very little in his opinion. This time, however, the committee also asked for a report on Einstein's work on the photoelectric effect. This was finally enough to sway the Academy's mind. They agreed to award Einstein a Nobel Prize in physics for his photoelectric effect theories and not the theories for which he was most well-known.

This isn't to say that Einstein's work on the photoelectric effect wasn't worthy; it certainly was Nobel Prize caliber science. In fact, it was the only paper that Einstein himself called revolutionary. However, it's ironic that the prize was awarded for work that was, within the physics community, far more controversial than his relativity theories. Both the special and general theories of relativity were accepted by scientists almost immediately after their publication, while Einstein's work on the photoelectric effect postulated that light was made up of discrete particles—an idea that physicists thought so absurd that no one accepted it for about fifteen years after it was first presented. Considering that Einstein's work in relativity was what catapulted him into the public eye and helped bring physics into the modern age, it was a bit weak-kneed of the academy not to honor it. Some scientific historians believe that the academy balked at relativity simply because they were under so much pressure to honor the idea. Since many leading scientists of the day were adamant that Einstein receive a prize, and there was still some consternation over the validity of his work in relativity, it was just easier to get Einstein out of the way by awarding him a prize for his equally good work on the photoelectric effect.

. . . and Yet, an Absent Einstein

So, in 1922 the academy decided to award Einstein the 1921 Nobel Prize in physics. But despite Einstein's fame, the general public didn't seem to take notice. While today, the Nobel Prizes are front-page news, in 1922 they were noted with two sentences in the *New York Times*. On November 10, on page four, column two, the paper's entire entry reads, "Nobel Prize for Einstein. The Nobel committee has awarded the physics prize for 1921 to Albert Einstein, identified with the theory of relativity, and that for 1922 to Professor Neils [sic] Bohr of Copenhagen."

Einstein had advance notice that he was finally to receive the Nobel Prize. His colleague Max von Laue (1879–1960), a professor of theoretical physics in Berlin, hinted at it in a September letter to Einstein, saying that "events may occur in November that might make it desirable for you to be present in Europe in December."

Possibly because of an annoyance at the committee's deliberations, or because there could be yet another delay, or possibly because, at this point, the world-famous Einstein didn't quite care about the Academy, Einstein continued on a planned trip to Japan. And so it was on an ocean liner, steaming far away from Europe, that Einstein learned he won the Nobel Prize. It didn't seem to make a huge splash: in his travel diary, there was no mention about the Nobel, and he and his wife Elsa did not return to Europe until the last week of December 1922.

When the winner of a Nobel Prize is absent, it is customary for representatives of the winner's country to accept the award on his or her behalf. But Einstein was claimed by two nations. He renounced his German citizenship back in high school, and he traveled under a Swiss passport. However, upon being nominated to the Prussian Academy of Sciences in 1913, he had been de facto granted German citizenship again. It was early in December, before the Einsteins returned from Japan, when Rudolf Nadolny, the German ambassador to Sweden, accepted the Nobel Prize in Einstein's name. In Nadolny's toast at the Stockholm banquet, he said, "it is the joy of my people that once again one of them has been able to achieve something for all mankind." He diplomatically added the hope that "Switzerland, which during many years provided the scholar with a home and opportunities to work, would also participate in this joy." After Einstein returned from his voyage, it was the Swedish ambassador to Germany who came to Einstein's home and handed him his medal.

Einstein finally gave his Nobel speech in July 1923 when he visited Gottenberg to attend a meeting of the Scandinavian Society of Science. He ignored the fact that he had won for the photoelectric effect and, instead, his speech was all about relativity. An audience of two thousand people was in attendance.

Despite Einstein's seeming indifference to the award, it's probable that he always believed he would win a Nobel Prize. One of the terms of his divorce from his first wife was that she would receive the entire monetary award should he ever win—terms that Einstein honored, sending Mileva 121,572.43 Swedish kronor, about $32,000 at the exchange rate of the time.

Olympia Academy

The Olympia Academy was created by Einstein when he was twenty-three. He and his "students" would sit and debate intellectual ideas, often while eating sausages. The "Akademie Olympia" was a farcical imitation of the self-important science institutions of the time, and it was a tonic to the floundering young Einstein.

In late 1901, Einstein was frustrated. He had his undergraduate degree and was working on his dissertation, yet time and again, he was unable to find an academic job. He also had a pregnant sweetheart whom his parents abhorred and the only job on the horizon was one at a Patent Office in Bern—and even that wasn't definite. Nonetheless, Einstein decided to move to Bern in February 1902. Hoping to earn some pocket money, he decided to tutor. He took out an advertisement in the local newspaper advertising "trial lessons free." What began as a search for employment ended up as one of Einstein's great joys: those tutoring lessons would grow into the Olympia Academy.

One of the first to answer the ad was Maurice Solovine (1875–1958). Solovine was a young Jew from Romania who had come to Bern to attend university but became disillusioned with its philosophy and physics professors. Later, Solovine recalled meeting Einstein for the first time, saying he climbed the stairs up to Einstein's small apartment and was struck by the spark in Einstein's large brown eyes. The two men had an immediate connection, beginning with their disenchantment with how physics was currently being taught. At that first meeting, the two men talked for over two hours, and then for another half hour out on the street.

Finally parting, they agreed to meet the following day. The tutoring sessions soon had a third member: Conrad Habicht (1884–1948). Habicht had known Einstein previously when Einstein was tutoring math in Schaffhausen. A bank director's son, Habicht had studied mathematics and physics at Munich and Berlin and was now working on his doctoral thesis at the University of Bern.

The two men were impressed with Einstein and his seemingly effortless ability to explain things clearly. The three threw themselves into the Academy. They had an extensive reading list, including Ernst Mach's *Analysis of Perception* and *Mechanics and its Development*, Karl Pearson's *Grammar of Science*, and Henri Poincarè's *Le Science et l'hypothese* (*Science and hypothesis*), as well as the philosophy of Spinoza, Sophocles, and Cervantes.

But the group was not all work and no play. According to Einstein's neighbors, the "intellectual" meetings were often loud, boisterous, and went late into the night. Solovine reminisced that they would sit around eating sausage, Gruyeré cheese, fruit, honey, Turkish coffee, and hard-boiled eggs. Once, Habicht and Solovine celebrated Einstein's birthday by buying him caviar, as Einstein was usually a rapturous eater. Unfortunately, the president of the Academy became so absorbed in explaining Galileo's principle of inertia that he gobbled down the expensive treat without even realizing what he was eating. A few days later the group splurged again, this time chanting over and over to themselves, "Now we're eating caviar!"

Eventually the position at the Patent Office came through and Einstein could send for his wife-to-be, Mileva. Solovine recalled that Mileva often attended sessions of the Olympia Academy. She didn't seem to enter into the discussions, but she felt at ease in their company. Indeed, Solovine and Habicht seem to be among the few people whom Mileva actually considered friends.

During meetings, Einstein used to tease Mileva by launching into risqué stories, knowing she would immediately leap in and scold him.

But Mileva could also be amused by the bawdiness of the group. Once, Habicht got a cheap, tin plate engraved with the title, "Albert Ritter von Steissbein, President of the Olympia Academy" that he fixed on the door of Einstein and Mileva's apartment. Einstein biographer Albrecht Fölsing wrote:

> "Ritter von Steissbein" might be loosely translated as "Knight of the Backside." The addition of "-bein" to "Steiss" turns it from the German for buttocks to "coccyx." But it also carries the indecorous suggestion of Scheissbein, or shit-leg. According to Solovine, Einstein and Mileva "laughed so much they thought they would die," and the name occurs elsewhere. Einstein sent an almost illegible postcard to Habicht reading, "Totally drunk—unfortunately both under the table. Your servant Steissbein and Wife."

When Einstein and Mileva were married on January 6, 1903, their witnesses were the other two members of the Academy, Solovine and Habicht. Although a few others became members of the Olympia Academy from time to time, the core was always Solovine, Habicht, and Einstein. A picture taken at the time shows three young men, all with moustaches, bow ties, and suits attempting to look official, but smirking at the camera. Almost half a century later, in 1948, Einstein reminisced to Solovine that the Academy was "far less childish than those respectable ones which I later got to know."

Oppenheimer, J. Robert
(1904–1967)

Julius Robert Oppenheimer is remembered as the father of the atomic bomb. A brilliant physicist, Oppenheimer organized the Manhattan Project at Los Alamos, New Mexico. Before that, he was known for his work in astronomy, applying Einstein's general relativity to the stars. He ended his days working at the Institute for Advanced Study at Princeton, where his office was one floor above Einstein's.

Oppenheimer and Einstein crossed paths many times throughout their lives, meeting at various scientific conferences, but Oppenheimer was of a younger generation of physicists—one who was educated after the revolution of the theories of relativity and quantum mechanics. Oppenheimer nonchalantly made use of both as he studied the insides of stars, attempting to understand what was happening deep in their fiery interiors. He wasn't part of the struggle to figure out the math behind the theories as Einstein did, and so from Oppenheimer's viewpoint, Einstein might as well have been an old man—one to be revered and respected, but nevertheless, one who no longer contributed new science to the field.

Oppenheimer was born in the United States but received his doctorate at the University of Göttingen. He went on to teach at the University of California, Berkeley. When World War II started, he was recruited to join the war effort to help develop an atomic bomb, and he became the director of the Manhattan Project. After the war, he landed at Princeton, and, with his top-security clearance he had to maintain a military guard on the safe in his Princeton office.

When he arrived in 1935, Oppenheimer, like Einstein, mocked the stuffy college town and "its solipsistic luminaries shining in separate and helpless desolation." "Einstein," wrote Oppenheimer, "is completely cuckoo." At the time, the physics community was openly disdainful of Einstein's rejection of quantum mechanics and his obsession with proving a unified theory to supplant it, and Oppenheimer was in agreement. Einstein, for his part, found Oppenheimer to be an "unusually capable man of many-sided education."

Unlike so many American physicists of the time, Einstein and Oppenheimer made their first impressions of each other only after World War II. The two men did not cross paths during the war, as Einstein was not part of the bomb-building project; the Federal Bureau of Investigation decided that he was a security risk because of his possible Communist ties. Einstein was never actually a member of the Communist Party, but, ironically, Oppenheimer was. In 2002, thirty-two years after Oppenheimer's death, letters were released that show he belonged to the American Communist Party in the late 1930s and early 1940s.

His wife, too, had been openly a member of the Communist Party and there was enough doubt about Oppenheimer during the Cold War to make him a target of the infamous McCarthy trials; U.S. senator Joseph McCarthy called the physicist in front of the senate committee in 1954. When Einstein heard the news, he laughed, saying that Oppenheimer had only to arrive in Washington, tell everyone they were fools, and leave. Ultimately, of course, this was advice that could not be followed, and Einstein was one of the many leading scientists of the day to stand up in support of his colleague. Despite their support, Oppenheimer's security clearance was withdrawn. Suddenly, he was no longer allowed to even read papers about the atom bomb that he himself had written.

The McCarthy trial did not affect Oppenheimer's job security, however, and he continued on as director of the Institute for Advanced Study, where, despite the fact that the two scientists disagreed on modern physics, Einstein and Oppenheimer always shared a mutual respect. Ten years after Einstein's death, Oppenheimer delivered a memoir that was later collected in a series of essays by Unesco titled, "Science and Synthesis." In it, Oppenheimer heralded Einstein's work both in creating the bomb and speaking out against it: "His part was that of creating an intellectual revolution, and discovering more than any scientist of our time how profound were the errors made by men before them. . . . his was a voice raised with very great weight against violence and cruelty wherever he saw them and, after the war, he spoke with deep emotion and I believe with great weight about the supreme violence of these atomic weapons."

Pacifism

Einstein was an outspoken pacifist, believing that militarism and war were the tragedies that destroyed his homeland, Germany. He spoke out loudly and often about his dismay over war and spoke of his love for Ghandi's peaceful dissention techniques. However, he also believed that there were extreme cases in which one should fight.

When young, Einstein seemed to have no qualms about the army. While finishing his last year of secondary school in Switzerland, Einstein showed up for his medical exam for military service—only to be rejected for flat feet.

Einstein moved to Germany in 1914, when he accepted a position at the new Kaiser Wilhelm Institute in Berlin and it was then that he began to give voice to his antimilitaristic opinions, speaking out against the nationalistic tendencies of Germany. Einstein's fears bloomed as the country rallied to war against much of the rest of Europe. During the First World War, nearly one hundred German intellectuals, including Einstein's friend the physicist Max Planck, signed a letter defending the conduct of Germany in the war. Einstein was one of three who countered with an antiwar statement. Actions like this landed Einstein on a list of suspected pacifists. Such rabble rousers, warned government officials, should not be allowed to travel abroad.

This did nothing to affect Einstein's vehemence on the subject, however. When the war was over, he strongly supported the foundation of the League of Nations, which was created with the charge to keep world peace. But Einstein was not in the majority. The postwar economic chaos in Germany created a fertile ground for finger pointing and the rise of militant, nationalistic German feelings. The country became politically unstable; in 1918, one of Einstein's lectures at the University of Berlin was actually "canceled due to revolution." As the leaders of the country enacted more and more restrictive, militaristic policies, Einstein spoke out all the more stridently.

This time, unlike during World War I, Einstein was more than a mere university professor. The furor over his theory of relativity granted him worldwide fame, and newspaper reporters called frequently to obtain the famous physicist's point of view on everything from the death penalty to global politics. Although Einstein was outspoken about his dislike for German politics, he, at least for a time, also defended his country. In 1921, he refused to attend the third Solvay Conference in Belgium because all other German scientists were excluded.

In 1922 Einstein joined the League of Nations' Committee on Intellectual Cooperation to work for peace. The League asked him to begin an intellectual dialogue with anyone of his choosing. Einstein chose a discourse with the father of psychoanalysis, Sigmund Freud, and asked the question: "Is there any way of delivering humankind from the menace of war?" The dialogue eventually became the book *Why War?*. Although it didn't achieve its objective—stopping the onset of World War II—the book became one of the early works espousing a new world order that emphasized peace over military strength.

Although he tried, Einstein's efforts at either calming German militaristic feelings or convincing others to support progressive German politics were for naught. World War II began, and as Nazism spread throughout Germany, Einstein moved across the Atlantic. In Princeton, New Jersey, he continued his activism, even speaking out against his beloved Israel when he felt the country relied too heavily on military might in its relations with the Palestinian people.

Throughout his life, Einstein heralded Mahatma Gandhi as the premier example of one who advocated resolving differences peacefully. He considered Gandhi's *Autobiography* one of his favorite books and kept a drawing of Gandhi hanging in his Princeton study. And yet, Einstein also distinguished himself from Gandhi, saying that at extreme times, there was reason to resort to war. In light of the atrocities of the Holocaust, Einstein's complete belief in nonviolence had wavered. He encouraged intervention, yet, when pressed, he stressed that if anybody should police a nation (even Germany) it should be an international entity that had no nationalistic ties.

> *I am a dedicated, but not an absolute pacifist; this means that I am opposed to the use of force under any circumstances except when confronted by an enemy who pursues the destruction of life as an end in itself.*
>
> —Einstein, in response to a Japanese letter on June 23, 1953

Proving this point, Einstein did do some work for the U.S. Navy during World War II. Even though it was merely technical and quite brief, he did voluntarily help a branch of the military.

However, Einstein had a slightly larger role in the application of atomic weapons. Not only did his theory that matter could be converted into energy lead some minds to conjure up images of immensely powerful bombs, but he also had a hand in getting the U.S. nuclear weapons program off the ground. Worried that the German government was close to creating such a bomb, he wrote a letter to President Roosevelt encouraging research on atomic weapons. Much has been made of the letter, and yet while it was significant in Einstein's life, it was but one of the considerations that spurred on the Manhattan Project. In addition, Einstein himself never saw his minor role in the creation of nuclear weapons as a moral weight on his pacifist conscience. He only ever stated that he regretted how mankind had chosen to use the weapons.

Einstein did what he could, however, to ensure that nuclear weapons would never be used again and he deplored the arms race between the United States and the USSR. He made many nominations for the Nobel Peace Prize and added his name and his fame to a number of political statements. His most noteworthy treatise on the subject was the Einstein-Russell Manifesto of 1955, a statement that sought to bring together Russian and Western peoples on the dangers of nuclear war. The manifesto became the foundation of the modern peace movement and the ensuing Pugwash Conferences on Science and World Affairs. It was published just a few months after Einstein died and it was the last article Einstein ever had a hand in—a fitting coda for a man who dedicated his life to the peace movement.

Parents

Einstein's parents, Hermann and Pauline Einstein, were liberal, non-practicing Jews of middle-class descent. Hermann had several businesses throughout his life, all of which failed, and the family was forced to move several times so he could find his next opportunity. Pauline came from a fairly wealthy family and had high hopes for raising a sophisticated son.

Hermann Einstein (1847–1902) came from Buchau, a small town in the German state of Württemberg. There, the Einsteins were part of long-established Jewish communities known as "meadow Jews" that were scattered through the small towns and farming villages of south Germany. There had been Einsteins, originally spelled Ainsteins, in Buchau since 1665.

Einstein's father, Hermann, was the son of Abraham Einstein and Helen Moos. (According to Jewish tradition, Hermann gave his son a name starting with "A" to honor Abraham's memory.) When Hermann was born, the Napoleonic reforms had begun and the emancipation of Germany's Jews was underway (although it took until 1862 for the kingdom of Württemberg to grant its Jewish subjects full civil rights). For Hermann, this meant that he could get an education in the big city of Stuttgart. He did well there, and his grades showed a clear mathematical bent. However, he needed to make a living, so he moved to the old cathedral city of Ulm and sold feathers for mattress stuffing.

When Hermann met Pauline Koch (1858–1920) she was eighteen years old and living with her fairly wealthy parents. Pauline's father, Julius Koch, worked his way up from being a baker to making a sizable fortune with his brother as a grain trader. Pauline grew up in a sprawling household where both brothers' families lived under one roof with each wife cooking during alternate weeks.

In 1876, twenty-nine-year-old Hermann married eighteen-year-old Pauline in the German town of Cannstatt. Hermann was older, but it was Pauline who was the sophisticate. She had a flair for music and the arts as well as a rather cool, sarcastic nature. The young couple remained in Ulm until around 1881, when they moved to Munich. In Munich, Hermann and his younger brother, Jakob (1850–1912), started a business installing gas and water lines. A few years later, the two brothers had an electrical business that, in 1888, supplied enough power to light the German town of Schwabing, which had about ten thousand people.

For a while, the Einstein household was happy and wealthy, but over time both business ventures failed. Ultimately, the family had to leave the villa where Einstein spent most of his childhood. His parents moved from Munich to Italy, where Hermann had another electrotechnical job. They left Einstein behind in the care of distant relatives so he could finish secondary school.

As the Einsteins' older child, and as a male, Albert Einstein carried the weight of his parents' hopes for upward mobility. To put a finer point on it, his mother pressured him to excel. While Hermann seemed to be an amiable failure, Pauline was bent on making sure her son was a success. For example, before Einstein was even in the first grade, Pauline showed him the way to navigate one of Munich's busiest streets. Then she sent him off by himself to do the journey again. Later, Einstein learned that Pauline had people secretly observing the four-year-old boy to check his performance.

Pauline also barreled forward on her son's education. Einstein had been slow to speak and because of this, in the beginning of his life, Pauline fretted that her child was retarded. With relief, she found that he was quite bright, and when he was five, she hired a woman to tutor him so he would advance quickly.

While Einstein clearly loved and revered his distinguished-looking father with his pince-nez and his heavy moustache, it was Pauline that Einstein resembled physically and feared emotionally. Pauline had a love of music, a commanding presence, a distinctive nose, and unruly hair. When the family was forced to move to Italy for financial reasons and Einstein stayed behind, he was miserable. He already detested the discipline of his secondary school and without his mother to demand that he attend, he left, surprising his parents by showing up suddenly at the house in Italy.

Immediately, Einstein's mother set about pulling strings so she could advance her son's schooling. She asked a family friend, Gustav Maier, to use his influence to get Einstein admitted early into the

Swiss Federal Polytechnical School, later to be known as the Eidgenössische Technische Hochschule, or the ETH. Although Einstein was allowed to take the test, he didn't pass until the next year.

While Einstein was studying at the ETH, the family finances once again took a turn for the worse. Ultimately, the young student had to rely on a modest allowance from wealthier relatives. He wrote to his younger sister, Maja in 1898, "What depressed me most is, of course, the misfortune of my poor parents who have not had a happy moment for so many years. . . . After all I am nothing but a burden to my family. . . . It would surely be better if I were not alive. Only the thought that I have always done what my feeble strength allowed and that year in and year out I do not allow myself a pleasure, a diversion except what my studies afford, keeps me going and must sometimes protect me from despair."

But while Einstein fretted about his parents' financial condition, he also went against their wishes by falling in love with, and eventually marrying, a young Serbian woman, Mileva Maric. Both of Einstein's parents bitterly hated Mileva.

Einstein's letters to Mileva from late July to August 1900 show his parents' dismay at their relationship. He described a scene between himself and his mother: when Pauline asked what was to become of Mileva, who had failed her physics exams, Einstein answered, "My wife." Pauline threw a fit. Einstein wrote, " Mama threw herself on the bed and cried like a baby. When she had recovered from the first shock, she immediately went on a desperate offensive: 'You are ruining your future and blocking your life's path . . . she does not fit in a decent family . . . you will be in a fine mess when she gets a child.'"

It wasn't just his mother who disapproved of the relationship; in a later letter Hermann scolded his son for his choices. Einstein wrote about it to Mileva: "I understand my parents very well. They consider a woman as a man's luxury which he can only afford after having found a comfortable position."

In 1902, Einstein's father fell ill. Hermann suffered from heart disease and it is likely that his many financial misfortunes had taken their toll. Einstein traveled from Bern to Milan to be with him. On his deathbed Hermann finally consented to his son's relationship with Mileva. On October 10, 1902, he died of heart disease. Einstein's friend and biographer, Abraham Pais, wrote, "When the end was near, Hermann asked everyone to leave so that he could die alone. It was a moment his son never recalled without feelings of guilt."

A few months later, on January 6, 1903, Einstein and Mileva married. Einstein's mother did not attend the wedding. Pauline went to live with her daughter, Maja, after she had married Paul Winteler in Lucerne, Switzerland. Einstein and his mother were estranged during his marriage to Mileva, although they did visit each other. During World War I, Einstein sent his mother an annual allowance of 600 marks.

But Pauline never gave up on managing her son's life. In fact, Einstein met the woman who would become his mistress, Elsa Einstein, when visiting his mother in Berlin in 1912. Pauline applauded Einstein's affair and celebrated when, in 1919, her son finally divorced Mileva and married Elsa. Perhaps Pauline was happy because Einstein seemed to have found a woman so similar to his overbearing mother. Elsa shared Pauline's traits of nagging Einstein about the little things, like table manners, while at the same time excusing his much broader swipes of bad behavior, such as his numerous affairs. Einstein's mother moved into Elsa and Einstein's Berlin apartment six months after they married, and Elsa nursed her mother-in-law through her last days. In March 1920, Pauline Einstein died of abdominal cancer.

Patent Office

One of the facts most cited about Einstein was that he burst on the scene, and changed the world of physics when he was nothing but a lowly patent officer in Switzerland. The brash young physicist was certainly disappointed that he couldn't find an academic job, but looking back, Einstein always claimed that the job at the patent office had been exactly what he needed.

The year 1901 was a time of indecision and failure for young Albert Einstein. Professionally, he failed time and time again to obtain a university position; he received no reply to his many missives to the prominent physicists of the day, and his doctoral thesis had been returned with the annotation that it needed more work. On a personal level, his parents were unstable financially and his college sweetheart was pregnant with his out-of-wedlock child.

While Einstein was teaching and tutoring secondary students in Germany, Marcel Grossmann, his friend and former classmate at the ETH, insisted that soon Einstein would get a spot at the Swiss Patent

Office. In February 1902, Einstein had had enough of teaching and moved to Bern, possibly to force the patent office to accept him, or possibly because he'd been told that the position was indeed about to open up.

Einstein found Bern a happy, comfortable, intellectually stimulating place. After a few months, the patent office finally came through with an offer, and he became a technical expert, third class, without tenure, at the respectable salary of 3,500 Swiss francs. The Swiss Patent Office was located on the upper floor of the new, somewhat pompous building of the Postal and Telegraph Administration on Genfergasse. Einstein reported for his first day of work on June 23, 1902, and stayed for seven years. He described the work he had to do there as methodical and mindless, the perfect way for a man whose thoughts were always trying to solve physics puzzles to spend a day. And yet, the patent office was not just drudgery; Einstein claimed to have enjoyed the work.

When Einstein first started, the head of the office, Friedrich Haller, gave him the following advice: "When you pick up an application, think that anything the inventor says is wrong." Haller warned that one could never just trust the words of the applicant, and that following "the inventor's way of thinking . . . will prejudice you. You have to remain critically vigilant." It was clearly good advice to someone who was questioning the very foundations and assumptions inherent in the physics of the day.

In addition, life at the patent office was familiar to the young theorist. His beloved uncle, Jakob Einstein, who taught him geometry and algebra as a young child, was an engineer. Einstein had grown up among technical drawings. So the patent office was a comfortable place that not only fit Einstein's contrarian nature, but encouraged and rewarded him for it. Of all the patents that Einstein reviewed during his seven years, only one has survived. It was the rule that after eighteen years, all papers of patent protection were destroyed, and so, even in the 1920s when Einstein was a world-renowned figure, the last papers he processed went into the shredder. The one that survived was preserved due to a court case and it called Einstein, "one of the most highly esteemed experts at the Office." It rejected a claim because, according to Einstein, the application was "incorrect, imprecise, and not clearly drafted."

Einstein climbed the professional ladder at the patent office slowly, even as he shot to the top of the scientific hierarchy. In 1904, he was passed over for a promotion to "expert second class." It's unlikely that Einstein was disturbed by the oversight, as the position went to his good friend Marcel Grossmann, who had such a hand in gaining Einstein's employment in the first place. In September of that year, Einstein received tenure and a slight raise to 3,900 francs. The next year, in a creative frenzy, he published five papers that lay the foundation for modern physics and the scientific community immediately took notice. But Einstein stayed at the patent office. In 1906 he finally was promoted to an "expert second class" and his salary went up to 4,500 Swiss francs. Einstein investigated obtaining another higher paid position either in the patent office or elsewhere in the building with the Postal and Telegraph Administration. But while these attempts were fruitless, he never seemed to resent arriving at his tall wooden desk each morning, even as he traveled to more and more conferences with the greatest physicists of the day.

Einstein finally left the patent office in the summer of 1909 for a position at the University of Zurich. The hiring was a bitter and prolonged affair, and Einstein wrote his good friend Conrad Habicht in the middle of the wrangling on December 24, 1907, "So now I am an official of the guild of whores." It's quite possible that Einstein, while realizing that he belonged in a university setting, always regretted having to leave the patent office behind. Years later, the great theoretician kept his hand in the "lowly" work of technology, serving as an expert or consultant on patents and having a few of his own inventions patented through his old haunt in Bern.

Pauli, Wolfgang Ernst
(1900–1958)

Wolfgang Pauli was a major contributor to the field of quantum mechanics and his work earned him the 1945 Nobel Prize in physics. Twenty years Einstein's junior, he collaborated with Einstein when the two scientists worked at Princeton. Pauli, however, had a fairly acerbic tongue and while he respected Einstein's early work on relativity, he was vocally disdainful of Einstein's later ideas.

Born in Vienna, Austria, on April 25, 1900, Pauli was introduced to the sciences at an early age by his chemist father, Joseph Pauli, and his father's friend, the physicist Ernst Mach (whose work influenced

Einstein as well). In high school, Pauli studied Einstein's special theory of relativity on his own, often hiding such papers under his desk and reading them during boring school lectures. Pauli went on to study at the University of Munich under the theorist Arnold Sommerfeld, who asked his young student to write an article on relativity theory for the *Mathematical Encyclopedia*. While this was an unusual task to entrust to such a young man, Pauli rose to the task, writing over two hundred pages describing the current state of the theory, as well as including his own interpretations. This article essentially put Pauli "on the map," as Sommerfeld enjoyed the article so much that he called it to Einstein's attention. Einstein himself complemented Pauli's "genius." Indeed, to this day, Pauli's *Mathematical Encyclopedia* article is credited with being a brilliant analysis that helped crystallize everyone's thinking on relativity.

Pauli finished up his Ph.D. in 1922 and went on to work with Niels Bohr in Copenhagen. It was in 1924 that Pauli developed the quantum theory that still bears his name: the Pauli Exclusion Principle. Essentially, this theory states that no two electrons in orbit around an atom can be in the exact same energy state. That is, neither can have the same amount of energy and move around the nucleus of the atom in the same orbit. As he developed this principle, Pauli realized he had to assign a new quality to electrons, a quality that he called "spin." Spin is fairly abstract when actually applied to a particle, but it can be thought of as a kind of angular momentum, describing how particles spin as if they were little tops. Pauli is also known for another great contribution to physics: in the late 1920s, he predicted the existence of an all-new fundamental particle, the neutrino. It wasn't until the 1960s that the existence of the tiny neutrino was proven conclusively, but Pauli sensed its presence based solely on mathematical necessity.

A less scientific effect was also attributed to Pauli—he seemed to have a bizarre influence on experiments around him. Machinery would suddenly break down in his presence. His friends referred to this as the "Pauli Effect" and Pauli seems to have taken great joy in his reputation. Despite this, as a scientist Pauli was known for being a perfectionist. He was even referred to as the "conscience of physics" because he took such joy in being a watchdog over his colleagues' science. Pauli was known to utter perfectly scathing commentary about the work of others, once saying of someone's scientific paper: "This isn't right. It isn't even wrong."

Even Einstein did not escape Pauli's sharp wit. While the two men were cordial, Pauli often mocked Einstein's scientific interests. Pauli was one of the many scientists who agreed with Niels Bohr when it came to quantum mechanics, accepting the interpretation advanced by Bohr known as the Copenhagen interpretation. Einstein, however, still refused to believe that quantum mechanics was complete. He was determined to find a new theory that included the mathematics behind the new physics—math that Einstein had to admit did an admirable job predicting the outcomes of experiments—and also improved upon it. Einstein referred to this longed-for theory as a unified field theory and Pauli was disdainful of this attempt to join up the two foundations of modern physics. Pauli liked to say, "What God hath put asunder no man shall ever join."

In 1932, Pauli wrote a fairly harsh review of Einstein's unified theory work, saying, "[Einstein's] never-failing inventiveness as well as his tenacious energy in the pursuit of [unification] guarantees us in recent years, on the average, one theory per annum. . . . It is psychologically interesting that for some time the current theory is usually considered by its author to be the 'definitive solution.'"

After Germany annexed Austria during World War II, Pauli moved to the United States. He worked at Princeton from 1940 to 1946, where Einstein also had his office. The two collaborated on only one paper together, published in 1943, on general relativity. But, despite Pauli's scorn for Einstein's unification theory work, the two men clearly respected each other as colleagues. In January 1945, Einstein sent a telegram to the Nobel Prize committee stating: "Nominate Wolfgang Pauli for physics prize stop his contributions to modern quantum theory consisting in so-called Pauli or exclusion principle became fundamental part of modern quantum physics being independent from the other basic axioms of that theory stop Albert Einstein." Later that year, Pauli indeed won the prize for work he had done over twenty years earlier.

Photochemistry

Photochemistry is the science of any chemical process that is initiated by light—anything from the photosynthesis of plants to photography. The fact that light could effect change was discovered in the early 1800s, but it was not until Einstein showed light was made of particles that scientists truly understood how to interpret those reactions. And so, Einstein is memorialized by photochemistry in two ways: an "einstein" is the unit of light energy absorbed by a molecule, and the second law of photochemistry is called the Stark-Einstein law.

In 1818, Christian J. D. T. von Grotthuss and, subsequently, in 1839, John W. Draper, showed that energy from light could cause chemical reactions. Their work became known in photochemistry as its first law, the Grotthuss-Draper law, which says that absorbed light causes a chemical change. What that chemical change might be depends on the substance; it could merely be raised temperature or it could be complete annihilation of the original substance. Toward the end of the nineteenth century, it was discovered that the chemical change varied in relation to the intensity of the incoming light. At that point, light was understood to be a wave and everyone assumed that incoming light waves could continually buffet a chemical process adding more and more energy.

In 1905, Albert Einstein first proposed that light might be interpreted not simply as a wave, but also as a stream of discrete particles, today called "photons." Each photon has a specific amount of energy and so when it knocks into something else, like an electron on a metal plate, it can only impart that specific amount of energy. On the other hand, if light were just a wave, an intense wave of energy would be able to add increasing amounts of energy as it continues to hit an electron.

The concept of photons was put to use by the German physicist Johannes Stark (1874–1957) in 1913 to apply to photochemical processes. Working with Einstein's ideas, Stark developed what is now known as the Stark-Einstein law, also categorized as the "second law of photochemistry." This law states that for each photon of light absorbed by a chemical system, only one molecule is activated. Einstein's idea that a photon is a discrete particle is crucial for this understanding. On a metaphorical level, if light always acted like a wave, it would be like a wave of water. If molecules were like billiard balls, the wave would wash over all of them. But because light acts like particles, a photon of light can be thought of just like a single ball and so it can only hit one molecule at a time.

See **Photons; Stark, Johannes.**

Photoelectric Effect

Einstein's work on the photoelectric effect was as revolutionary as his work in relativity, since it was one of the seminal theories that helped create quantum mechanics. The popular mind has deemed it not as sexy—or as memorable—as his other theories, but it is actually the work for which Einstein won the Nobel Prize in 1921.

At its most basic, the photoelectric effect describes what happens when light aimed at a sheet of metal knocks electrons out of the metal, inducing electric current. But at the beginning of the twentieth century, the understanding of how light moved was completely at odds with what actually happened when someone conducted a photoelectric experiment. In 1905, Einstein's so-called "miracle year," he published a paper offering a solution that relied on the fact that light could be understood as being made of discrete particles. This was a radical idea, but one that is thoroughly accepted today.

The History

Heinrich Hertz (1857–1894) first noticed the photoelectric effect in 1887 when he blocked all extraneous light from an electricity experiment he was performing. Hertz discovered that the electric sparks created by the apparatus were weaker without additional light; thus, light itself aimed at a metal plate was inducing electricity. By the end of the nineteenth century, it was understood that this electricity was very specifically made of electrons being knocked out of their atoms by the burst of energy imparted by the incoming light.

In 1902, the German physicist Philipp Lenard (1862–1947) identified some problems with Hertz's idea. Lenard believed, along with all his contemporaries, that light was a wave. Consequently, one would expect several outcomes: energy with greater light should convey more energy to the electrons; feeble light should take a while to impart enough energy to the electrons in the metal to knock some of them free; and no matter what frequency the light was moving, one would expect the same result. Lenard discovered that nothing of the kind happened. As he aimed stronger and stronger beams of light at the metal, the electrons always came off with the exact same amount of energy—there may have been more of them, but that was the only change. In addition, electrons always flew off the moment the light reached the plate, unless the light was at a low frequency, at which point nothing happened whatsoever. Lenard brought these problems to the public attention (and won a Nobel Prize for it), but he wasn't destined to be the one to solve them.

Elsewhere in the physics community, Max Planck (1858–1947) was also working on radiation. To solve a completely different set of problems, he hypothesized that perhaps energy only came in specifically sized packets. Instead of a stream of radiation (light, X-rays, and so forth) being a continuous beam, radiation was made of quanta of energy. In other words, energy was less like a sluice of water being shot out of a water gun, and more like a continuous series of Ping-Pong balls. By introducing this radical concept, Planck managed to make the math for his studies work. That didn't mean he necessarily believed energy only came in discrete packages; he thought at first that this was merely a neat math trick to help him out of a jam.

How Einstein Explained It All

Einstein, on the other hand, took Planck's work to heart and was willing to accept that this mathematical trick might represent an actual physical reality. On March 17, 1905, he published a paper entitled "On a Heuristic Point of View Concerning the Production and Transformation of Light." Einstein hypothesized that light was not, in fact, a wave as was currently accepted. Perhaps light was indeed physically made of light "quanta;" perhaps light was made of particles not unlike electrons themselves.

If one could make the conceptual leap to accepting light was made up of particles, everything seemed to make sense. Instead of a light beam adding continuous energy to the electrons in a metal plate, now one had to interpret the photoelectric effect as if each individual photon could affect only one electron at a time. This explained each of the problems that had plagued contemporary scientists.

The first problem was that light coming in with more energy didn't correspond to electrons coming out with more energy. With Einstein's solution, one could see that changing the amount of energy in a light wave simply meant that it had more photons. More photons translated to knocking more electrons out of the metal, but didn't imply that any single electron should have more energy.

The second problem was that low energy light waves didn't take a while to knock electrons out of the metal, but did so immediately. Again, a low-energy light wave could now be understood to simply mean that there were fewer photons in the light beam. While fewer photons means fewer electrons, an individual photon is nevertheless going to have no problem kicking an electron free the moment it hits the metal plate. There is no need for multiple waves of energy to build up over time, giving the electron enough energy to finally break away.

The third problem was that within the light wave theory one wouldn't have expected a change in frequency to affect the outcome when, in fact, it did. The explanation here lies in the fact that the amount of energy in each individual photon is directly related to its frequency. Below a certain frequency, a photon quite simply didn't have enough energy to affect an electron, no matter how many photons slammed against the plate. (Remember, the photon theory allowed for just one photon to affect just one electron; no longer could a light wave send continuous energy into the metal plate, letting it build up over time.)

Einstein's theory did more than just offer explanations for the crises of the photoelectric effect; it also offered ways of being tested. His theory implied that there was a correlation between the frequency of the light and the energy imparted to the electrons. This correlation was one that could be measured.

Despite the fact that one could verify this correlation and that Einstein's hypothesis successfully explained the photoelectric effect, it took quite some time for the scientific community to accept that it wasn't just a math trick. Even Einstein took a few years before he committed to the idea that light was truly a beam of particles. Another scientist, Robert Millikan, performed experiments nearly a decade later in order to disprove the theory, and despite results that continually supported the quanta hypothesis Millikan nevertheless refused for years to believe that there wasn't an alternate explanation.

By the 1920s, it was almost universally accepted that light was indeed made up of quanta, despite the fact that it also appeared to be a wave. This fundamental "wave-particle duality" of light would turn out to be one of the cornerstones of quantum mechanics, a field that always intrigued Einstein much more than relativity.

See **Lenard, Philipp; Light; Millikan, Robert; Miracle Year; Photons; Quantum Mechanics.**

Photons

The idea behind a photon seems simple enough: they are the discrete particles that make up light and Einstein postulated their existence in 1905. But the way photons behave is far from simple and their odd characteristics ensured that it was almost two decades before they were fully accepted by the physics community.

In 1905, Einstein published a paper titled "On a Heuristic Point of View Concerning the Production and Transformation of Light." It described

what is known as the photoelectric effect, in which light knocks electrons off a sheet of metal. The paper suggested that the only way one
could understand the photoelectric effect was if light came in "quanta"
of energy; that is, energy packets of a very specific size. Einstein's theory
suggested that each packet of energy of light corresponded to just one
electron knocked out. Even though this agreed with what was actually
seen in the photoelectric effect better than any other theory, contemporary scientists believed too firmly that light was a wave and that these
waves of light traveled through space much the way a sound wave travels through air. Scientists had accepted the wave theory of light ever
since the 1800s and the theory successfully explained just about all phenomena seen up to that point. One of the most convincing pieces of
evidence was that when you directed two beams of light at a screen, they
created interference patterns (rings of light and dark) that could only
occur if light were a wave. The photoelectric effect, in which light
knocked electrons off the metal sheet, was one of the few places where
the wave theory broke down, and scientists were not inclined to discard
what seemed to be a firmly established law of physics in the face of a single example of contrary evidence.

In fact, even scientists who thought Einstein's science was otherwise far-reaching and insightful still rejected light quanta. In 1913,
four scientists, including Max Planck (who was the first person to create
equations in which energy came in discrete quantities, but who was
still reluctant to believe in their physical reality) recommended
Einstein for membership in the Prussian Academy of Sciences. They
wrote a glowing recommendation of the young man, but then added,
"That he may sometimes have missed the target in his speculations, as,
for example, in his hypothesis of light quanta, cannot really be held
against him, for it is not possible to introduce really new ideas even in
the most exact sciences without sometimes taking a risk."

Einstein also had issues with the light quanta since he couldn't
quite get his head around just what they were. He, too, knew that light
often behaved as if it were a wave; in the same year that he published
his light quanta theory, he also published other papers in which he
assumed that light was a wave. It wasn't until 1909 that Einstein began
to think of these quanta as physical particles. However, in a paper
written that year, he stated quite clearly that this didn't mean the
wave theory was untrue. The "emission theory," as he referred to his
quanta idea, should not be perceived as "incompatible" with the wave
theory.

Over the twenty years after they were first postulated, Einstein's particles of light were slowly accepted. Ultimately, scientists decided that light quite simply could be both—or either—particle or wave depending on the circumstances. While this might seem contradictory, it fit in well with the modern physics then being devised: quantum mechanics. Not only did quantum mechanics embrace the idea that energy came in quanta, but the early creators happily accepted numerous "contradictions" of this sort.

> *All these fifty years of pondering have not brought me any closer to answering the question, "What are light quanta?"*
>
> —Einstein, in a letter to Michele Besso, December 12, 1951

The word "photon" itself was coined in 1926, twenty-one years after Einstein suggested its existence. A scientist named Gilbert Lewis wrote a paper titled "The Conservation of Photons," in which he claimed that light was made up of "a new kind of atom . . . I propose the name photon." ("Photo" being the Greek for "light.") The word stuck, and Einstein's "light quanta" had become a fully sanctioned part of modern physics.

See **Photoelectric Effect.**

Pipe

Like his dearly loved violin, Einstein's pipe was never far out of reach. It is said that Einstein once fell overboard off a sailboat but refused to let go of the pipe in his hand. In his later years, he would seem especially contemplative as he sat in a comfortable chair for hours smoking his pipe, methodically cleaning and refilling it over and over.

Once asked by an observer why he spent more time cleaning his pipe than smoking it, Einstein replied, "My aim lies in smoking, but as a result things tend to get clogged up, I'm afraid. Life, too, is like smoking, especially marriage." Einstein had recently been required to give up his favorite fat, black cigars because his doctors warned him they were no good for his heart. And so, it's quite possible that at that time, Einstein was in the midst of yet another row with his wife, Elsa, over his smoking.

Indeed, while smoking brought him great joy, many tried to deny him the pleasure. When his doctor told him that he was no longer allowed to buy tobacco because it was bad for his heart, Einstein took him at his word. From then on, he merely took other people's tobacco.

In the biography of Einstein *Einstein, a Life* by Denis Brian, one of Einstein's neighbors, James Blackwood, recalled a night in 1934. Einstein was fiddling with his pipe, taking it from his pocket, toying with a match, and then tossing the unstruck match and sucking on his unlit pipe. Blackwood's mother told the scientist that he should feel free to smoke, a comment that caused the female side of the Einstein household—Elsa, stepdaughter Margot, and secretary Helen Dukas—to erupt into laughter. Elsa explained that she had told Einstein that he smoked too much and he responded that he could quit anytime he wanted to. When she needled him further, he announced he wouldn't smoke until New Year's Day.

> *Pipe smoking contributes to a somewhat calm and objective judgment of human affairs."*
> —Einstein, upon accepting life membership in the Montreal Pipe Smokers Club in 1950

Elsa reportedly added, "And he hasn't smoked since Thanksgiving." Einstein responded, "You see, I am no longer a slave to my pipe, I am a slave to *dat voman.*"

Planck, Max
(1858–1947)

In the world of physics, Max Planck is father figure to Einstein. Planck was the first to predict that energy came in bite-sized chunks called quanta, an idea on which Einstein capitalized when he theorized that light came in similar packets, today known as photons. The father figure metaphor extends beyond this, however. The two men were exceedingly close and Planck's encouragement was a boon to Einstein, as the older physicist helped promote the theory of relativity and took an active interest in advancing his career.

Max Planck's breakthrough contribution to physics came in 1901, when he solved a problem known as the Ultraviolet Catastrophe. Scientists had discovered that when it came to light and radiation, the classic mechanical laws they inherited from Isaac Newton quite simply didn't work. One example is so-called blackbody radiation. If one had a perfect black body that absorbed radiation, then one should be able to measure the heat spectrum it gave off. But Newtonian mechanics predicted that ultraviolet wavelengths should increase infinitely, something which not only sounded improbable but did not actually happen in experiments. Planck, who was quite mathematically creative, stepped up with a solution that assumed that radiation could only exist in specific bits, or quanta, of energy. Instead of being a continuous wave of energy like a sound wave, Planck suggested that the energy was discontinuous—sort of how a water wave is actually made up of tiny water molecules, even if these are not visible to the eye. Once these quanta were introduced, Planck's theory corresponded to what was actually seen in blackbody radiation. The Ultraviolet Catastrophe was no longer an issue.

But Planck didn't quite know how to interpret his new description of radiation, or even whether his innovative math technique should be applied to any other situation. Indeed, he claimed that he had only introduced these quanta in "an act of despair." In 1918 Planck won the Nobel Prize for this work that founded a new branch of science: quantum physics. But he was a reluctant revolutionary and didn't take the next step: to try to figure out just what this new quantum idea meant. That was left to Einstein. Years later, Einstein recalled that he read Planck's innovative paper while he was at university and it left a deep impression on him. Einstein realized that neither of the two fundamental theories of the day—Newtonian mechanics and Maxwell's electromagnetic theory—exactly described the universe. Einstein spent much of the next few years occupied with trying to solve this problem. Ultimately, in 1905, he incorporated Planck's ideas into a completely new theory of light. Einstein's theory said that visible light, just like ultraviolet radiation, came in quanta.

This concept is what would eventually win Einstein the Nobel Prize, but it was also the theory that took the longest for anyone else to accept. At first, much like Planck before him, Einstein did not definitively state that his "light-quanta" were anything more than a mathematical tool. However, within a few years he truly believed that light came in particles just the way electrons did.

It is to Planck's credit that he was partially responsible for Einstein's inventive—almost "fringe"—paper being published. Planck was an editor of the prestigious German journal *Annalen der Physik*. He ran his section with an amazingly open mind—if an author had been published before, he was almost guaranteed a spot for any subsequent papers, no matter what Planck himself thought of the work.

In this case, Planck was not particularly receptive to the new theory. Einstein, of course, saw the roots of his theory in Planck's work, but Planck himself took time to accept the idea. Directly after the first Solvay Conference in the fall of 1911, Einstein wrote to a friend, "I largely succeeded in convincing Planck that my conception [of light quanta] is correct, after he has struggled against it for so many years." While Planck did eventually accept the existence of photons, he always maintained something of a distance from the quantum physics that he had spawned, leaving his younger colleagues to hammer out the details.

A Mentor and a Champion

When it came to the special theory of relativity, however, Planck was less reticent. The same year that Einstein published his theory of light-quanta, he also published his unprecedented paper on special relativity. By that fall, Planck was giving lectures on the details of Einstein's new theory. Planck was, of course, a preeminent scientist, and for young Einstein to have this backing was a major coup. In 1910, Planck went so far as to compare Einstein to Copernicus, saying, "This principle [of relativity] has brought about a revolution in our physical picture of the world, which, in extent and depth, can only be compared to that produced by the introduction of the Copernican system."

And yet, Planck was not above gently mocking Einstein. Upon reading Einstein's attempt to write a simplified description of general relativity for a lay audience, Planck said that Einstein seemed to think that he could render a complicated sentence understandable simply by inputting frequent interjections of "Dear Reader."

Planck also went on record to say that he didn't necessarily accept the general theory of relativity. Nevertheless, Planck was by and large a champion for Einstein. This was true when it came to Einstein's career as well. Planck helped get Einstein a job at the new Kaiser Wilhem Institutes in Berlin and even helped argue for Einstein's raises. Planck was also the secretary of the Prussian Academy and was devoted to advancing German science. As German anti-Semitism and nationalism increased, Einstein promised Planck, who was by now a dear friend, that he would not abandon Berlin unless it was absolutely necessary. Einstein did, in fact, leave Berlin and resigned from the Prussian Academy in 1933, just after Hitler was granted full and total authority over Germany. By then even Planck had to admit that it was "the only possible way out."

The Damage of War

Planck, however, stayed in Germany and retained his position in the Academy. As the Nazis began to attack Jewish science and Jewish scientists, Planck tried desperately to stem the tide. In 1933, even after Einstein was ousted from the Prussian Academy, Planck praised Einstein and his work, announcing: "Herr Einstein is not just one among many outstanding physicists, but Herr Einstein is the physicist through whose essays, published in our Academy, physical knowledge in this century has been deepened in a manner whose importance can only be measured against the achievements of Johannes Kepler or Isaac Newton." Later, Planck met with Hitler to argue that his campaign against the Jews was damaging to Germany's scientific advancement. Planck's pleas fell on deaf ears.

Despite a lifetime of prestige in Germany, wartime was personally brutal to Planck. His son was killed by the Gestapo in 1944 as punishment for being involved with a failed assassination attempt on Hitler's life. Three of Planck's children and his first wife had died previously and this was the final blow. While his second wife and their son were still in Planck's life, he seemed to have become but a shadow of his former self. He lived only three more years, dying at age eighty-nine.

While always a leader in the scientific community, Planck did not contribute significant physics papers after his 1901 quanta breakthrough. His writing turned more and more to philosophy and he is known for a succinct description of how scientific theories change: "A new scientific truth does not triumph by convincing its opponents and making them see the light, but rather because its opponents eventually die and a new generation grows up that is familiar with it." Planck was writing at a time when several other philosophers were developing ideas of how science develops, ideas that are still enmeshed in current philosophical thought—but Planck's principle does seem to apply to quantum mechanics. Planck and Einstein were two of the few physicists who raised their voices against the new physics, while a young crop of twenty-somethings embraced it wholeheartedly. After the deaths of Planck and Einstein, the quantum mechanics they founded—but always questioned—was taught with the force of accepted theory to each new crop of physics students.

See also **Germany; Quantum Mechanics.**

Poincaré, Henri
(1854–1912)

Mathematician Jules Henri Poincaré has gone down in history as the man who almost discovered relativity. As it was, Einstein clearly spent many hours reviewing Poincaré's theories before having the eureka moment that led to his famous 1905 paper on the subject. For a period of time, there was some discussion on whether Einstein should have attributed Poincaré's ideas, but subsequent analysis shows that Einstein clearly realized a profound insight into Poincaré's work that may have escaped the man himself.

Einstein and Henri Poincaré had a notably chilly relationship. Poincaré never accepted Einstein's relativity theory and Einstein never directly said he was building on Poincaré's work. On the other hand, Poincaré did recommend Einstein for one of his first jobs, calling him "one of the most original minds I ever came across."

In the early 1900s, the Frenchman was the world's foremost mathematician. He developed the modern qualitative theory of dynamic systems, created the field of topology (the study of shapes) and used it to prove that the solar system is stable, and was also the chairman of the Bureau of Longitudes and coauthor of its exceptionally accurate maps.

As for relativity, Poincaré and the Dutch physicist Hendrik Antoon Lorentz regularly exchanged theories and papers on the nature of time. Lorentz had worked out equations in which time seemed to be different for different observers. However, Lorentz saw this assumption as a mathematical tool, not as a true representation of reality. Poincaré tried to come up with what this change in time within the equations corresponded to in the real world. He suggested that they could be interpreted as clocks synchronized by light signals; since light would take some finite amount of time to travel from one clock to the other, clocks in different systems would show a different time. In 1904, Poincaré included a section devoted to the relativity principle—the idea that things like time were relative depending on which system an observer was in—in a lecture called "On the Present State and the Future of Mathematical Physics." It was the first text in which not only the subject of relativity but also the name appears.

But within the lecture, Poincaré backed off of this idea, adhering to Lorentz's original idea of there being only one "true time." He wrote, "the clocks synchronized in that manner do not therefore show the true time, but what one might call 'local time' so that one of them is slow with regard to another. This does not matter much, as we have no way of determining it." (This 1904 lecture by Poincaré also contained some other hints at the future development of physics. Poincaré put forth the first indication that the velocity of light could play a major role in physics, structuring theory not only in optics and electrodynamics but also in mechanics.)

At the time, Einstein was working at the Swiss Patent Office, and was in the midst of stimulating conversations with his friend Michele Besso, as well as his friends Conrad Habicht and Maurice Solovine in their farcical Olympic Academy. Solovine later noted that Einstein had the Academy spend several weeks reviewing Poincaré's *La Science et l'hypothèse (Science and hypothesis)*. Poincaré's book reduced the ether to a hypothesis, which was merely "convenient for the explanation of phenomena" and even predicted that "one day the ether will undoubtedly be discarded as unnecessary."

So, all of this was percolating in Einstein's brain as he talked to his friends and thought about the nature of light. However, when he published the special theory of relativity (after a sudden moment in 1905 when it all coalesced and he announced one morning to his friends not to worry, he had completely solved the problem) the only footnote on the paper was one thanking Besso.

In defending his lack of attributions, Einstein says he was not acquainted with either Lorentz's 1904 paper or Poincaré's June 1905 work that discussed relativity. "In that sense," Einstein claimed, "My 1905 paper was independent." Einstein's relativity theory rapidly spread throughout the scientific community, and most scientists quickly accepted the theory. But Poincaré stayed particularly quiet. He did not actively reject Einstein's ideas; he simply ignored them. The two men met only once, at the First Solvay Conference in 1911. Later Einstein wrote, "Poincaré was simply negative (toward the relativity theory) and with all his perceptiveness showed little understanding for the situation."

Poincaré passed away in 1912 at the age of only fifty-eight. Long after his death, Einstein did speak about him, in a lecture to the Prussian Academy of Sciences in Berlin—but it wasn't about relativity. Instead, he hailed "the acute-minded and profound Poincaré" on his connecting physics and geometry.

Popular Works

Unlike many of his contemporaries, Einstein didn't write solely for other scientists. He wrote numerous articles for a lay audience, not only about his scientific theories but also on his opinions about peace, Judaism, politics, fascism, freedom, and his friends. He wrote volumes of editorials to newspapers and magazines, gave thousands of speeches, crafted obituaries of prominent scientists and thinkers, wrote introductions to other people's books, and contributed to television programs.

Einstein's first published statement on a nonscientific subject came in 1917, when he wrote against the mandatory graduation required of all German students. Teaching independent thought and not a rote list of facts was just one of Einstein's pet topics. He had little use for staying in the ivory tower of academics simply because it was expected. After this first paper, Einstein's career as a commenter on everything around him was off and running.

Speaking out for peace was one of Einstein's oft-repeated platforms. A lifelong pacifist, Einstein early on used his scientific stature to promote the cause. One well-publicized essay was a collaboration between Einstein and Sigmund Freud entitled *Why War?*. Although it wasn't successful in its stated aim of deterring World War II, it and Einstein's other works on peace and pacifism were collected after his death into the book *Einstein on Peace*. Published in 1960, this influential compilation became a boon to those with a pacifist agenda, as it helped advance calls against the United States's war in Vietnam as well as bolster the influence of the United Nations.

Another of Einstein's most prominent topics was the cause of Zionism and the creation of the State of Israel. Einstein was not shy about working out his ideas in public. He would happily publish different opinions at different times. While he always remained committed to the Zionist cause, which he viewed as a way of instilling pride and belonging in the Jewish people, he was less definite in his beliefs on Israel. In his writing, he sometimes decried its nationalistic stance, but also cheered when the state was founded.

Einstein wrote popular works about his science, too. He did this from the very inception of his theories. In 1916 he not only published the general theory of relativity in a scientific publication, he also published a fifty-page booklet titled *Relativity*. In the preface Einstein writes, "The present book is intended, as far as possible, to give an exact insight into the theory of relativity to those readers who, from a general scientific and philosophical point of view, are interested in the theory, but who are not conversant with the mathematical apparatus of theoretical physics."

Whether or not Einstein succeeded in clearly explaining the special and general theories of relativity is in question. The acknowledgment that space and time are easily twisted is not an easy concept. In an addition to the fifteenth edition of the book, published in 1952, Einstein is still clarifying his views with befuddling statements such as, "I wished to show that space-time is not necessarily something to which one can ascribe a separate existence, independently of the actual objects of physical reality. Physical objects are not in space, but these objects are spatially extended. In this way the concept of 'empty space' loses its meaning."

Loses its meaning indeed! And yet one has to applaud Einstein's lifelong attempts to engage the public in important scientific

So I'm just writing, always dissatisfied with what I have written, yet unable to improve on it.

—Einstein, in a letter to his friend Otto Nathan, February 17, 1949

and political discussion. He was ever hopeful in this endeavor—the forward to *Relativity* ends with his wishes. "May the book bring some one a few happy hours of suggestive thought!"

Positivism

Early on in Einstein's career he wholeheartedly embraced a philosophy known as positivism. It insists that meaningful science can only be based on events or objects that can be directly experienced and measured. Over the course of his lifetime, however, Einstein fell away from this strict view and believed that science should embrace a "realist" philosophy, meaning it should attempt to describe reality, even if it had to resort to intuitive jumps and abstract concepts.

The development of Einstein's special theory of relativity shows clear signs of his youthful positivism, while his later general theory of relativity shows his veering towards realism. The realism view clearly helped in Einstein's breakthrough in developing a complete theory of relativity, but it also led him to reject the consensus among modern physicists when it came to the theories of quantum mechanics.

Like so many philosophical debates, the validity of positivism has been rigorously argued, both for and against, since the ancient Greeks. In the early 1900s, however, positivism was largely associated with a scientist whose work held great influence over Einstein's thinking: Ernst Mach. Mach believed that if something wasn't able to be directly experienced through one of the five senses, then it could never be considered a true picture of reality. Abstract concepts like energy and light waves, said Mach, must be constantly questioned; to believe that you had an absolutely correct idea of what they were was to be "dogmatic," or closed off from new understandings.

While it sounds like Mach was dismissing anything that was not concrete, in truth, his view of the world had a great deal of subjectivity in it: things that do not exist on a material plane can be (indeed *should* be) constantly reinterpreted, lest one mistakenly think it to be an accurate description of reality.

Einstein's acceptance of Mach's positivist doctrine was what led to his creative leap in developing the special theory of relativity. As Einstein worked, he thought specifically—and only—about what one could observe and measure. He realized that people moving at different speeds would measure the timing of events in completely different ways: a person standing on a train platform would measure the time that the train arrived differently than a person on the moving train. Since, according to positivism, all that mattered was what one directly perceived, Einstein was able to make the jump to understanding that time itself indeed varied for different observers. It's a concept that lies at the heart of the special theory of relativity.

But being too strict of a positivist can lead one into cul-de-sacs of thought: scientific dead-ends. After all, Einstein did draw a conclusion from the sensations of observers in the train station, a conclusion that by its very nature of being a theory ceases to be connected to direct experience.

An example of the problem with positivism is the discovery of the electron. Just six years before Einstein published the special theory of relativity, two men, J. J. Thomson and Walter Kaufmann, both did experiments in which they measured the ratio of electric charge to mass in electric currents. Kaufmann reported that he had found the ratio of electric charge to mass. Thomson, on the other hand, made the breakthrough: that this precise ratio correlates to a new particle and that the current was not a single beam of energy, but made up of electrons. Thomson later won the Nobel Prize for discovering the electron. Within the world of science, it seems, if one remains strictly positivist, then one can do little more than catalogue facts of nature, never understanding the "hows" and the "whys" behind them.

In the twentieth century, physics veered away from studying the macroscopic world of friction, gravity, and pulleys of early physicists, and it became harder and harder to come up with meaningful theories if one wasn't willing to make assumptions. Einstein may not have even realized initially that he, too, was veering away from Mach's positivism as he began to work on the general theory of relativity. But he quickly found that he could not devise a new theory of gravity with only a short logical leap from empirical data to hypothesis. Einstein ultimately had to rely on abstract concepts of space and time as well as a great deal of math.

Developing the general theory of relativity led Einstein down the path of "rational realism," a philosophy that chafes under Mach's insistence that things like space and time might be subjective. Einstein grew to believe there was an absolute reality in the universe, a reality that it was the physicist's job to interpret and understand. One still had to take care to use a logical progression from the facts one could perceive to developing theories, but one nevertheless could, and should, hypothesize about abstract concepts.

This change in Einstein's views resulted in two interesting developments. The first is the reaction of Mach himself. Much to Einstein's surprise, Mach rejected the general theory of relativity out of hand. He had indeed praised Einstein's earlier special theory of relativity, but the general theory was too much for him. A theory that relied so heavily on untouchable, unseeable things like gravitational fields and space-time was simply too absurd for Mach's positivistic mind.

The second area in which Einstein's rejection of positivism came into conflict with others was quantum mechanics. The founders of quantum mechanics began their work focusing on what one could measure—and that alone. They did not attempt to describe what was happening in an atom any further than what they could observe. What they observed, it turns out, was that atoms and other particles all behaved in inherently random ways; for example, one could never predict exactly which way they'd move. So quantum mechanics theorists were content to merely predict the likelihood that a particle would travel in one direction or another. And indeed, they came up with very accurate rules for making these predictions. But Einstein resisted the idea that this randomness was somehow a true representation of what was happening on a physical level; he insisted that this randomness showed that theories of quantum mechanics were incomplete—there had to be an underlying theme that would explain all this randomness.

Through quantum mechanics, positivism was in direct conflict with realism. Many physicists accepted quantum mechanics theories because they were derived from basic observations and gave accurate descriptions. Einstein agreed with that. He knew quantum mechanics was a useful tool, he just didn't think the fact that these observations were correct meant that they were an accurate representation of what was truly happening. Most physicists were content to stop with quantum theory, while Einstein wanted to take it further and explain what he thought was really going on. He wanted to know the truth about physical reality, even if that meant making creative leaps and accepting amorphous concepts about particles.

Numerous scientists who saw Einstein as a spokesperson for positivism were surprised. A classic example is Werner Heisenberg (1901–1976), who couldn't believe Einstein's discomfort with quantum mechanics. In his book *The Part and the Whole* Heisenberg told of trying to convince Einstein that he should accept quantum mechanics for the simple reason that it was a science based solely on what one could measure, just as Einstein's own special relativity had been. Einstein responded, startled, that he may have once relied on this kind of philosophy, but that he now believed it to be nonsense.

By 1930, Einstein had consciously rejected the positivist philosophy of science, writing to Moritz Schlick: "Physics is the attempt at the conceptual construction of a model of the real world and of its lawful structure. To be sure it must present exactly the empirical relations between those sense experiences to which we are open; but only in this way is it chained to them." Einstein had embraced realism, and he never wavered again.

See **Mach, Ernst; Quantum Mechanics.**

Princeton

Einstein arrived at Princeton in 1933 with his wife, Elsa, his secretary, Helen Dukas, and the mathematician colleague he called his "calculator," Walther Mayer. Einstein was fifty-four and he began what would be his last job at the Institute for Advanced Study, living out the rest of his life quite contentedly in the bucolic college town.

Einstein's move to the United States was part of a mass emigration of European scientists out of Europe in the 1930s. Most of his colleagues probably would have expected Einstein to go to California, where he had been warmly received and had given many lectures over the course of the last few years. But during one visit to Caltech, Einstein met Abraham Flexner. Flexner was drumming up financial and administrative support for his Institute for Advanced Study, a soon-to-be created research center in New Jersey.

Einstein was clearly the preeminent physicist of his time, and landing him would put the institute on the map. At the time, Einstein was in negotiations with Caltech for a permanent position there. One sticking point was his demand for a full position for his assistant, Mayer. As those conversations dragged on, Flexner made Einstein an attractive offer and in the summer of 1932, the physicist accepted. At that time, the deal was just for Einstein to spend six months at Princeton and then to return to his full-time position at the Kaiser Wilhelm Institutes in Berlin. Although he still spoke publicly of returning to Berlin, Einstein certainly suspected as early as 1931 that he would soon be leaving Germany permanently. So, although Einstein's appointment in Princeton was officially as a visiting professor, it was in every other way a permanent move.

Arrival

Flexner was pleased that he had attracted the great Einstein to his new institute and he was almost obsessed with keeping the physicist focused on Princeton and away from the general public. Einstein and his wife, Elsa, were settled not into Princeton's fancy Inn, because that would have raised attention, but instead a more modest hotel near the university. Elsa, however, with her usual decisiveness, quickly moved them into Apartment 2, Library Place, a small apartment in an elegant residential area across from the Princeton Theological Seminary.

Einstein almost immediately found the small town of Princeton to his liking although, as ever, he was amused by self-important academics. In a November 20 letter to his regal pen pal, the Belgian queen Elisabeth, Einstein wrote, "Princeton is a wonderful piece of earth and at the same time an exceedingly amusing ceremonial backwater of tiny spindel-shanked semigods."

Unfortunately, Einstein's patron Andrew Flexner seemed to have just one of those semigod complexes. From the beginning, Flexner tried to control the actions and interactions of his famous acquisition. He appointed himself Einstein's guardian and not only discouraged his participation in pacifist rallies, discussions, and fund-raisers, he telephoned the organizers of such events, saying he was speaking on Einstein's behalf and berated them for wasting the great man's time. The breaking point came when Flexner, who also opened all of Einstein's correspondence, tersely dismissed an invitation for Einstein to dine at the White House.

When Einstein heard of Flexner's actions he not only immediately accepted the White House invitation, he also dressed down Flexner. In writing of his plight to his friend Rabbi Wise who had organized the invitation, Einstein listed his address as "Concentration Camp, Princeton." He also sent the institute's trustees a long list of Flexner's actions. As a result, Flexner was directed to remove himself from Einstein's affairs and, seemingly, the two had very little conflict from then on. On the other hand, without Flexner's championing Einstein's concerns, Einstein ended up having very little influence in running the institute.

But the only such concern of Einstein's was to find ways to help Jewish scientists escape Nazi Germany. As the world marched toward war, Einstein used his position at Princeton to bring bright students to the Princeton campus as their entrance to more permanent positions in the United States.

Settling In

With the rise of Hitler, it was now clear to Einstein that Princeton would become his new home. He accepted an early offer to make his position at the institute permanent and in August 1934, Elsa moved her husband and his secretary into the small clapboard house that would be their final home: 112 Mercer Street.

The little, unassuming white house with black shutters was in the same neighborhood as Einstein's previous apartment and only a short bicycle ride to his office on the Princeton campus. In the morning, he would meet his coworkers in his office, Room 209, Fine Hall, to discuss mathematics and physics. He would then return to Mercer Street and, after lunch and a nap, sit in his study with Dukas, writing and answering correspondence.

Just months after the family moved, Elsa fell ill and passed away. Without Elsa, the driving force behind his rather rigorous traveling and lecture schedule, Einstein soon spent all of his time shuttling between the institute and his home. It was a life that suited the scientist, as he said in a 1936 letter to his friend Max Born, "I have acclimated extremely well here, live like a bear in a cave and feel more at home than I ever did in my eventful life."

And yet, Einstein was far from a hermit. Thanks to the world-renowned reputation of the institute, his Princeton period was one of many collaborations with other, often younger, scientists.

But I also found Princeton fine. A pipe as yet unsmoked. Young and fresh. Much is to be expected from America's youth.

—Einstein, as quoted in the *New York Times*, July 8, 1921

The Institute for Advanced Study quickly became a center of higher thought and every mathematician of account spent time there. In fact, the institute was so focused on mathematics that for five years, Einstein was its only physics professor. This changed after World War II when one of its other famed inhabitants arrived: the physicist Robert Oppenheimer, who worked in an office one floor up from Einstein. The two interacted infrequently and Einstein's removal from other physicists seemed to suit him. At the time, and, truly, for the rest of his life, Einstein was happily out of step with his fellows when it came to new theories in the field.

One person who did stand out as a similarly-minded scientist was the graduate student Nathan Rosen (1909–1995) with whom Einstein wrote his first joint collaboration while at Princeton: the Einstein-Podolsky-Rosen argument was a commentary on quantum mechanics that still gets attention today. This was the first of four papers that Einstein wrote with Rosen, making him one of Einstein's most frequent collaborators.

As Einstein settled more and more into his set ways, the people of Princeton seemed to go out of their way to protect the physicist's privacy. One visitor described the reception of the town when he came, unannounced, to speak to Einstein. When he asked at the hotel desk how to get to 112 Mercer Street, the desk clerk asked, "Are you expected?" When he found the answer was no, the clerk kindly but insistently asked him to come back in one hour. When he returned, the clerk was all smiles, saying, "It's all been arranged." Then, when the visitor told the cab driver he was going to 112 Mercer Street, the cab driver immediately asked, "Are you expected?"

See also **Dukas, Helen; Oppenheimer, J. Robert; United States.**

Quantum Mechanics

As physicists in the twentieth century discovered the whole host of tiny particles that make up our universe, they developed theories about how particles moved and interacted, a body of science now known as quantum mechanics. Coupled with the theory of relativity, quantum mechanics is one of the foundations of modern science, and Einstein had a sure hand in laying that groundwork. But Einstein soon found himself marginalized from the rest of the community, as other scientists accepted a version of quantum mechanics that he rejected.

The first mention of a "quantum" of energy was in 1900, by Max Planck (1858–1947). Planck was studying an experiment that has come down in history as the black body experiment because it describes how a perfectly dark body absorbs radiation. As the body heats up, it radiates energy, but not in the way classical physics predicted. Using science as it was then understood, the amount of radiation would scale up to infinite amounts, something that clearly didn't happen in real life. Planck wasn't a radical thinker in any sense of the word; he was very comfortable with classical physics exactly as it was and wasn't looking to overturn it. However, he was particularly good with math, and he used a breakthrough mathematical technique to solve the problem. He imagined that the energy didn't travel in a continuous stream, but instead could only move in clumps of specifically-sized packets, or quanta. It's as if the milk you're pouring has curdled; instead of a liquid, the milk can only pour out in lumps. Planck discovered that if he assumed that the energy streaming off the black body was strictly limited to moving as if it were made of these lumps, then the way that the black body gave off radiation suddenly made sense.

When Planck presented his ideas, he didn't completely know what this new mathematical solution meant. He would not have suggested that energy truly was limited to discrete particles like this; he just thought he had come up with a mathematical solution. As such, nobody expanded on Planck's ideas for several years—until Einstein.

In 1905, Einstein published a paper entitled "On the Heuristic Viewpoint Concerning the Generation and Transformation of Light." It was "heuristic" since Einstein thought he was writing about an idea that couldn't necessarily be tested or proven, but was simply a different conceptual way to think about something—namely, light. Capitalizing on Planck's earlier work, Einstein suggested that despite the last hundred years of experiments and theories showing that light was a continuous wave, perhaps light should actually be interpreted as being made up of "light quanta," little packets of energy. Einstein used his light quanta to fight his way out of another physics problem facing scientists at the time: the fact that no one could quite make sense of the way light and matter interacted. When light hit matter such as a metal plate it caused electrons to jump out of their atoms, a phenomenon known then and now as the photoelectric effect. But theory and practice didn't match up—the wrong number of electrons were invariably released. Einstein solved this problem with his light quanta hypothesis. With his new version of light, light made of grains of energy instead of a stream, the amount of electrons knocked off of the metal plate matched up with the theory.

Much like Planck before him, Einstein didn't instantly take the math and try to turn it into an interpretation of reality. The fact that thinking of light as quanta solved an intellectual problem did not automatically translate to the theory that light was indeed made of particles. But within a few years, Einstein became more and more convinced that his "light-quanta" were very real indeed.

First Wave of Quantum Mechanics

While just about everyone in the know initially rejected the light-quantum, many of Einstein's contemporaries did begin to play with the idea of quanta in general. In 1913, Danish physicist Niels Bohr (1885–1962) used energy quanta to devise one of the first theories of how an atom worked. Before Bohr, Ernest Rutherford (1871–1937) had drawn up a model of the atom that looked like a mini-solar system, with a nucleus at the center and electrons in orbit around it. But this model had crucial faults. As the electron radiated energy, it should slow down and spiral into the nucleus for a fiery death. If Rutherford's model was accurate, it would mean that all atoms were inherently unstable. Bohr came along and superimposed the brand new concept of energy quanta onto this very classical physics model. In Bohr's version, the electrons were stuck in very specific orbits, since they were also stuck with very specific amounts of energy. Suddenly, the atom was stable: constrained to specific paths, the electron could never move from the lowest orbit all the way into the nucleus.

Bohr's model of the hydrogen atom was not pretty. It solved one problem but was nevertheless a complicated description that his colleagues believed needed, and soon received, refinement. But the model of the atom was nevertheless an important step, as it was one of the first times this nascent quanta idea was associated with matter. Material things, on the other hand, were already understood to come in finite particles; at that point everyone believed in the existence of atoms. But energy itself had long been thought of as continuous and fluid. What Bohr (and Einstein and Planck before him) did was to show that there was also value in imagining radiation as particles. As physicists began to explore the energy inside an atom—the world of protons, neutrons, and electrons—it seemed that one had to jettison classic mechanical descriptions such as the perfect gravitational orbits of the solar system. Instead, an all new science based on energy quanta might just be the key to understanding how the microscopic world worked.

Einstein continued working on energy quanta. Not only did he believe in his light quanta, or "photons"—an idea that Bohr was one of the last to accept—but he applied quantum theories to understanding specific heat and the ways in which matter absorbs radiation. Einstein, however, was beginning to notice a distressing side effect of this new atomic physics. While incorporating quanta of energy into their models did wonders to explain why molecules gave off radiation, the new theories couldn't answer a whole host of other questions. What led to this spontaneous emission? In which direction would the emission go? Quantum theories accounted for how the atom behaved, but they didn't offer answers for the specifics. One could never, using these new rules, be able to predict the details.

Einstein was concerned with this issue perhaps before anyone else. As early as 1917, he wrote in one of his papers that there was a weakness in these theories: they "leave time and direction of elementary processes to chance." Einstein was as caught up in the power of the new dynamics as everyone else. They were all together on the forefront of a new kind of science. As soon as a new particle was discovered—the electron had been found in 1899 and the proton in 1911—these twentieth-century physicists pulled together theories to explain the mysterious atomic world. It was an exciting, if unsettling time. Einstein wrote in 1949 in his *Autobiographical Notes*: "It was as if the ground had been pulled out from under one, with no firm foundation to be seen anywhere, on which one could have built."

And they were devising a science that seemed to work. Quantum theory explained all that the experiments showed. Yet, to Einstein, it seemed obvious that there was a large hole. There were plenty of things that quantum science could not explain—there was work to be done to find a truly complete theory.

Quantum Mechanics Comes Together

The 1920s and 1930s were the decades when quantum mechanics truly formed into a cohesive whole. In the early part of the 1920s, scientists continued to publish papers that we now consider to have been tangents, off track, or wholly incorrect—but soon the community was focusing more and more on an agreed set of rules. If Einstein and Planck were the first to cement the quanta into the scientific consciousness, then it was Werner Heisenberg (1901–1976) who figured out exactly how to put it to use. In 1925, he devised a set of mathematical tools referred to as "matrix mechanics" that helped crystallize all the work published until then. Heisenberg's mechanics could make predictions about that problematic "timing and direction" of the radiation that gave Einstein pause, but only in a probabilistic way. That is, the mechanics could tell you what chance there was that radiation might go off in this or that way from an atom, but it couldn't tell you for sure what would happen. It was essentially as if an atom acted like a roulette wheel—Heisenberg's math could tell you that it would be black 50 percent of the time, odd 50 percent of the time, the number 23 would come up 2.7 percent of the time, but it couldn't tell you exactly where the marble would land on any specific spin of the wheel.

Heisenberg's math was quickly heralded as a great stride forward in understanding quantum mechanics, but it only emphasized Einstein's qualms. Einstein agreed with the rest of the scientists that matrix mechanics did a great job at making probabilistic predictions. Here was, truly, a wonderful new tool to analyze the world of atoms, but Einstein thought it couldn't possibly be the last word. A theory that only offered statistics about the most fundamental particles in nature was not yet good enough. A year later, Erwin Schroedinger (1887–1961) published another set of mathematical tools, relying on wave mechanics to provide a foundation for quantum mechanics, and Einstein hailed this as something he hoped to be more on track. Because Schroedinger's version stemmed from a physical concept people could visualize (the movement of waves) Einstein hoped this would offer a more precise description of what was actually occurring in an atom.

It was soon shown, however, that Schroedinger's work and Heisenberg's were equivalent, and Einstein was once again left feeling that the rest of the physics community was off course. Knowing of the resistance from Einstein and a few other greats, Heisenberg wanted to do more than just create a mathematical model; he had to correlate his math to a physical description of what was happening. What was needed was a holistic picture of the particle world, and for that he was lucky enough to work with Niels Bohr.

Together, Heisenberg and Bohr created what is known as the Copenhagen interpretation of quantum mechanics, named after Bohr's home city. The two men knew the math they'd created could do no more than make predictions about how particles behaved. Einstein believed this to mean that someday soon someone would devise a theory that could, in fact, determine *exactly* how particles behaved. Heisenberg and Bohr, however, put forth the concept that the math could only make predictions because the behavior of the particles themselves was fundamentally unknowable. Even if one had supreme insight and knew precisely at any given moment all the variables in any given system (how fast an electron was moving, where it was going, what atom it was about to collide with) there would be no way to determine exactly what would happen next. There were guidelines, of course. It was likely that it would go this way, or that, and the math could help you narrow down the possibilities, but frankly, there was always the minutest chance that the electron would just disappear completely and show up the next moment in Hawaii.

In 1927, Heisenberg developed an additional theory called the Uncertainty Principle, which stated that not only were there limitations on predicting the future behavior of particles, but one couldn't even know with clarity what a particle was doing in the present. The Uncertainty Principle stated that one could only ever know certain attributes of a particle with clarity. If you knew its speed precisely, for example, you could never know its position particularly well. Again, this was not, claimed Heisenberg, a limitation of the theory, but an accurate description of what was happening in the particle itself. An electron that travels at a set speed simultaneously has a position that is spread out in space. An electron with a point-like, perfect position in space, on the other hand, doesn't have a defined speed.

None of this sat well with Einstein. He had been inculcated from his youth with a profound belief in the innate cause-and-effect nature of the world. As Heisenberg and Bohr began to propound their idea that the atomic world was fundamentally random, Einstein was not the only one to balk. But that would soon change.

Einstein versus Bohr

The tide turned in October 1927 at the sixth Solvay Conference. The physicists at the meeting were divided into two camps: those on Einstein's side, including Schroedinger, and those on Bohr's side, including Heisenberg. Einstein had been invited to give a lecture on the current status of quantum mechanics, and this was eagerly awaited since everyone knew Einstein had a very particular viewpoint. But Einstein withdrew from the honor, knowing not only that he had a bias, but that this bias perhaps kept him from keeping on top of all the literature on the subject. He wrote to the conference moderator, H. A. Lorentz (1853–1928), that he had not been able to delve into the modern development of quantum theory as much as he needed to for such a lecture, "partly due to the fact that I do not approve of the purely statistical interpretation upon which these new theories are based."

But once he arrived at the conference, it was clear that Einstein was indeed well-versed in the new theories. Every day he threw a new criticism of quantum mechanics at Bohr over breakfast. He devised wonderful thought experiments—thought experiments that still get discussed to this day in physics classes around the world, that Bohr credited with helping crystallize his own thinking on quantum physics—and that Bohr managed to discredit by nightfall without fail. The pattern continued all week. Einstein kept thinking up arguments against quantum mechanics. Most of the other participants ignored him, claiming that his thought experiments didn't really represent problems, but Bohr felt that the foundations of his new mechanics depended on solving these riddles. By dinnertime, he'd present Einstein with a solution to show that his Copenhagen interpretation remained triumphant.

For those who had long known Einstein, there was some irony in all of this. Many of the other attendees had been at Einstein's first Solvay Conference in 1911, when he was the one doing the convincing. His special theory of relativity, his theory of light-quanta, and an early version of the general theory of relativity had all been published, and Einstein found himself in the position of having to convince his elders of the veracity of his work. Now, sixteen years later, Einstein was part of the old guard who rejected the new physics. Einstein's friend Paul Ehrenfest (1880–1933) even went so far as to jest at Einstein's expense, saying: "I am ashamed for you."

Whether due to Bohr's continued rebuffs of Einstein's critiques or simply because the young scientists assembled had such enthusiasm for the modern science they'd created, the momentum of the conference turned in favor of the Copenhagen interpretation. Later, Heisenberg described the experience: "I would say that a change had taken place, which I can only express in terms of lawsuits. That is, the burden of proof was reversed." Instead of Heisenberg and his colleagues being forced to convince Einstein of their interpretation, it was Einstein who was put on the offensive, trying desperately to convince everyone else they were wrong.

Einstein versus the World

It is important to note that Einstein never believed quantum mechanics to be incorrect. He saw how accurately it predicted atomic behavior and its math seemed impeccable. But Einstein saw it as something akin to thermodynamics. Thermodynamics can accurately describe how heat and pressure will affect a given system, but it doesn't attempt to describe just which atom of gas will travel where. Einstein felt that quantum mechanics was similar. It was very useful so far as it went. He wrote, "There is no doubt that quantum mechanics has seized hold of a beautiful element of truth and that it will be a touchstone for a future theoretical basis." But the current picture of quantum mechanics could never describe, he claimed, a full physical picture of what was going on.

However, Einstein's admiration for those who'd created the statistical tools of quantum mechanics was quite genuine. He remained in correspondence with most of them—Niels Bohr was always a great favorite of his—and over the years, he nominated many of the founders of quantum theory, including Heisenberg, for Nobel Prizes.

For their part, the rest of the physics community always felt pained that the man many of them saw as their unspoken leader was unable to accept a theory they embraced. The day Ehrenfest realized he had to side with Bohr against Einstein was a grim one for him—it actually brought tears to his eyes. Bohr, for his part, never gave up trying to convince his friend. Their last visit together took place in the United States on a sailboat, and Bohr spent the entire trip lecturing on the subject. His colleagues never knew why Einstein was so adamant, though many blamed it on the stubbornness of old age. Einstein himself wrote to Born in 1944: "Even the great initial success of the quantum theory does not make me believe . . . although I am well aware that our younger colleagues interpret this as a consequence of senility."

Einstein's position on the matter, however, was firm. The universe, he insisted, was not random. It did not, could not, run like a roulette wheel, with no way of knowing what number would show up next. Perhaps one needed to know an improbably large number of details—how fast the wheel was spinning, how hard the marble had been thrown, what temperature the room was—to make accurate predictions, but ultimately all of those details added up to a precise level of cause and effect. If one could somehow miraculously know all the details, one could say with certainty where the marble would fall into its hole—and just how an electron would travel. "God," Einstein repeated to anyone who would listen, "does not play dice."

Reference Frames

A reference frame is really nothing more than a way to describe a place. It's the particular environment in which one is at rest—sitting in a chair, sitting in a moving airplane, standing on the surface of the rotating Earth. Reference frames are very important in Einstein's theories, because his work depends on the fact that the laws of nature must be the same in every reference frame.

There is no spot in the universe where one can say definitively, here I am at rest. Even standing still on the sidewalk, your reference frame is hurtling through space because you're standing on a moving planet. Everything in the universe is moving in relation to something else. In each case, one may feel at rest but will appear to be moving to someone in another reference frame. A friend who dropped you off at the airport would tell you that your reference frame in the plane is moving, and a friend on a rocket ship would tell you that your reference frame standing on the surface of the Earth is moving.

Until Einstein presented his work, physicists assumed there was some basic state of rest in the universe; not necessarily a center, but a backdrop, an absolute space, through which everything else moved. In fact, this assumption was crucial for the contemporary understanding of light, which was assumed to travel like ocean waves through a mysterious substance called the ether. Ether was the primary stationary reference frame of the entire universe, but experiments in the late 1800s failed to find it and new theories needed to be found.

It is unclear whether or not Einstein knew of these experiments. He contradicted himself on the subject, but it's certainly clear that he dismissed ether and its ultimate state of rest when developing his theory of special relativity. In that theory, he claimed that the speed of light wasn't merely constant with respect to some stationary ether, but was constant no matter your reference frame. That is, a person on a moving train will measure light as traveling 186,000 miles per second and a person standing at the train station will also measure it at that speed, *not* 186,000 miles per second plus the speed of the train.

The reference frames Einstein considered for his special theory of relativity were limited to what are called inertial reference frames: frames that were either still or moving in one direction at a constant speed—no acceleration allowed. These are called "inertial" because they are ones where Newton's law of inertia (in the absence of outside forces a body at rest stays at rest and a body in motion stays in motion) holds true.

For an example of a noninertial reference frame, imagine being in a car with dice hanging from the rear view mirror. You are at rest in the car, so the moving car is your reference frame. There are only two forces acting on the dice: gravity, pulling the dice down; and the tension in the string resisting the force of gravity, keeping the dice attached to the mirror. As the car moves at a steady pace in one direction, the dice never move—Newton's laws hold true. But when the car makes a right turn, the dice swing out toward the left. With respect to the car's reference frame, the dice have just made a very definite movement, though no force has acted on them. Occurrences in a turning car, therefore, do not follow Newton's inertia laws and this is not an inertial reference frame.

Einstein went on to explain the physics in these noninertial reference frames with his general theory of relativity. He firmly believed that the laws of physics must hold for all reference frames whether they are inertial or not, so he set himself the task of developing rules that would correspond both to straight cars and turning cars. With this initial goal—and over a decade of analysis—Einstein developed general relativity. The theory provides a new way of understanding gravitational forces so they are equivalent for all reference frames, no matter whether they are still, moving, or accelerating.

See **Relativity, General Theory of; Relativity, Special Theory of.**

Relativity, General Theory of

The general theory of relativity was Einstein's crowning achievement. It revolutionized the theory of gravitation and initiated the new field of cosmology, the study of the universe. Einstein pumped out the special theory of relativity in a quick five weeks—in contrast, the general theory took him almost ten years from first version to final eloquent equations.

Almost immediately after crafting the special theory of relativity, which described the nature of how light moved, Einstein realized it was applicable to only a limited range of phenomena in the universe. Special relativity tackled the different experiences of two observers moving with respect to each other at a constant speed. These observers are said to be in "inertial" reference frames stemming from Newton's concept of inertia, in which a body at rest stays at rest and a body in motion stays in motion. Being at rest or at a constant speed feels essentially identical.

The special theory of relativity relies on the fact that these two states are the same for any observer. There is no preferred reference frame, says the theory, no intrinsic difference between the state of moving at a constant speed versus sitting still and having the world move along at a constant speed underneath you. If you're moving in a car, there is no definitive test for figuring out which of the two scenarios is indeed happening. From this starting point, and making the assumption that the laws of physics must be the same for observers in both reference frames, Einstein created the special theory of relativity.

But, if your car suddenly drove around a corner—changing speeds or changing direction, both of which are considered "accelerating" in physics parlance—you'd notice. The feeling of accelerating feels substantially different from simply sitting still. Perhaps there was something about accelerating reference frames that did make them different from each other. How could Einstein reconcile this with his belief that the laws of physics should be identical, no matter what?

Just as the universe should always be the same for two people moving with constant velocity, the laws of physics should be the same for two people even if one is speeding around a corner or if one is accelerating towards the earth after jumping out of a plane. But accelerating reference frames and gravity just didn't fit into his previous theories.

Einstein first hit upon a solution to this issue, with what he described as the "happiest thought of his life," toward the end of 1907. He had been asked to write a review of relativity for a German journal, and he decided to include something about his current thoughts on acceleration. As he pondered how best to extend what was then the one and only "theory of relativity" to noninertial reference frames, a startling image appeared to him. As he later told a Japanese audience on a lecture tour in Kyoto, "I was sitting on a chair in the patent office at Bern when all of a sudden a thought occurred to me: 'If a person falls freely he will not feel his own weight.' I was startled. This simple thought made a deep impression on me."

Does Gravity Exist?

It is a simple enough thought, but a very profound one. If you have just jumped out of a plane, you will start accelerating toward Earth at the rate of 32 feet/s^2, but if you were blindfolded and couldn't hear the wind rushing past you'd have no way of knowing that you were accelerating. There is no actual sensation of being pulled down toward Earth. With that simple thought experiment, Einstein realized a fact about accelerating reference frames that he had learned long ago about inertial ones: it doesn't matter whether you perceive yourself as moving or as still. There is fundamentally no difference between moving or not moving, even if you're accelerating. Suddenly, Einstein was able to make the leap to an all new equivalence principle. There is no inherent difference between falling toward the ground versus standing still and having the ground hurtle toward you.

When it came to the feeling of gravity under our feet while standing on Earth, for example, there would be no difference between standing on Earth versus standing in an elevator that accelerates upward at just the right rate of 32 feet/s^2. What that meant is that the concept of gravity itself was suspect. There was no force per se acting on the person or the earth, merely a rate of movement. The door was open for Einstein to create a new theory of gravitation.

In that first 1907 paper, Einstein only tackled a handful of concepts regarding gravitational fields. He stated emphatically that "we shall assume the complete physical equivalence of a gravitational field and the corresponding acceleration of the reference frame." In other words, there was no fundamental difference between analyzing a body being moved by gravity and a body that was simply accelerating. The equivalence principle of inertial reference frames, so crucial for the existing special theory of relativity, had just been extended to noninertial frames as well. He also stated for the first time that if gravitation wasn't a force acting on objects with mass, then it would also have effects on light, even though it was massless. Einstein predicted that light would be affected as it traveled through intense gravitation fields no matter what was making those gravitation fields, now that he was trying to do away with the old concept of Newton's force-at-a-distance gravity. As light traveled through a gravitation field it would change frequency, becoming redder to the eye. This is known today as "gravitational redshift" and Einstein would revisit and perfect the concept before it was completely accepted.

Here, however, Einstein stopped. He was just entering the first part of what was to be a topsy turvy decade. His theories had gained him notice in the academic community, and for the first time he began to be courted for bona fide university positions. He took a series of jobs that carried him to Prague to Zurich and ultimately to Berlin. Whether due to the strain of constantly moving (or having to teach, or his dissolving marriage, or his dislike of the cities in which he found himself) or simple disinterest, Einstein did not revisit relativity until 1911. At which point he set about to present his ideas more eloquently.

In this later paper, he made the realization that if light could be affected by a gravitational field, then it should bend around a star or the sun the same way an asteroid does, caught for a short time in orbit around the gigantic object. Never mind that light had no mass, it should bend just as if it were being pulled in towards that star by a force. And *that*, said Einstein, was testable. He made a prediction for just how much light would be deflected as it passed by our sun, thus setting up a challenge to all the astronomers out there to prove or disprove his new equivalence theory.

With the 1911 paper, Einstein once again became enraptured with relativity theory. He knew he had just scratched the surface, announcing some of the manifestations of an original gravitation theory without hammering out the details of that theory. But the next steps were going to be tough. He knew he was attempting to perfect an all-new definition of space-time and for that, he would need to access all new types of math.

Geometry Reinvented

In 1912 Einstein lived in Zurich, teaching at his alma mater, the ETH. There he was reunited with his best friend from college, Marcel

Grossmann. While Einstein's physics sense may have been unerring, he needed a little help pulling together the ideal math for his new physics, and he set Grossmann the task of gathering research. After a day in the library, Grossmann presented Einstein with the details of a little-studied nineteenth-century geometry known as Reimann geometry. Its detail perfectly equipped it to handle multiple dimensions, including time, as Einstein cast about for a new way to describe space. It is a kind of math from which one can derive what's known as "tensors," a mathematical beast that incorporates pointing in a specific direction.

Grossmann is also said to have told Einstein that this Reimann geometry was so tough that physicists really ought not to mess with it, and so the two worked together to fit this old math to the new theories. Einstein wrote of this time: "In all my life I have not labored nearly so hard, and I have become imbued with great respect for mathematics, the subtler part of which I had in my simple-mindedness regarded as pure luxury until now." Together, Einstein and Grossmann published a paper in 1913 based on the tensor math they'd rediscovered. While the paper is mostly just a footnote on the way to the full theory—it does not contain a complete or accurate description of gravitation—it is notable for the fact that the Reimann geometry, together with what is known as the Ricci tensor, became the tools that would forever serve as the language of relativity theory.

Einstein plugged on with the new math—his 1914 paper on the subject spent as much time describing tensor analysis as it did describing his physics theory. That paper was coalescing on an idea, however.

> As an older friend I must advise you against it for in the first place you will not succeed, and even if you succeed no one will believe you.
>
> —Max Planck, after Einstein showed him early—and disorderly—versions of general relativity, 1913

Einstein understood at that point that while a given mass didn't send out an attracting force the way Newtonian gravity suggested, the mass still caused the gravitation. The mass changed the space around it, thus causing incoming objects to accelerate. Not a complete solution yet, but Einstein was getting closer.

At this point, it seems that even Einstein wasn't completely convinced that he was going to come up with a replacement for Newton's gravity theories. In April of that year, he was asked to write about his work for the German newspaper *Vossische Zeitung*, and he spent most of the article discussing special relativity. He only briefly stated at the end that there was a chance that it was but "the first step" towards a much larger theory. However, he said, "On this point, the views even of those physicists who understand relativity theory are still divided."

Tear it Down and Start Over

That division would soon come together, however, as Einstein was on the verge of a breakthrough. In the fall of 1915, he quite suddenly realized his work so far had been on the wrong track. He wrote a spate of letters to friends about a mistaken assumption he had made in his earlier papers and then he set to work righting the problem. November of that year was a time of great focus. Einstein said it was one of the most strenuous times of his life, but in the end he was successful.

He finally pulled together the correct equations for a new theory of gravitation. Throughout the entire previous year, he constantly updated the Prussian Academy of Sciences on his progress, thus immortalizing into the Academy's records all of his wrong turns as well as his final successes. He was well aware of this and even mocked himself, saying: "That fellow Einstein suits his convenience. Every year he retracts what he wrote the year before." But in many ways, this was Einstein's strength. He would continue throughout the years to publish papers that he would later deem incorrect. It was his ability not to worry about making public mistakes that surely led him to take so many risks in his theories.

Regardless, on November 18, he was able to present to the Academy one of his greatest triumphs. With his new improved theories of gravitation, he could accurately predict the orbit of Mercury—an accomplishment that Newton's law of gravity couldn't achieve. The problem with Mercury had been known since the mid-1800s. By and large, Newton's gravitation theory jibed perfectly with planetary orbits, but Mercury was ever so slightly off by 43 seconds of an arc per century (a second is $\frac{1}{3600}$ of an angular degree). Einstein's new equations solved the problem completely. When he used his gravitation theory to map Mercury, there was no longer even the slightest discrepancy. It was the first showing that he was on to a correct theory. Finding that proof was apparently a near-religious experience for Einstein, who later said that not only was he overjoyed—but that he felt as if something had snapped inside him.

While Einstein may have been hesitant about his theories before, everything changed that November. Mercury showed him he was correct, and he never doubted again. He knew in his bones that he had produced the theory of gravitation that would replace the one Isaac Newton wrote down nearly three centuries earlier. Einstein presented the final gravitation equation, $G_{\mu v} = 8\pi T_{\mu v}$, to the Prussian Academy on November 25, 1915.

The New Theory of Gravitation

The rest of the scientific community seems to have agreed with Einstein's assurance. By January of the next year, Karl Schwarzschild (1873–1916) made the first significant contribution to the field of general relativity, describing the gravitational field around a star. Schwarzschild made a second dramatic offering to the field: the metaphoric images we use to understand general relativity.

Einstein, after all, had simply offered the world an equation to describe how space is affected by a mass. By itself, that equation does not offer a description of the universe that the average person can relate to daily experience. The first half of the equation, the G, contains information about how shape curves while the second half, the T, contains information about the mass that is doing the curving. Einstein knew what that equation represented, but in a fairly mathematical way.

By applying the equation to a specific object, however, Schwarzschild took the math and gave it a real-life scenario that was easier to understand. Schwarzschild described how an idealistic model of a star (he described a nonrotating sphere) would cause a gravitational field around it. The best image of what's happening here is of an adult standing in the middle of a trampoline. The adult represents the gigantic star, and the trampoline itself is space. The adult naturally curves the surface of the trampoline, creating a great valley in the center. Now if you put a child on the trampoline he'd have a hard time staying up on the sides—he'd slip and slide down toward the bottom of that valley. Even if he could manage to stay upright, he'd nevertheless feel the pull down the slope toward the adult. A star, says Einstein's general relativity, does to space what the adult does to the trampoline. Space twists around it, causing passing objects to "fall" into it.

Note that there is no force actually pulling the child toward the adult on the trampoline, just as there is no force acting at a distance pulling passing asteroids toward a star. It is simply the slope of space that causes two objects to gravitate toward each other.

Warped space means that light, too, will turn as it passes a large object. Einstein had figured this out some eight years earlier, but using his early equations he came up with the wrong prediction for just how much that light would bend. On November 18, 1915, he also presented the Prussian Academy with a new prediction. This would turn out to be the crux of the next major proof of relativity four years later.

Following It Up

There seems to have been a qualitative difference in Einstein after he'd determined the final equations. Their simplicity and beauty gave him the sense that he was finally finished—in a way that the previous eight years of struggling with gravity clearly never had. With the encouragement of his colleagues Max Planck (1858–1947) and Paul Ehrenfest (1876–1964), Einstein published a comprehensive article on general relativity in March 1916, in a version that was meant to be understood by a wider audience.

By and large, Einstein's ability to use his new theory of gravitation to solve the Mercury problem was enough to convince most scientists that the theory was correct. Other scientists like Willem de Sitter (1872–1934) and Alexander Friedmann (1888–1925) began to apply the work to other aspects of astronomy, attempting to understand the implications for the universe as a whole. Sometimes in collaboration with Einstein and sometimes in papers that Einstein loudly disparaged, other physicists took the general theory of relativity and turned it into a whole new field of cosmology: the study of the origins and ends of the universe.

While general relativity was accepted in the hearts of the scientific community, it had one last hurdle to overcome. Einstein made very specific predictions about the way light bent, and the challenge was on to figure out if he was correct. Scientists in England made it a point of pride to be the ones to prove whether Einstein was right or wrong. If their beloved scientific hero the British Isaac Newton was destined to be overturned, at least let the English be the ones who got credit for the great experiment that would bring the proof. They wanted to see if light from a distant star bent as it traveled by the closest large enough object we have—the sun. But starlight is obscured during the day, so the only way to perform the test was during an eclipse.

The timing had to be just right. In 1919, Sir Arthur Eddington traveled to Principe Island off the west coast of Africa to take photographs during an eclipse, and he found the right amount of curvature in the light rays from a star as they passed the sun. This was essentially the second confirmation of general relativity, since Mercury's orbit was the first. However, it was a much larger, more profound test, and it is often considered the definitive proof of Einstein's theories. Einstein was pleased, dashing off a postcard to his mother that he had received "joyous news" that Eddington had demonstrated the deflection of starlight. But Einstein also never feared that the outcome might have been different. When asked how he would have felt if Eddington hadn't confirmed relativity, Einstein responded: "I would have felt sorry for the Dear Lord—the theory is correct."

Further Confirmation

While Mercury's orbit and the eclipse expedition proved the general theory of relativity to the confidence of just about everyone, Einstein nevertheless made two additional predictions ripe for testing: redshifting and gravitational waves.

Light, said Einstein, would shift toward the red end of the spectrum as it traveled through a gravitational field. In 1920, when he wrote a popular description of his theories, *Relativity: The Special and the General Theory,* he stated that it was still an open question as to whether the effect existed, but that "astronomers are working with great zeal towards the solution." Indeed they were. Within four years, the phenomenon was spotted on the light streaming from massive white dwarf stars. Observations collected in 1924 of Sirius B (a star 8.6 light years away and 61,000 times denser than the sun) showed that the light coming from Sirius was redshifted because the star's gravitational field is 30 times greater than that of our sun.

Einstein was not alive, however, for another celebrated redshift experiment conducted in 1960 by Robert Pound and Glen Rebka. The pair shot a beam of gamma rays up a seventy-four-foot-tall elevator shaft at Harvard University. In a masterfully sensitive measurement, they found that the beam was affected by Earth's gravity and had a redshift of two parts in a thousand trillion—within 10 percent of what Einstein's relativity theories predicted. Again, the general theory of relativity held up to examination.

The last test for relativity offered by Einstein, however, the existence of gravitational waves, has yet to be conclusively proven. Since electromagnetic fields produce waves, which we perceive as light, Einstein hypothesized that gravitational fields should do the exact same thing. Traveling through the universe, as fast as the speed of light, should be ripples in the very fabric of space-time, created by accelerating objects. But they are tough to measure; much as light from a distant star seems dim to us, these waves diminish in strength the farther they travel. In the 1970s, researchers measured the effect of what they perceive to be gravitational waves in a binary pulsar system. One of the pulsars is slowing down at the rate of 75 microseconds per year, just the amount of energy it would be losing if it were giving off gravitational waves.

But no one has yet been able to measure these waves directly. One current massive collaboration on the lookout for gravitational waves is called LIGO, the Laser Interferometer Gravitational Wave Observatory. With exquisitely sensitive machinery, LIGO hopes to detect gravitational waves as they pass through Earth. So far none have been detected. But if LIGO, or some other such experiment succeeds, relativity will have passed one of its last great tests.

See **Cosmology; Gravitation; Reference Frames; Relativity, Special Theory of.**

Relativity, Special Theory of

The best-known of Einstein's achievements is his special theory of relativity. It's not his most complicated theory or his only revolutionary work. It's not even what he won the Nobel Prize for. But it is the source of all the famous tidbits generally known about Einstein's science. The special theory of relativity introduced the equation $E = mc^2$, and the concepts that nothing can travel more quickly than the speed of light, and that time slows down the faster you move.

Special relativity boils down to this: the speed of light never changes and this leads to some quirky differences in the way that people who are standing still or moving will perceive the same beam of light. The only way to explain these differences without dismantling the laws of physics, according to the theory, is to realize that as any person or thing moves, time progresses more slowly and space contracts. We don't notice this in our daily lives because the effects are noticeable only at incredibly high speeds.

How Einstein Figured It Out

The details of this theory came as the culmination of many years' worth of puzzles that rattled around in Einstein's brain. He wrote later: "I was 16 when the image first came to me: What would it be like to ride a beam of light? At 16 I had no idea, but the question stayed with me for the next 10 years. The simple questions are always the hardest. But if I have a gift, it is that I am as stubborn as a mule."

He was given the tools to begin to answer this question from his teen years when he was at the University of Zurich in 1898, first studying Maxwell's equations (the body of rules that govern how light moves). Although there were various issues with the theory of light at the time, exactly where the problem lay was unclear. Maxwell's equations stated that light always appears to move at the exact same speed, namely 186,000 miles per hour. This is unlike any other moving object in the world: toss a ball while in a 75 mph train and it will appear to go a slow 10 mph to you, but a fast 85 mph to anyone standing on the side of the train tracks. But if you shine a flashlight while sitting on the train, you'd measure it at 186,000 miles per hour and so would the person outside the train—not 186,000 plus 75 mph. But if this were true, then the person who is moving would deduce completely different laws of physics than the person who is standing still—and that's unacceptable. The laws of physics should be the same for everyone, regardless of whether they happen to be on a train or not.

So scientists decided there must be some medium, some *ether*, that was permanently at rest. They thought that light must travel through ether the way a water wave travels through water. This ether was also thought to be a fundamental background to the whole universe. Earth, the sun and the planets all traveled through this ether, so when it came to light there was expected to be a reference frame that truly could be proven to be "at rest" while the larger bodies in the solar system were truly proven to be moving.

But it wasn't so. No matter how they set up an experiment—the most famous one, tried numerous times over many years, is called the Michelson-Morley experiment—no one could find this mysterious ether.

Without even being sure what was wrong with the current theories, Einstein knew that they were incomplete. His goal had always been to understand *exactly* how the universe worked, and he wanted to nail down how light moved. Years later in a letter to his friend Erika Oppenheimer, he explained his dilemma. He wrote that experience shows that all systems are equivalent (i.e., the laws of physics are deduced the same way, no matter whether the system is moving or not) in mechanics, in optics, and in electrodynamics. However, this equivalence in electrodynamics, unlike the others, could not be explained by current theories. "I soon reached the conviction that this had its basis in a deep incompleteness of the theoretical system. The desire to discover and overcome this generated a state of psychic tension in me that, after seven years of vain searching, was resolved by relativizing the concepts of time and length."

Those years of searching grew to a head by the spring of 1905. The pieces were slowly, subconsciously, coalescing into a solution. Einstein knew he was on the brink of solving the jigsaw puzzle that plagued him, so he asked for help from his friend Michele Besso, who worked with him at the Swiss Patent Office. The pair played hooky for the day and brainstormed over all they knew about light and electromagnetism. They ended the day exhausted and believed they were no closer to understanding the mystery. Einstein went home close to despair, convinced he was never going to understand the "true laws" of the universe. But somehow during the course of that night, things became more clear. He woke up with a sudden understanding; his subconscious had finally pushed new ideas to the forefront of his mind. His waking mind knew how light moved and how its movement affected the very nature of space and time.

Light and Space and Time

To begin with, Einstein focused on this oddity that light always travels at the same speed, regardless of whether you're moving or not. This isn't true of a baseball, a bird, or even of sound. Let's say you're in a sailboat and a bird flies overhead. Someone sitting on a dock might see the bird flying calmly at five miles an hour as it floats along looking for a fish to catch. But you're on a sailboat that's moving in the opposite direction at about the same speed. To you the bird is moving away from you at ten miles per hour. On the other hand, a person who is perched somewhere outside of Earth but who can still see that same bird might see that the whole Earth is hurtling along through space in relation to the sun at 66,600 miles per hour. To this extraterrestrial, the bird appears to be moving at 66,605 miles an hour, which is no lazy pace at all.

The point is that speeds measured by people traveling at different rates will result in completely different measurements. This is true for everything in the world except light. If we replace that bird with a light beam from a lighthouse, then no matter what speed or "reference frame" you're in, that light is moving at 186,000 mph. The person at the dock will measure it at that speed, you in your boat will measure it as that speed (not 186,000 +5 mph as it was for the bird), and an extraterrestrial will measure it at that speed (not 186,000 + 66,600 mph). Light, quite simply, always travels at the exact same speed. Experiments have verified this again and again and it is one of the most well-confirmed facts of physics.

The second tenet that Einstein assumed for his relativity theory was that no matter the reference frame, the laws of physics will always be the same. It doesn't matter whether you're moving or how you're moving. The laws are consistent.

Einstein held true to these two principles and followed the logic and math associated with them strictly, no matter how bizarre the results. He found that if you're going to keep the speed of light constant, then you have to adjust some of the *other* things in the world that have always been thought of as "constants." These are things that seem to be extremely unchangeable at first glance, like time and space. If we insist that light stays constant, then at high speeds time itself slows down and space contracts.

Dilated Time and Contracted Space

An example to explain this takes place on a train. (Einstein liked to use examples on trains, and convention dictates that they're almost always used when describing relativity.) Imagine you are standing on a station platform watching a train go by. Your friend is standing at the back of the train as it speeds past. Just as she passes you, a conductor at the front of the train, say, 500 feet away, turns on a flashlight. From your perspective, the flashlight beam reaches you several moments later, the exact amount of time that it would take light to travel 500 feet, which is technically 0.000005 seconds, since light travels extremely quickly. Just take it on faith that you can measure time frames this small. However, as you watch, your friend has continued moving along in the train, rushing toward the light beam at the same time that it is streaming toward her, and the beam *reaches her first*.

But there's a problem here. As far as your friend is concerned, she's not moving at all. After all, she knows that there is no reason for your reference frame to be any better than hers, so she figures she's at rest and you're the one who's moving. She thinks that the light beam traveled 500 feet (the distance from the front of the train to the end) from the conductor's flashlight to her and she knows it should have taken 0.000005 seconds. But it didn't. She measured that it took that long to get to *you* as you moved away from her, but somehow it got to her more quickly. Since she knows that, according to the laws of physics, any object moving at 186,000 miles per hour should travel 500 feet in 0.000005 seconds, this is somewhat confusing.

What Einstein did to solve this confusion was to switch around the very definition of what was happening. Since you saw your friend moving toward the light beam, you, in essence, perceived the distance the light had to travel as getting shorter. So, instead of that merely being your "perception," said Einstein, it is in actuality what's happening: when an object is moving, space itself shortens. By making this assumption, then both your friend and you will still come up with the same laws of physics. Your friend no longer has to worry that it took the beam of light such a short time to get to her because according to special relativity, the beam didn't actually travel a full 500 feet. Because it was moving so fast, space contracted and it traveled a shorter distance.

Of course, there's nothing that insists that only space needs to change. As far as your friend is concerned, it could be that the light beam did, in fact, travel a full 500 feet, but that her method of marking time is wrong. If she could slow down her clocks, she could measure the light beam as having taken the full .000005 seconds. This, too, saves her from the problem of having to assume that something is wrong with the laws of physics.

As Einstein worked out the equations to describe these phenomena, he realized that a combination of both happens. As that light beam travels towards your friend at such a high speed, it experiences both a shorter distance and a longer time.

In fact, the closer one gets to traveling at the speed of light, the closer one gets to having time stop altogether. Einstein described this in a beautiful thought experiment that follows from his first teenaged question of what would it be like to travel on a beam of light. He reasoned that if you started your journey at a big bell tower clock at noon and began racing away at the speed of light, when you looked back, you would always and forever see that clock with its two hands pointing right at the twelve. After all, no new beam of light showing a new time would ever be able to catch up to you. In essence, as you traveled on the beam, time itself would have stopped for those you left behind. Of course, as they watched you speed away, they would think that you were the one for whom time stopped while they continued to live their lives at a normal pace.

This contracting of space and shortening of time led to some very specific, testable phenomena. For example, imagine a short-lived, tiny particle speeding around a particle accelerator in a physics lab. Many particles decay within a matter of microseconds and yet, they can last much longer as they whiz around and around in the innards of the accelerator. The explanation is that since they're moving so fast, time itself passes more slowly for the particle than it does for those watching. If you could somehow zoom along at the same speed with the particle, you would only experience a few moments before it decayed and disappeared. It's only to an outside observer that the particle lasts for such a (comparatively) long time.

Scientists have also sent atomic clocks (known for their incredible precision) into orbit around Earth at fast speeds. When the clocks come back down to Earth, they have lagged behind the clocks that stayed behind. These experiments have been rigorously conducted, making sure that the clock didn't break down in any way. The only reason the atomic clock runs slower than the clock on Earth is because it is moving so quickly, and so time itself slows down.

Debut of the Theory

The morning that Einstein woke up with the insights that led to the theory of special relativity, he told Besso, the man with whom he'd brainstormed the day before, simply: "I've completely solved the problem." For the next five or six weeks, he intensely scribbled out his ideas into a cohesive paper, and in June 1905, he mailed the manuscript to the German physics journal *Annalen der Physik*. Then, exhausted, he lay in bed for the next few days recuperating from his feverish work.

The paper was published in the September 26, 1905 issue of the journal with the title, "On the Electrodynamics of Moving Bodies." It was the third paper (and there would be two more) that Einstein published in the prestigious journal that year, a year often referred to as his "miracle year" based on his prodigious output. The paper was qualitatively different from his others in one bizarre way: there were very few footnotes or attributions. Unlike so many papers that are legacies of the surrounding scientific literature, Einstein's first relativity paper seemed to have come completely out of his own head.

This is not to say, looking back, that one can't see how the paper emerged from contemporary scientific understanding. In fact, descriptions of the emergence of relativity always describe the Michelson-Morley experiment's inability to find the mysterious ether, and Lorentz's equations that showed length contracting when things moved as being the catalysts that nudged Einstein toward his conclusions. But while the scientific milieu around Einstein must have served as an important backdrop for his ideas, it does not seem to have had a direct influence. Decades later, Einstein insisted that while his equations, in the end, mirrored Lorentz's, he had never seen that aspect of the older scientists' work. Einstein's other papers in that miraculous year of 1905 showed meticulous documentation of previous sources; it is unlikely that he would have neglected to give proper acknowledgments here. Instead, special relativity seems to be a true break from previous thought.

Einstein knew this work was fairly surprising, not simply for its strange notions of altering space and time, but because it questioned Newton's sacrosanct laws. (Special relativity does not, in fact, outright contradict Newton's mechanics. If you use the equations for relativity for objects and people traveling at slow speeds, the only speeds Newton encountered, then they look just like the equations for Newtonian mechanics. So, the special theory of relativity encompasses Newton's work and then expands it, applying to an even greater realm of phenomena.) Tackling the great Isaac Newton might well have resulted in a furor, but no letters or rebuttals came to the journal. As it was, only a very few scientists even understood how important the paper was. Max Planck (1858–1947), already an established physicist, wrote a note to Einstein early in 1906 asking for clarification on a part of the theory—but for some time that was the only nibble that made its way to the author.

Planck's interest, however, grew. He sent his assistant, Max van Laue, to meet Einstein and to get more information from the young man. Within a few months, Planck began to teach relativity theory in his classes at the University of Berlin. Over the next few years, Planck even wrote a few papers expanding on Einstein's idea. Einstein always said it was Planck's interest that nudged the theory of relativity into the spotlight. By 1908, slowly but surely, Einstein's new theory had captured the minds of every modern physicist.

Mass and Energy

Even before others caught the bug, Einstein continued to plug away at his new concept of cosmic reality. In the summer of 1905, he realized another consequence of his work: much the way space and time were connected, mass and energy were connected as well. He wrote to one of his closest friends, Conrad Habicht: "One more consequence of the paper on electrodynamics has also occurred to me. The principle of relativity, in conjunction with Maxwell's equations, requires that mass be a direct measure of the energy contained in a body; light carries mass with it. A noticeable decrease of mass should occur in the case of radium. The argument is amusing and seductive; but for all I know the Lord might be laughing over it and leading me around by the nose." Despite worrying that he might be on the wrong track, Einstein followed through with his idea that the amount of mass in an object would have a direct correlation to its energy.

In November 1905, he wrote about this topic for his fourth *Annalen der Physik* paper of the year. It was a slight two pages long and was published as a footnote to the previous paper. In this paper, Einstein shows a little more hesitancy than in his previous ones, phrasing the title in the form of a question: "Does the Inertia of a Body Depend upon its Energy Content?" It wasn't until 1907 that Einstein became convinced the Lord was not in fact laughing at him and he realized that the correlation he noticed between energy and mass was even stronger than he first supposed. They were, in fact, two sides of the same coin—mass was a form of energy and they were related by the now-famous equation $E = mc^2$.

Postscript

It was not until 1915 that this body of work got its name. Einstein initially referred to his idea simply as the "principle of relativity." It became known as the "theory of relativity" in 1907 when that name was used by physicist Paul Ehrenfest. (Others suggested the "theory of invariants" because in many ways the point is that despite relativity the laws of physics remain the same no matter how an object is moving. However, this title never caught on.) It finally became the "special theory of relativity" in 1915 to distinguish it from the later "general theory of relativity."

See $E = mc^2$; Electrodynamics; Ether; Light; Michelson-Morley Experiment; Miracle Year; Relativity, General theory of.

Religion

Albert Einstein never embraced an organized religion. Born Jewish, he shed the customs and traditions of Judaism when he was twelve, and never associated himself with conventional religion again. However, it would not be true to say that Einstein was not religious. He often expressed a deep awe and appreciation for what he described as "the mysterious," which he claimed was the essence of any religion.

When Einstein was an adolescent, German law required that every student have official religious education. So, his fairly unobservant Jewish parents hired a distant family member to tutor him in his heritage. Around eleven years of age, young Albert embraced Judaism with a ferocity. Much to his parents' surprise (and perhaps, chagrin), Einstein threw himself into Jewish traditions, including refusing to eat pork. He would later describe this phase as his "religious paradise." But, the phase would not last long.

At the age of twelve, Einstein discovered the world of science and the Bible stories he had so enjoyed now sounded like lies told to children. He reversed completely his previous religiousness and rejected the world of what he now perceived to be fairy tales. For the rest of his life, Einstein seems to have understood religion in similar terms, describing a belief in a personal god or a belief in an afterlife as being crutches for the superstitious or fearful. He never again participated in a traditional religious ritual: he refused to become a bar mitzvah at thirteen, his marriages were civil, he never attended a service, and he chose not to have a Jewish burial.

Nevertheless, Einstein described himself as religious. A story is told of a party in Berlin in 1927 where a guest made sarcastic comments about religion and God all evening. The man, a literary critic named Alfred Kerr, was reprimanded that such comments probably shouldn't be made in front of Einstein. Kerr turned incredulously to Einstein to ask if he was indeed so religious. Einstein replied, "Yes, you can call it that. Try and penetrate with your limited means the secrets of nature and you will find that . . . there remains something subtle, intangible and inexplicable. Veneration for this force beyond anything that we can comprehend is my religion. To that extent I am, in point of fact, religious."

Einstein believed in something he called, "cosmic religion." In studying the universe, he felt that humans were inherently limited to only a partial understanding of nature. There would always be a level of existence that humans could not comprehend: something complex, unexplainable, and subtle. Respect and love for this mysteriousness was the "cosmic religion."

Ever the scientist, Einstein analyzed this assumption. In a November 9, 1930 article he wrote for *New York Times Magazine* called *Religion and Science*, he presented three stages of religious evolution. At the beginning, he said, people faced the simple fear of the dangers of the universe, and this led to a belief that there must be something powerful whose whims dictate human fate. Next comes the idea of an anthropomorphic God who can punish or reward, thus leading to concepts of morality as well as answering questions about life after death. Beyond this, said Einstein, is the cosmic religion, a feeling of human impotence and futility in the face of nature and the "world of thought." He wrote that the universe and its workings are what inspires awe. In this kind of religiosity, the practitioner wishes to experience being part of the universe in a much more holistic way, as opposed to being an individual separate from it. Einstein cited works from Buddhist scripture to the Psalm of David to Schopenhauer's writings as examples of this kind of mystical experience. Ultimately, he insisted that this feeling was so universal, so free of dogma, that no single church could encompass it. Thus "cosmic religion" is inherently separate from organized religion—and it is this type of religion that Einstein embraced. Indeed, said Einstein, it was the highest purpose of all science and art to inspire this intense level of feeling. Moreover, if one could not achieve a sense of the mysterious, one may as well be dead. Clearly, religion—albeit a very specific definition of religion—was a crucial part of Einstein's being.

Religion and Science Go Together

In addition to religion being an important part of a human's existence, Einstein insisted that a connection between religion and science was crucial. His 1930 "Religion and Science" article was one of his first public declarations of how he viewed science and religion. Not only did Einstein point out, as mentioned above, that science can, and should, lead to religious feeling, he offered reasons as to why the traditional "conflict" between science and religion was small-minded. Einstein said that while, historically, religious peoples have feared the stark causality inherent in scientific thought—for if nature and man are constrained to certain absolutes of cause and effect, what need is there for a god to step in and offer rewards or punishments?—religion should not rely on this rationale for moral behavior. Einstein belived that morality was not based on the idea of "divine punishment," but instead, should stem from compassion.

This article was met with a mixed response. It was published shortly before Einstein made his second trip to the United States and he was surprised by how many people wished to discuss his ideas on religion. Some of the reactions were as one would expect. The strongly conservative side derided him. A Catholic priest said that Einstein had made a mistake by including the "s" in his "cosmic religion." On the other hand, some liberal Jewish rabbis applauded Einstein's thinking. (Of course, there were Jews and Christians who took the opposite points of view as well.) The article came at a time when the nature of twentieth-century science was being shaped and so, naturally, there would be those who resisted science's attempt to answer questions previously the purview of religion and those who disliked Einstein's introduction of religion into the scientific world.

> *Science without Religion is blind;*
> *Religion without Science is lame.*
>
> —Einstein, speaking at a 1941 symposium
> on science, philosophy, and religion

Nonetheless, Einstein would always hold that science and religion benefited from mutual association. In his opinion, the best that religion could be stemmed directly from the scientific impulse. He wrote, "The further the spiritual evolution of mankind advances, the more certain it seems to me that the path to genuine religiosity does not lie through the fear of life, or the fear of death, and blind faith, but through striving after rational knowledge." It was the search for knowledge itself that Einstein believed to be the basis of religion.

Relativity and Religion

While Einstein clearly saw his love of science and awe in the presence of the universe as his religion, he did not confuse the laws and rules of science with the tenets of religion. When relativity and quantum mechanics were introduced in the beginning of the twentieth century, numerous theologians and philosophers naturally attempted to incorporate the "new science" into their worldviews. At first glance, the fields of relativity and quantum mechanics seem to allow for a less deterministic world than the hard and fast rules of Newtonian mechanics. According to Newton, a thrown ball always goes up and down at the same speeds; in quantum mechanics, objects don't always go where they're thrown. In actuality, these sciences are also bound by their own rules and laws, but it cannot be denied that they don't jibe with everyday experience. Consequently, it is easy (if one is so religiously inclined) to see the fields of twentieth-century physics as pointing toward a sense of the "mysterious" in what might otherwise be a cut-and-dry mechanistic universe.

Einstein denied the connection wholeheartedly. When asked in 1921 by the Archbishop of Canterbury how relativity affected religion, he replied that it did not. Relativity, he insisted, was wholly scientific and had nothing to do with religion.

Nevertheless, relativity has often been brought to bear on the world of religion, usually by using the metaphors and rhetoric of the science to support the metaphors and rhetoric of religion. Einstein's introduction of a fourth dimension, for example, has been used to support the idea that there is an alternative to our mundane reality: add a fourth dimension and our worldly existence is transformed into eternal life. In addition, the $E = mc^2$ component has been used to support the existence of the divine: since energy is equivalent to mass, this is seen as "proof" that there is a life force inherent in every material object. Needless to say, such associations may be interesting tools for religious discussions but are in no way rigorous scientific proofs.

Roosevelt, Franklin D.

Shortly after the world-famous Einstein immigrated to the United States in the fall of 1933, he and his wife were invited to dine with President Roosevelt on January 24, 1934, and they spent the night in the White House. Later, the two men famously collaborated in beginning the Manhattan Project to create the atom bomb.

Einstein's initial invitation to the White House came at the insistence of the American Rabbi Stephen Wise. Incensed at Germany's racial policies, Wise believed that Roosevelt had "not lifted on behalf of the Jews," and so to get Einstein to plead his people's case to the American president, Wise contacted a Roosevelt adviser and soon an invitation was in the mail.

That first invitation was declined, but not by Einstein himself. Abraham Flexner, the head of the Institute for Advanced Study in Princeton, New Jersey, where Einstein had just begun working, opened all of Einstein's mail. Flexner turned down the President's invitation, telling Roosevelt that Einstein came to America for seclusion, and accepting one invitation would mean he would then have to accept more and not be able to work. Einstein was furious when he heard of Flexner's interference and, soon, a second invitation was forthcoming.

> *I'm so sorry that Roosevelt is president—otherwise I would visit him more often.*
>
> —Einstein, according to his friend Frieda Bucky

The meeting between Einstein and Roosevelt was pleasant but apparently unremarkable. Neither party ever commented extensively on their conversation, although later Elsa remarked to a friend that Roosevelt asked her husband to accept what two U.S. Congressmen were proposing—an honorary United States citizenship. But Einstein declined special treatment.

While that first meeting was of little consequence, Einstein's later contact with Roosevelt put the physicist at the forefront of the atomic age. Discoveries in 1938 had physicists buzzing about scientific developments in the study of uranium. Comments from German scientists to American colleagues about their new techniques in splitting uranium atoms and harnessing their massive energy worried those who were concerned about the possibility of Nazi Germany obtaining an uber-weapon. Knowing of the new research and fearful of Germany's destructiveness, Einstein wrote a letter of warning to the president. Although the letter didn't lead to immediate action, it certainly marked the first time that Roosevelt was made aware of the fact that modern physics had opened the door for a brand new kind of bomb. Over the next few years, as the United States became embroiled in World War II, Roosevelt eventually began the massive Manhattan Project that ultimately developed the first atomic bomb. However, Einstein, with his pacifist leanings and Communist connections, was deemed a security risk by the U.S. military and not asked to participate, thus ending Einstein's involvement with Roosevelt.

Russell-Einstein Manifesto

What came to be known as the Russell-Einstein Manifesto was a short statement signed by eleven prominent scientists, declaring their concern over the arms race between the United States and the USSR. It was released on July 9, 1955, in London a few months after Einstein's death. It was Einstein's last political statement.

The manifesto was the outcome of a longstanding collaboration between Einstein and the writer, pacifist, and winner of the Nobel Prize for literature, Bertrand Russell. In a February 11, 1955 letter, Russell wrote to Einstein, "In common with every other thinking person, I am profoundly disquieted by the armaments race in nuclear weapons . . . I think that eminent men of science ought to do something dramatic to bring some notice to the public and governments the disasters that may occur. Do you think it would be possible to get, say, six men of the very highest scientific repute, headed by yourself, to make a very solemn statement about the imperative necessity of avoiding war?" Einstein's reply came five days later. He endorsed Russell's sentiments, readily agreeing that something must be done by the scientific community to denounce the stockpiling of arms by the world's superpowers.

We invite this Congress, and through it the scientists of the world and the general public, to subscribe to the following resolution:

"In view of the fact that in any future world war nuclear weapons will certainly be employed, and that such weapons threaten the continued existence of mankind, we urge the Governments of the world to realize, and to acknowledge publicly, that their purpose cannot be furthered by a world war, and we urge them, consequently, to find peaceful means for the settlement of all matters of dispute between them."

Max Born
Perry W. Bridgman
Albert Einstein
Leopold Infeld
Frederic Joliot-Curie
Herman J. Muller
Linus Pauling
Cecil F. Powell
Joseph Rotblat

Bertrand Russell
Hideki Yukawa
            —*The Conclusion of the Russell-Einstein Manifesto*

Russell drafted a statement that began by saying the current arms race was "the tragic situation which confronts humanity." He went on to state: "We feel that scientists should assemble in conference to appraise the perils that have arisen as a result of the development of weapons of mass destruction, and to discuss a resolution in the spirit of the appended draft." The resolution urged the governments of the world to publicly denounce the existence of nuclear weapons and to find a peaceful means for settling disputes.

Russell sent a draft of the manifesto to Einstein, who all along had been suggesting names of prominent scientists he believed would support their cause. Einstein replied to the draft by writing what would become his last completed correspondence: "Dear Bertrand Russell, Thank you for your letter of April 5. I am gladly willing to sign your excellent statement. I also agree with your choice of the prospective signers. With kind regards, A. Einstein"

Of the eleven signers of the document, ten either were or would become Nobel Prize winners, including Linus Pauling, Joseph Rotblat, Leopold Infeld, Hideki Yukawa, and Max Born.

Schroedinger, Erwin
(1887–1961)

Erwin Schroedinger was an Austrian physicist who helped create the foundations of quantum mechanics. Like Einstein, Schroedinger didn't agree with the extremes to which others took the new science. He was one of the few physicists who aligned himself with Einstein against quantum mechanics, trying to search for a unified theory that would improve upon the theories everyone else espoused.

Einstein and Schroedinger worked together in the early 1930s as professors at the Kaiser Wilhelm Institutes in Berlin. Both men stood out in the extremely formal university as professors who treated their students as equals. The two spent time together walking and sailing and they became close friends.

Like so many of their contemporaries, however, Einstein and Schroedinger began writing to each other about their work long before they met face to face. In the 1920s, the entire physics community focused on a new kind of science that had become known as quantum mechanics, since it was based on the idea that light and energy were not continuous streams, but made up of particles or "quanta." Einstein was the first to suggest that light was made of these quanta, and so he was involved in quantum mechanics from the beginning. But the field had begun to take what Einstein and Schroedinger agreed was a bizarre turn.

As more and more was learned, it seemed that quantum mechanics did away with the laws of cause and effect, insisting that atomic processes were so random, one could never predict exactly what would happen next. In 1925, Werner Heisenberg (1901–1976) put forth a new kind of matrix mathematics that could be used to make probabilistic predictions about how an atom might react to any given situation. This was hailed, rightly, as a boon to the fledgling science, but it also entrenched the notion that one could only make "guesses" about how an atom moves.

New Math

The next year, Schroedinger came up with what he hoped was a better alternative. He devised another set of mathematical tools to help with quantum theory, called wave mechanics. Einstein rejoiced. Schroedinger's math, referencing the physical qualities of waves as it did, seemed to hold out hope that there was a physical reason behind the oddities of atomic behavior. Einstein, always unhappy with Heisenberg's probabilities, wrote to his friend Michele Besso in May 1926: "Schroedinger has come out with a pair of wonderful papers on the quantum rules."

But Einstein's elation was not to last. Almost immediately, it was shown that Schroedinger's math, so different from Heisenberg's at first glance, was in fact identical. Schroedinger had essentially confirmed the inherent randomness that other scientists were avidly touting. He was as displeased with this turn of events as Einstein, going so far as to say that if he had known what his papers would unleash, he might not have published his work at all. As it happened, the contention over whether to use Heisenberg's matrix mechanics versus Schroedinger's wave mechanics became somewhat heated. Even though he disliked the way others interpreted his math, Schroedinger argued for the superiority of his own work, thus annoying Heisenberg, who wrote to his friend Wolfgang Pauli in 1926: "The more I think about the physical portion of Schroedinger's theory, the more repulsive I find it. . . . What Schroedinger writes about the visualizability of his theory 'is probably not quite right,' in other words it's crap." As it is, today, Schroedinger's math is more commonly used.

Despite his major contribution, Schroedinger had reservations about quantum mechanics all his life. He is famously known for a thought experiment called Schroedinger's cat, in which he mocked the new science that insisted nothing in the atomic world could be known unless—and until—it was measured. The thought experiment went like this: Imagine putting a cat in a sealed box with a sample of radioactive material with a 50 percent chance of decaying in, say, one minute. If it decays, it will set off a poisonous gas into the box that will kill the cat. So, in any given minute, there is a 50 percent chance that the cat will die. Of course, quantum mechanics states that we can't know whether or not that radioactive material has decayed until we measure it. In fact, for the minute while we're waiting, the material is in two states simultaneously: one in which it hasn't decayed and one in which it has. The material is not forced to be in one or the other definite state until one actually looks at it and measures it. If one accepts this, asked Schroedinger, how do we interpret the state of the cat waiting in its sealed box? If, for a full minute, the radioactive material is simultaneously both decayed and not decayed, then is the poison simultaneously both released and not released? Is the cat both dead and alive at the same time? Is the cat neither? And is it in whatever amorphous state it is until someone actually opens the box and looks inside? The obvious absurdity of this concept was one of the reasons Schroedinger thought the theory of quantum mechanics was not yet well enough understood.

A Collaboration . . .

Regardless of their frustrations regarding the abandon with which the community embraced quantum mechanics, both Einstein and Schroedinger knew that the theory did a fantastic job of predicting the probabilities of atomic events. Schroedinger's work in wave mechanics was a crucial part of that success, and Einstein was one of several people who nominated Schroedinger for a Nobel Prize many times. Schroedinger finally won the physics prize in 1933.

Because Schroedinger, like Einstein, did not believe that quantum physics was complete, he joined Einstein in the quest to come up with a new theory. Einstein referred to this as a unified field theory, since it would be a grand overarching theory to unify all of physics. Consequently, in the 1940s, when Einstein was living in Princeton and Schroedinger had left what he deemed the hatefulness of Germany to live in Ireland, Schroedinger was one of the few people with whom Einstein shared his ideas. "I am sending [this] to nobody else," Einstein wrote Schroedinger in 1946, "because you are the only person known to me who is not wearing blinders in regard to the fundamental questions in our science." But, the collaboration took a turn for the worse when Schroedinger announced that he had solved the problem completely. He was convinced he had found the unified field theory through the use of a type of math called Affine geometry. He announced his new findings on January 27, 1947—not to a scientific journal, but with great fanfare at an event attended by reporters and even Ireland's prime minister, Eamon De Valera.

...And an Accusation

Much to Einstein's surprise, the work was nearly identical to his own. While Schroedinger had devised a new method of attaining them, the equations he'd announced were the same as ones Einstein had already found and discarded as not being complete. Einstein made several scathing comments to the *New York Times* that such overly hyped announcements as Schroedinger's did a disservice to scientists, because "the reader gets the impression that every five minutes there is a revolution in science, somewhat like a coup d'etat in some of the smaller unstable republics."

Schroedinger sent an apology to Einstein, attempting to explain how he made such a colossal mistake, but Einstein wasn't swayed. Einstein wrote Schroedinger to say that they should take a break from writing each other and instead concentrate on their work. It would be another three years (and just a few years before Einstein's death) before they began their correspondence again.

Solvay Conferences

The Solvay Conferences were a series of scientific meetings in Brussels attended by some of the greatest physicists of all time. Numerous crucial disputes were hammered out there, most notably the interpretation of quantum mechanics.

A wealthy industrialist and chemist from Brussels named Ernest Solvay founded the conferences. He made his fortune by developing a process for producing sodium carbonate. Solvay admitted that he didn't understand the puzzling contradictions posed by the new atomic physics, but he said his goal was to create, "a personal exchange of views of these problems between the researchers who are more or less directly concerned with them."

Einstein, Max Planck, and Marie Curie were some of the twenty-one European scientists who attended the first Solvay Conference in November 1911. Eleven papers were presented and followed by rather intense scientific discussion. Einstein, only thirty-one years old at the time, had the honor of giving the closing lecture as well as a summation of all the earlier scientific discourse. This, and all following Solvay Conferences, were chaired by the Dutch physicist Hendrik Lorentz. As Einstein later told a Geneva colleague, Lorentz "needed all this vast scientific knowledge, mastery of languages, and incomparable tactfulness, to keep the discussions focused . . . and yet allow each participant's views to come through."

The conference let Einstein discuss his startling theories of relativity with leading physicists like Henri Poincaré, who was overwhelmingly negative; Planck, who was also doubtful; and Curie, who, while initially not convinced, was impressed enough with Einstein's abilities as a physicist to subsequently recommend him for a university position.

Photos of the first Solvay Conference show these three leading theoreticians sitting in the place of honor—the center of the group. Einstein, the youngest attendee, is off to one side looking away from the camera's lens. A similar photo from over a decade later offers a wonderful visual description of how far Einstein had come. Now that Einstein's theories had become not only accepted, but were evolving into entirely new fields of physics, he is shown sitting dead center, staring directly at the camera.

At that, the Sixth Solvay Conference in 1927, the tables were turned, and it was Einstein who was resistant to new theories. Max Born and Niels Bohr attended with the hope that they would be able to convince Einstein to accept Heisenberg's Uncertainty Principle. Earlier that same year, Werner Heisenberg published a paper stating that the more precisely one knew specific characteristics of a particle, the more uncertain other characteristics would be. For example, if one measured the speed of a particle very carefully, one wouldn't be able to determine its position particularly well. This didn't mean that the position was simply hard to measure, but that it truly didn't exist in a definite sense. Even a supreme being wouldn't be able to measure both characteristics perfectly. This Uncertainty Principle, of course, flies in the face of everything one experiences in real life, where trains and boats and people are usually definitely all in a specific space and moving at a specific speed. It was an idea that Einstein hated.

At the conference, Einstein and Bohr debated whether Heisenberg's theory was correct, an argument they never resolved. Physicist Otto Stern recalled that every day, Einstein would come to breakfast with a thought experiment he believed exposed a logical flaw in quantum mechanics. "Pauli and Heisenberg were there," Stern remembered, "[they] did not pay much attention [saying] '*Ach was, das stimmt schon, das stimmt schon.*' They dismissed Einstein's concerns, saying, 'Ah, well, it will be all right, it will be all right.' But Bohr took Einstein's challenges seriously, and by dinner, Bohr would have a solution." The next morning over breakfast, Einstein would present another objection. It was the beginning of a discussion between the two physicists that would continue for the rest of their lives. But Einstein was alone in his subbornness—this sixth conference is famous since most physicists left agreeing that Heisenberg's theory and Bohr's interpretation of quantum mechanics, known as the Copenhagen interpretation, was correct. It is ironic that Einstein spent the first conference convincing the older scientists that his relativity theory was correct, but now, he was the one dragging his feet.

In all, Einstein attended four of the six Solvay Conferences held from 1911 to 1930. To this day, those early conferences are held in reverence by the science community as the place where great minds solved some of the biggest problems in twentieth-century physics.

See **Bohr, Niels; Heisenberg, Werner; Lorentz, Hendrick Antoon; Quantum Mechanics.**

Space-Time

In day-to-day experience, one sees moving through space and time as very separate, distinct things (one cannot, after all, move around time backwards and forwards and sideways, with the ease one moves around in space). Einstein, however, with his two theories of relativity, changed this notion completely, showing that space and time were, in fact, intimately connected. Ultimately, a new combined concept was born: space-time.

After Einstein published the special theory of relativity in 1905, one of his former professors, Hermann Minkowski (1864–1909), expanded on the theory and nailed down its implications for space and time. In the beginning, no one was more surprised than Minkowski that Einstein had produced such interesting theories. Minkowski knew his former student had always skipped lectures and he said that he "really would not have believed him capable of it." But Minkowski didn't hold Einstein's earlier academic misbehavior against him. His mathematical mind took to Einstein's relativity with a flourish. The special theory of relativity insisted that there was no absolute space and time, and that both were dependent on the person who was perceiving them. Moving through space could actually change time, and so Minkowski set out to produce a mathematical framework to help describe this. He created a new concept: the space-time continuum— a four-dimensional continuum where everything is defined by both its position in space and its position in time.

That means that, rather than describe a person by saying he is standing at 77° longitude and 38° latitude and at seven feet above sea level, Minkowski pointed out that one needs to add that he is also at 5:17 in the afternoon. Bringing time into the scenario is crucial for describing events. Imagine that person is standing at that spot when his girlfriend gets angry and throws a book at him. If his space-time coordinates are correct, he's going to get a thwack on the head. But if she throws it at 5:18 and he's moved, then his space-time coordinates will have changed and he will avoid the blow. This may seem fairly simple and obvious, but by defin-

> *Henceforth space itself and time by itself are doomed to fade away into mere shadows, and only a kind of union of the two will preserve an independent reality.*
>
> —Hermann Minkowski, *Space and Time*, 1908

ing objects with space and time coordinates, Minkowski opened up the door for ways to mathematically determine whether one action can ever affect another action—i.e., whether, given the time and speeds of the people involved, that thrown book could ever hit her boyfriend. This becomes all the more important as objects begin to travel closer to the speed of light. Einstein's special theory of relativity showed that space and time change depending on how one is moving through space-time and so it's all the more important to have a mathematical way to interpret these fluctuating entities.

What else Minkowski could have done with his mathematical creation is not known, since he died at the age of fifty-five of a burst appendix in 1909. It is likely apocryphal, but his last words are said to have been, "What a pity I have to die in the age of relativity's development."

Yet Minkowski probably would have been pleased to know that Einstein made much use of the space-time continuum in creating the general theory of relativity. Having the ready-made math at his fingertips helped Einstein create a theory that showed that great masses warped space and time, twisting it in unusual ways. Gravitation, it turns out, is dependent on these space-time gymnastics, and Minkowski's mathematical contribution was crucial.

Spinoza, Baruch (Benedictus)
1632–1677

Baruch Spinoza was a Dutch philosopher whom Einstein claimed as his favorite philosopher of all time. Einstein read and reread Spinoza's work throughout his life and often quoted the philosopher when trying to describe his own understanding of the universe.

Einstein seems to have first encountered Spinoza during his autodidactic days in Bern just after he'd left university. He and his friends in the Olympia Academy read and discussed Spinoza's *Ethics*. Einstein certainly read numerous other philosophers as well (he was given to quoting Kant and Hume, too), but later in life, he always said that Spinoza was his favorite. It's not surprising that Einstein should see a somewhat kindred spirit in Spinoza—they were both educated, well-respected Jews who had distanced themselves from the organized religion of their birth. They both had minds steeped in a scientific rationalism, choosing to perceive the world based on what one could actually sense. And, as a result, both men dismissed the idea of an anthropomorphic god, the existence of a soul, and magical occurrences without obvious causes.

Spinoza's view of God and religion dovetailed quite nicely with Einstein's. In 1929, New York City rabbi Herbert S. Goldstein wrote a telegram to Einstein with the succinct message: "Do you believe in God? Stop. Prepaid reply fifty words." In a mere twenty-nine, Einstein summed up: "I believe in Spinoza's God who reveals himself in the orderly harmony of what exists, not in a God who concerns himself with fates and actions of human beings." This exchange, quoted that year in the *New York Times,* may well have been the first time that Einstein was linked to Spinoza in the public mind. The association stuck and numerous journalists at the time and scholars since have explored just how Einstein's image of God related to that of Spinoza's. Spinoza believed there was no personal God, but that Nature itself was a manifestation of the divine—a concept referred to as pantheism.

Einstein himself was occasionally contradictory on the subject of whether he embraced Spinoza's God. In an interview for the book *Glimpses of the Great* published in 1930 by George Sylvester Viereck, Einstein was asked specifically if he believed in the God of Spinoza. He said, "I can't answer with a simple yes or no. I'm not an atheist and I don't think I can call myself a pantheist . . . I am fascinated by Spinoza's pantheism, but admire even more his contributions to modern thought because he is the first philosopher to deal with the soul and body as one, not two separate things."

> How much do I love that noble man
> More than I could tell with words.
> —Einstein, in *"Zu Spinozas Ethik,"* a
> poem he wrote for Spinoza

Spinoza affected Einstein in another important way, because his writings describe a world that relies emphatically on cause and effect; nothing happens that cannot be explained by a previous chain of events. Einstein believed that Spinoza was the first to take this notion to an extreme that governed not just nature, but all of human activity as well. With this level of determinism, there was simply no room for a soul. Einstein also embraced this extreme kind of causality. Whether he learned it originally from Spinoza per se or from elsewhere, Einstein certainly relied on Spinoza to back up his own thoughts on the subject. Ultimately, Einstein's reliance on causality led him not just to question the existence of a soul and a God who interfered with human events, but also some of the science of his day: quantum mechanics. The modern interpretation of quantum mechanics allows for a universe that is fundamentally random, and this was a fuzziness Einstein abhorred.

Much has been made of Einstein's philosophies and his approach to philosophers. It is certainly clear that he turned to fields outside of physics to create his world view, but it would be a stretch to say that the work of any one philosopher drove his scientific instinct. Einstein once said that "everyone had their own Kant," since everyone interpreted that philosopher's work to their own ends. Indeed, Einstein seemed to have had the same attitude towards Spinoza, knowing that the value he placed on the Dutchman's writings were uniquely personal. Einstein was careful not to read more into Spinoza (or his own understanding of Spinoza) than was prudent. In 1932, the three-hundredth anniversary of Spinoza's birth, Einstein was asked to write an essay on the philosopher but he refused. He was not equipped, he said, to give a thoughtful scholarly analysis.

Stark, Johannes
(1874–1957)

Johannes Stark was a German physicist who won a Nobel Prize in 1919 for discovering that in an electric field, light could be split into spectral lines—a phenomenon now known as the Stark effect. As Einstein began his rise to fame, he corresponded steadily with Stark. In 1913 Stark modified Einstein's photo-equivalence law into what is today called the Stark-Einstein law. After World War I, however, Stark fervently embraced Nazi politics, calling for an all-new "Aryan" science and mounting a scathing campaign to discredit Einstein's "Jewish" relativity theory.

In 1907, Stark, who was then a professor at the Technische Hochschule in Hannover, asked Einstein to write a review article on relativity for *Jahrbuck für Radioaktivität und Elekronik*, (*Yearbook of Radioactivity and Electronics*). During this period of time, and for the next several years, Einstein and Stark carried on a correspondence that was fairly cordial. One ex-

> *People who have been privileged to contribute something to the advancement of science should not let [arguments about priority] becloud their joy over the fruits of common endeavor.*
>
> —Albert Einstein, in a letter to Johannes Stark, February 22, 1908

ception during those years came when Einstein was living in Prague and wrote a paper on photochemical processes that Stark believed drew from one of his own papers. Stark attacked Einstein on the pages of the German journal *Annalen Der Physik* and Einstein responded in the journal, successfully showing that Stark had missed the point.

In 1913, Stark modified a theory on photons that was published by Einstein in 1906. The final version, now called the Stark-Einstein law or the second law of photochemistry, states that each molecule involved in a photochemical reaction absorbs only a single quantum of the radiation or light that causes the reaction. That year, Stark also discovered an effect of light that has been named after him ever since. Scientists already noticed what was called the Zeeman effect, in which magnetic fields split radiation from particles into so-called spectral lines. These lines depend on how fast a given atom or ion is oscillating and can be useful in identifying exactly what particle is doing that oscillating. Stark managed to produce similar spectral lines using an electric field instead of a magnetic one. Ultimately, the Stark effect proved to be more complicated to analyze than the Zeeman effect, and it is less often used today to analyze atomic structure. Nevertheless, this was Nobel-caliber work, for which Stark won the prize in 1919. In his acceptance speech, Stark showed the first inklings of his later politics. The talk begins with the concept that the Germans were carrying on the great legacy of the ancient Greeks in understanding atomic structure. His point, again and again, was how he contributed to German physics as a whole. The seeds of nationalism had clearly taken root.

After the Nobel Prize, Stark's biography takes a dark turn. He is not remembered for science during the second half of his life, but for his politics. Just what turned Stark against his former colleagues and their science is unclear, but in the 1920s Stark fully absorbed and accepted the Nazi rhetoric of the glory of the Aryan race and began a campaign to undermine modern physics, complete with a spiteful campaign against Einstein. In 1922, now a professor at the University of Wurzberg, Stark wrote a book denouncing modern physics called *The Present Crisis in German Physics*. He claimed that subjects like relativity were obviously subversions, and Jewish subversions at that, of pure rational thought.

Although Nazi anti-Semitism may have been taking hold in Germany, Stark was still ostracized by his former academic colleagues. His statements led to his resignation from his professorship and he had to make a living by starting a porcelain factory. By 1924, Stark declared full allegiance to Hitler and continued to attack "Jewish" physics as a science that ignored objective experiments or observations of facts. In the 1930s he worked with Philipp Lenard, another Nobel Prize winner with extreme nationalist tendencies who had turned on Einstein, trying to create "pure" German science, much the way Hitler was trying to create a "pure" German race.

Stark became president of the Imperial Institute of Physics and Technology from 1933 to 1939, where he had an even higher platform for his rhetoric that all science should be dedicated to supporting Nazi philosophies. He claimed that Jews, with their blatant disregard for truth, were unfit for physics. Worse yet, they didn't limit themselves to the proper channels. He wrote: "the dogmatic zeal and propagandistic drive of the Jewish scientist leads him to report on his achievements not only in scientific journals but also in the daily press and on lecture tours." In general, Stark's attacks on modern science were not rationally presented; he simply stated that relativity was so contrary to daily experience and common sense that it must be wrong.

After World War II, a denazification court in Bavaria put Stark on trial. By then, Einstein was long gone from Germany, but other physicists spoke out against Stark: Max von Laue, Werner Heisenberg, and Arnold Sommerfeld all testified. The court labeled Stark a "Major Offender" and sentenced him to four years in a labor camp. Although the sentence was suspended, the last of Johannes Stark's days were not happy ones. He worked alone in a private laboratory in a country home in Upper Bavaria until he died in 1957.

Switzerland

Einstein was born in Germany, but became a Swiss citizen in 1901. He adored his adopted homeland, for it was where he had some of his most fertile scientific successes and where he and Mileva Maric settled as newlyweds for their joyful first few years. While Einstein did eventually obtain German citizenship again when he became a professor in Berlin in 1914, his Swiss passport would prove of infinite value to the Jewish scientist as Germany grew more and more anti-Semitic under Nazi influence.

Einstein first came to Switzerland in 1895 when he took a final year of high school in Aarau, a small town on the bank of the Aar River. In 1896, he was admitted to the Swiss Federal Polytechnical School, later to be known as the Eidgenössische Technische Hochschule, or the ETH. While a student there, Einstein applied to become a Swiss citizen and he was granted Swiss citizenship on February 21, 1901. He maintained and cherished his Swiss citizenship for the rest of his life.

Post-World War I Germany, however, was eager to claim Einstein as its own. The German government wanted to improve its image in the eyes of the world after its devastating losses during the Great War and lured Einstein to Berlin. The government made him a member of the Prussian Academy of Science, thus de facto reinstating him as a German citizen. Although Einstein was probably more loyal to Switzerland when he won the Nobel Prize for physics in 1922, it was the German ambassador who accepted the prize on his behalf. (Einstein himself was on a trek to Japan and the Far East.) Ever diplomatic, the German ambassador did give a nod to Switzerland during his acceptance speech.

There were also some significant benefits to traveling under a Swiss passport. Einstein's status as a neutral alien protected him from conflicts with military authorities in Berlin and also gave him the ability to travel to neutral countries from Berlin. As German citizens, especially Jewish ones, had more and more of their rights to travel curtailed in the 1920s and 1930s, Einstein had a fairly luxurious amount of freedom. And so, despite Einstein's citizenship in Germany and even later, when he renounced Germany and became a U.S. citizen, he never renounced his Swiss citizenship.

There is a postscript to Einstein's Swiss connection. Many Jews and others persecuted by the Nazis tried to safeguard their money by opening Swiss bank accounts. During recent times, Switzerland has been in the spotlight for being lax about returning the original funds to the rightful heirs after World War II. The name "Albert Einstein" is one of the names on a list of 21,000 dormant bank accounts, though there is no concrete proof that it is the physicist's account.

Regardless of such details, Einstein clearly cherished all that Switzerland represented. In 1948, after living in the United States for fifteen years, Einstein wrote, "I love the Swiss because by and large, they are more humane than the other people among whom I have lived."

Thought Experiments

While just about everyone plays "what-if" games in their head to try to solve a conundrum, few use it to such advantage as Einstein did. Einstein took these gedankenexperiments, as he called them, to new heights, creating unique ways to envision a problem that didn't require actually conducting a physical test.

Thought experiments were nothing new to scientists, though few took them to such an art form as Einstein. One of Einstein's heroes, the German Ernst Mach (1838–1916) also relied extensively on such mind games, and it's possible that Einstein emulated him from a fairly early age. In his *Autobiographical Notes*, Einstein describes one of his most fruitful thought experiments, which he first toyed with when he was sixteen. He imagined what it would be like to ride a light beam. Traveling at such incredible speeds— the same speed as the light itself— what would one see? What would the electromagnetic wave look like? Would it appear frozen in movement? What if one was riding this beam of light away from a clock? Looking back, the clock would be frozen, since new light waves showing you a time change could never catch up with you. What did this mean about time itself?

> *I will a little think.*
>
> —What Einstein, when trying to solve a problem, often said before standing up and pacing the room

Ideas like this rattled around in Einstein's head for years and were finally answered in 1905, when in several fitful weeks he lit upon the special theory of relativity. His new theory stated that even if you were traveling close to the speed of light, you would never perceive light to be frozen. Instead, it would seem to be moving away from you at 186,000 miles per second as it always did. The theory also said that if time appeared to be frozen behind you, then from your perspective that reference frame was frozen, stuck forever at that point.

Einstein's general theory of relativity also got a germ of a start from a thought experiment—one that Einstein referred to as "the happiest thought of his life." After the publication of the special theory of relativity, which described how light moved so well, Einstein wanted to apply the concept to gravitation. The problem was that gravity caused acceleration and so it seemed markedly different than light which traveled at a single speed. Much like the previous one, this vague problem stayed on the edges of Einstein's mind for years. One day he imagined what it would feel like to be in a free fall. Much like riding the light beam, he envisioned riding the force of gravity and realized that when in free fall, one wouldn't actually feel gravity. For example, if Alice closes her eyes while going down a long rabbit hole and isn't able to see the various tea party accouterments in the shelves as she falls past, and if somehow she couldn't feel the wind blowing past her, she will not notice that she is in fact, falling. She isn't just moving at a steady speed, mind you; Alice is getting steadily faster, accelerating due to gravity. Regardless, she would feel as if she were simply suspended in space. If Alice's movement felt just the same to her as if she were standing still, then Einstein suddenly had the starting point for how to relate her accelerating reference frame to the one of someone at rest watching her. If the two reference frames felt identical, Einstein could create equations assuming they *were* identical. The general theory of relativity was born soon after.

After the general theory of relativity, Einstein devoted attention to atomic physics and put his thought experiments to use once again. He is remembered to this day for his lively disputes with Niels Bohr regarding how to interpret the new quantum mechanics, and invariably Einstein used thought experiments to support his view. From light beams traveling through slits to boxes dangling on a scale, Einstein employed as many scenarios as he could in an attempt to convince Bohr and his colleagues. One of Einstein's last great papers is a thought experiment known as the EPR paradox, in which he envisions two particles that are taken miles away from each other and yet somehow are able to communicate faster than the speed of light. This, like so many of his quantum thought experiments, was answered by Bohr in a way that didn't necessarily satisfy Einstein, but did satisfy the rest of the community. Many of Einstein's thought experiments about quantum physics eventually helped cement the new dynamics into the minds of its proponents—the exact opposite of what Einstein intended.

Science historian Gerald Holton, who has studied Einstein exhaustively and has attempted to describe just what made his brain so creative and fruitful, believes that these thought experiments are one part of the answer. Einstein had the ability to visualize solutions to hypotheses so vividly that he could solve complex problems in his head. Thought experiments may well have been the key to his genius.

See **Bohr, Niels; Quantum Mechanics; Relativity, General Theory of; Relativity, Special Theory of; Solvay Conferences.**

Time Travel

*In 1895, ten years before Einstein published the special theory of rel-
ativity, H. G. Wells published his famous book The Time Machine. With
one manuscript, Wells embedded the concept of time travel into society's consciousness; it became fashionable cocktail party conversation.
And so, many people naturally believed that Einstein's relativity equations, with their groundbreaking implications for space and time, might
be applied to the idea of time travel.*

Into the Future

If one is comfortable with the basics of special relativity, it's simple to
understand how it allows for time travel into the future. Imagine sending a friend off to circle the Earth for a month in the space shuttle, but
traveling much faster than the current shuttle can go—somewhere
close to the speed of light. According to Einstein, that speeding friend
is experiencing time at a much slower rate than you are. Thanks to the
special theory of relativity, time slows down the faster you move. So
you live your life merrily along at the same pace you always do, while
your friend's clock, heartbeat, and perception of time slows down substantially. When a month has elapsed and your friend comes back
home, he or she has aged, say, half the time that you have because it
took only two weeks to "travel" a month into the future.

Traveling to the Past

Now while your friend may use this technique to travel into the future,
he or she would be stuck there. At least that would have been the case if
Einstein had stopped after producing the special theory of relativity. The
general theory of relativity, which incorporates a more complex vision of
space and time, also allows for someone, in theory, to travel into the past.

A handful of people over the course of the twentieth century have
explored this possibility. One of the earliest "time machines" was theorized by W. J. van Stockum in 1937. Van Stockum described an
incredibly dense, infinitely long, rotating cylinder. If you were to
travel around that cylinder, you would naturally be pulled into the
past because the intense gravity would slow time down. In essence, by
the time you got around the cylinder, the past would have been mov-

ing so slowly that it wouldn't have gotten very far and you could basically catch up with yourself. Of course, there aren't a lot of infinitely long cylinders lying around the universe, so this is not a time machine one is likely to just stumble upon.

In 1948, Kurt Godel (1906–1978) at the Institute for Advanced Study in Princeton suggested that if the universe rotated and didn't expand, a person who traveled in one direction would eventually reach his or her own past. This is an interesting solution to Einstein's field equations, of course, but not one that is particularly relevant since the universe does expand and does not spin. Nonetheless, Godel's solution showed that there is nothing inherent in relativity to forbid time travel. When Einstein heard about Godel's solution to the field equations, Einstein said he found it troubling that his theory allowed for such shuffles through time.

In the 1960s and 1970s, almost all theories for a time machine revolved around objects that, well, revolved. Massive objects spinning quickly were believed to be the one way to travel into the past. Frank Tipler produced the best known of these in 1974. He ran with Stockum's cylinder idea of thiry years earlier, determining that the cylinder might not have to be infinitely long, but did have to be incredibly strong and dense.

Despite these ideas, few scientists paid much attention to time travel. However, the idea blossomed in the minds of science fiction writers. Television shows like *Dr. Who* and *Star Trek*, books like *Planet of the Apes* by Pierre Boulle, *Slaughterhouse Five* by Kurt Vonnegut, and *Time and Again* by Jack Finney, as well as hundreds of other books, movies, and TV shows incorporated the idea of time travel, entrenching it in the modern mind as both a familiar concept while still one thought to be fantastic and out of this world.

Nonetheless, it was science fiction that helped push time travel toward legitimate science. Astronomer and author Carl Sagan wrote a now-famous book called *Contact* in 1985. In 1997 it was made into a movie starring Jodie Foster. While writing the novel, Sagan used his knowledge of gravitational theory to devise a black hole through which his heroine could travel to the other side of the universe. He was using this as a literary device which he knew to be fantastical, but Sagan nevertheless wished his science to be as accurate as possible. So he had his colleague Kip Thorne (1940–), a cosmologist at Caltech, look over what he'd written. Thorne knew that no one could possibly survive a trip through a black hole, but he realized to his surprise, that perhaps Einstein's equations did allow for space travel via a "wormhole."

Wormholes, if they exist, are space-time tunnels that open into two widely different places in space. They were conjectured within months of Einstein's 1916 publishing of the general theory of relativity. In 1935, Einstein and Nathan Rosen (1909–1995) developed a more complete model of these tunnels, which are now referred to as Einstein-Rosen bridges. Such things were not expected to exist for more than fleeting moments in time—flashing into existence for a second and then disappearing as quickly. But Thorpe theorized that an infinitely advanced society might have some way of holding such a wormhole open, and if so, it would be a reasonable shortcut through space and time. It is a portal to vastly different spaces by definition, but turning it into a way to travel through time as well is a little more complicated. Thorpe envisioned that an advanced society could drag one end of the wormhole into the future by moving it at incredibly fast speeds. Then a traveler could go through it in either direction, effectively moving through time.

In the late 1980s, Thorpe researched the idea more thoroughly and published his theories. Soon, other scientists realized time travel research was not quite as ludicrous as they thought. This is not to say that it has completely hit the mainstream. Just because time travel is not forbidden by relativity does not mean it is required. Einstein's laws of relativity led to the conclusion that black holes *must* exist. But those same laws only mean that it's *possible* for wormholes to exist, and no one's gotten anywhere close to finding an actual wormhole anywhere in the universe.

Even if you could find a real-life wormhole, hold it open, and move one end into the future, there is still one small hitch. You could only travel back as far as the time you found the wormhole. For example, if you found a wormhole on Tuesday, you couldn't use it go to Monday. But if you waited until Friday, you could pop through the wormhole and go back to Tuesday. So if this kind of time machine were ever built, one could still never go back to a time period before mankind was technologically advanced enough to build time machines. (This might explain why we never encounter time travelers from the future.)

Perhaps a technologically advanced society could create and manipulate a wormhole. Perhaps not. Regardless, there are still quite a number of scientists who believe the concept of time travel is far too rife with problems and paradoxes to be physically allowed. For example, what if you go back in time and accidentally kill your grandfather before he has children. How, then, would you ever be born? These scientists believe someone will eventually interpret our understanding of physics or discover new physics to prove that time travel is impossible.

See **Wormholes.**

Twin Paradox

The twin paradox is one of the classic thought experiments illustrating the oddities created by special relativity. The basic idea is this: twins decide to part ways for awhile. One remains on Earth while the other boards a rocket ship that travels at incredibly fast speeds away from Earth. Upon his return, he finds himself younger than the twin who stayed home.

In accordance with the laws of relativity, the traveling twin moves so quickly, he experiences a shorter time span than the one who stays on Earth. This explains why he's younger. But, this is not the paradox; this is a verifiable fact, as shown by similar experiments using extremely precise atomic clocks. The paradox is to figure out why the traveler is the one who ages more slowly; after all, relativity states that all reference frames are equivalent. So, the traveler could claim that he had stayed still while Earth and his twin sped away.

Einstein himself introduced the concept at the heart of the twin paradox in his 1905 paper that first described the special theory of relativity. He noted that if two working clocks set to the same time were separated (one kept still, the other moving at some velocity), the moving clock's time would lag behind the time shown by the clock that stayed at rest. (Of course, he cited some specific math to support this: the moving clock will lag two times the time the clock was moving, times the squared quantity of the velocity the clock was moving, divided by the speed of light, or $2\ t(v/c)^2$.)

The idea that time moves more slowly for a person in motion is difficult for the average human being to grasp, since he or she never experiences such things during daily life. This is because the effect isn't noticeable unless someone travels close to the speed of light. Nonetheless, experiments in which scientists sent atomic clocks flying around the Earth at fast speeds show that Einstein's prediction is correct. Atomic clocks are amazingly precise, and yet two clocks that began in synch are out of synch when the traveling clock comes back.

It is important to note here that atomic clocks are not based on any kind of mechanical watch works; rather, an atomic clock measures time through the inherently constant motions of atoms. If an atomic clock shows a time loss, it is because the atoms themselves were moving more slowly. Therefore, Einstein did not describe an artificial human construct of what "time" is, but, even more startling, he described the slowing down of the very pace of nature itself.

Both theory and experiment, therefore, suggest that if we substituted two twins for our clocks, a moving twin would age more slowly. For example, if we began with two seven-year-olds and sent one off on a journey to Proxima Centauri (some 4.3 light years away) at 75 percent the speed of light, the space traveler would come back nearly thirteen years old, while the child who stayed at home would now be nearly sixteen.

But again, why on Earth should it be the traveling twin who aged? The main premise of the special theory of relativity is that no frame of reference is any better than any other. From the space traveler's perspective, she could insist that she had stayed still the whole time while the Earth sped away from her for nine years. She has every right to expect her twin brother waiting at home to have aged more slowly. This, then, is the crux of the paradox.

If one can do the math, however, the answer is clear. It lies partly in general relativity, which describes the forces of gravity, an area that special relativity doesn't tackle. But the simple reason is that the two reference frames are *not* identical because the traveling twin turns around and comes back. The experience of decelerating and accelerating is simply not one that the twin on Earth feels. The forces felt by the traveling twin make her experience unique and ensure that she is the one who has aged more slowly. If, on the other hand, she traveled forever and ever in one direction, the paradox remains and we would never be able to say for sure that one twin had aged more slowly than the other.

See **Relativity, Special Theory of; Thought Experiments.**

Uncertainty Principle

The uncertainty relations, also known as the Uncertainty Principle, are one of the fundamental tenets of quantum mechanics—fitting in well in a field that abounds with counterintuitive truths. The principle, devel-

oped by Werner Heisenberg in 1927, claims that there are certain attributes of a particle that can't be measured. Specifically, if something like position is known with a great deal of accuracy, then its momentum (for all practical purposes, its speed) is not well-defined. This doesn't mean that it's just difficult to measure both a particle's position and its speed, but that a given particle quite simply cannot have a precise speed while having a precise position, and vice versa.

Einstein, who was always frustrated with what he considered the fairly fanciful ideas within quantum mechanics, completely rejected the uncertainty relations. He believed theories like this showed that quantum physics was incomplete. Quantum mechanics, thought Einstein, was an infant science still in need of some overarching theory that would eventually eradicate oddities like the Uncertainty Principle.

One of Einstein's favorite forms of mental gymnastics was to develop "thought experiments" that helped to crystallize one's thinking. To refute Heisenberg's Uncertainty Principle, Einstein developed a thought experiment that began with a box full of light. The box sat on a scale so it could be weighed perfectly. This scale was so sensitive that it measured not just the box but the weight of the light inside. Because photons are energetic, they have mass according to Einstein's equation $E = mc^2$ which states that energy and mass are essentially the same thing. So, by measuring the mass of the box and its contents, one can, in essence, measure the energy of the light inside.

Taking the thought experiment one step further, Einstein then imagined hooking up a very precise clock to the box. At precisely noon, the box will let a single photon escape. At that moment, the weight, measured by the scale, changes by exactly the mass of one photon. Looking at the weight change of the box, an observer now knows, very precisely, the mass of that one missing photon. But measuring mass, as we've already seen, is the same thing as measuring energy. Aha, announced Einstein, I have just developed an experiment in which we simultaneously, precisely, measured both time and the energy of a photon—just what the uncertainty relations claim I couldn't do.

Einstein presented his light box experiment to Niels Bohr (1885–1962), a physicist who firmly embraced all the peculiarities of quantum mechanics. Bohr managed to refute Einstein's argument using Einstein's own theory of relativity. Bohr pointed out that when that lone photon escaped, the box of light would naturally recoil, and thus, the box would move in space. Relativity theory states that movement inherently affects time, and so that moving box would experience time in a slightly different way than the stationary reference frame of the observer. That is to say that by removing one photon of light, and consequently moving the box, the time in the box's reference frame was not exactly noon. And so, measuring the time at which that photon escaped wasn't so precise after all.

Almost all physicists today accept the Uncertainty Principle and quantum mechanics, quirks and all. The uncertainty relations fly in the face of common experience, but nevertheless, they hold up in experiment after experiment. Einstein, however, despite Bohr's counterargument, which Einstein had to agree was logically sound, never accepted that the uncertainty relations were an accurate description of reality.

See **Heisenberg, Werner; Quantum Mechanics.**

Unified Theory

Einstein spent the last thirty years of his life seeking one theory that would explain all of physics—something he called a unified theory. Einstein had been at the forefront of two major revolutions in modern physics—relativity and quantum mechanics—but he didn't believe these were the final word. He was convinced that one day scientists would find an overarching theory that would include all previous physics and offer the ultimate explanation for how the world worked.

Einstein's initial motivation to find a unified field theory was simply to devise a theory that would explain both gravity and electromagnetism, the two known forces at the time. His goal changed slightly, however, in reaction to the discovery of quantum mechanics. The rest of the scientific community felt they had solved all questions about electromagnetism with the advent of quantum theory, but Einstein believed it was nothing more than a useful tool. Quantum physics, he thought, was useful to predict what might happen with electrons and photons, but it didn't accurately describe the physical reality of how particles behaved. Einstein was searching for a new theory that incorporated all the successes of quantum mechanics but offered a deeper—and, in his mind, correct—explanation for how particles interacted.

In 1929 Einstein produced his first major stir on unification, publishing a six-page manuscript that summarized over a decade of thought on the subject. Newspaper reporters camped outside his house in Princeton trying to get information about the newest "breakthrough" from the famed genius. Einstein tried to ignore them, but after a week, he finally gave in to requests for interviews. He was quoted as saying "The purpose of my new work is to . . . reduce to one formula the explanation of the field of gravity and of the field of electromagnetism. . . . Now, but only now, we know that the force which moves electrons in their ellipses about the nuclei of atoms is the same force which moves our Earth in its annual course about the sun, and is the same force which brings to us the rays of light and heat which makes life possible upon this planet."

But Einstein's belief that he had come up with a single explanation for such diverse effects as light rays and the gravity of planetary orbits was optimistic. His colleagues all agreed that his new equations failed to incorporate his own relativity, and they all rejected his new unified theory. Einstein seemed fairly unconcerned and went off to tackle the problem again. He published various papers on it throughout the years, focusing on unification almost exclusively the last decade of his life.

But the path to unification was not easy. For one thing, in the early twentieth century, as physicists began to understand the inner workings of the atom more and more, they discovered new forces. Now there was the weak force that held neutrons and protons together and the strong force that held quarks together. A unified theory would have to unite these forces, too.

Second, very few other scientists held Einstein's zeal. One of the few who also actively searched for a unified theory was Erwin Schroedinger (1887–1961), another founder of quantum mechanics. For a time in the 1940s, Einstein and Schroedinger corresponded about their respective work and Einstein praised his friend, saying that he was the only one he could talk to about this important topic since the rest of the world had blinders on about quantum mechanics, accepting it unquestioningly.

Besides Schroedinger, however, the community's support was lukewarm at best. While Einstein had far too much prestige for his ideas to be dismissed out of hand, he was intrigued by a subject that simply failed to capture his colleagues' imagination. Wolfgang Pauli, twenty years Einstein's junior and also a professor at Princeton, was particularly outspoken. Pauli publicly mocked the fact that Einstein seemed to have a new theory every year, and Einstein once wrote to

Schroedinger about a new tack he had taken: "Pauli stuck out his tongue at me when I told him about it."

Indeed, even Einstein was aware that he was riding a bit of a roller coaster. On several occasions he announced to his friends that he believed he was on the right track to a unified field theory at last, only to follow up several months later with an admission that everything he had been working on was wrong. In 1952, Einstein was seventy-three years old and beginning to accept that he was not having any success. He said to his colleague George Wald, "someone else is going to have to do it." But the nagging hope that a unified theory was just around the corner dogged him until his end. In 1955, on his death bed in Princeton, Einstein called for his notes and continued to work on the task he had started over thirty years earlier. In all, during Einstein's last ten years, he published eight papers on unified field theory.

Unfortunately, Einstein did not live to see others caught up in the excitement about a unified field theory. In the 1960s, Sheldon Glashow (1932–), Abdus Salam (1926–1996), and Steven Weinberg (1933–) finally connected the weak force to the electromagnetic force, and now it is referred to as the electroweak force. Today, there are numerous physicists trying to find the place where the electroweak force intersects the strong force and everyone in the community would like to see gravity connected up as well. Modern string theory, first developed in the 1970s and 1980s, does incorporate all four forces, but has the disadvantage of neither having been tested experimentally nor of anyone knowing how to test it experimentally with current technology.

While Einstein was spurred on to develop the unified theory because of his difficulties with quantum mechanics, most scientists today accept quantum mechanics in a way that Einstein never did. However, they also agree that there should be some additional theory that connects all the forces together. But, as Einstein discovered, it is not an easy search. An accepted unified field theory has yet to be found.

See **Kaluza-Klein Theory; Schroedinger, Erwin.**

United States

Einstein moved to the United States in 1933 and ultimately settled in New Jersey where he lived for the last twenty-two years of his life. He enjoyed his life in the United States, happy to be in a country with freedoms that his native Germany denied, but never one to keep silent, he was as outspoken when he perceived injustice in America as he was about anything else.

Einstein's first visit to the United States was not as a scientist, but as a spokesman. In 1921, Einstein traveled with Chaim Weizmann on a whirlwind tour of the United States, raising money for the World Zionist Organization. Einstein was given a hero's welcome, including a motorcade in New York City, lectures at the National Academy of Science in Washington, D.C., and (as Einstein described it) "one happy half hour" with scientists at Cleveland's Case Institute of Technology.

Einstein returned to America in 1931 to work for two months at the California Institute of Technology. He was greatly interested in the discoveries being made at Caltech's Mount Wilson observatory which seemed to support many of his theories. Like the previous trip, Einstein's visit made headlines not only because of his science, but because of his support of political causes. At Einstein's stopovers in New York City before and after his California post, he spoke out against the current Nazi regime in Germany and for pacifist causes overall, causing great consternation back in Berlin.

Einstein also provided support for America's increasingly powerful scientific presence. During his early visits to California in the late 1920s, he discussed relativity with Caltech cosmologists and spoke often with scientists. One of many noteworthy meetings was with Albert Abraham Michelson (1852–1931) of the Michelson-Morley experiment, which finally disproved the existence of ether.

Einstein made several more trips to the United States. His affinity for the United States and the discoveries being made by its scientists, as well as the increasingly fascist polices in Germany, led him to decide to leave Europe. He recorded his freedom from Germany in his travel diary on December 2, 1931 while aboard a boat on his way to the United States for another stint at Caltech. Looking up at the seagulls flying overhead as the ship pulled away from the European coastline, he wrote, "Today I resolved in essence to give up my Berlin position. Hence a migrating bird for the rest of my life!"

Up to and during World War II, there was a near exodus of European scientists fleeing the repressive politics and, ultimately, war that raged across the continent. Einstein, as the most famous scientist in the world, was clearly a catch for any country. Many of his fellow Zionists strongly believed that Einstein should settle in Palestine and teach at the Hebrew University; after all, it was Einstein's support that helped to create the university in the first place. But apparently, Einstein was more at home in the United States and, quite frankly, Princeton made the best offer.

However, some people did not want Einstein to come to America. As Einstein prepared for the third of his visits to Caltech, a group of American women patriots protested Einstein's request for a U.S. visa, claiming he was a communist, but their evidence was not enough to keep such a well-renowned scientist out of the country.

Einstein himself seemed to waffle at the finality of leaving Europe. Despite his confession to his travel diary that he wanted to move, he publicly only announced his departure from Berlin in stages. When he arrived in New York harbor in December of 1932, unlike every other arrival, his whereabouts were kept secret. Often when Einstein traveled, his arrival in a city would be a celebrated occasion with an overwhelming number of banquets and speeches. But the trip to Princeton was a cloak-and-dagger affair. As the ship, the *Westerland*, arrived, the Einstein troupe—Einstein, his wife Elsa, secretary Helen Dukas, and Walther Mayer—were off-loaded in New York harbor onto a boat, quickly processed through immigration, and sped off to New Jersey. The Institute's director, Flexner, who wanted a great deal of control over his new prize, had organized the secret arrival. It was unexpected. In fact, the mayor of New York City was waiting at the Twenty-third Street pier ready to herald the coming of the world-famous scientist with a parade. The bait-and-switch could have been thanks to anti-Communist concerns, the rise of Nazi Germany, or Flexner's controlling behavior; it's likely the secrecy was a combination of all of those factors and more.

The only justifiable purpose of political institutions is to assure the unhindered development of the individual. . . . That is why I consider myself particularly fortunate to be an American.

—Einstein, in a "Message for Germany" given on December 7, 1941

Einstein's decision to stay in the United States, however, was not made official until the winter of 1933. He was giving a lecture in California on January 30—the day Adolf Hitler came to power in Germany. He went back to Europe for a brief visit, which was to be his last. After getting his affairs in order, Einstein made his way back to the United States.

In 1935, Einstein made his U.S. citizenship official. As he had arrived on a visitor's visa, he had to apply for immigration at a consulate abroad. And so the entire Einstein household, Einstein, wife Elsa, stepdaughter Margot, and secretary Helen Dukas, made a sea trip to Bermuda in May. The brief trip was the last time Einstein left the United States. He would take his oath as an American citizen in Trenton, New Jersey on October 30, 1940.

Still Outspoken

Coming to the United States didn't stop Einstein from speaking out or becoming involved in national politics. One of his earliest moves was in 1939 when he wrote a celebrated letter to President Roosevelt, encouraging him to begin work on an atomic bomb. While Einstein did not help work on the Manhattan Project per se (since he was not granted the security clearance necessary due to a letter in his FBI file suggesting he was a Soviet sympathizer), he did quite happily and openly assist the American war effort. This fact was made all the more dramatic by Einstein's history as a pacifist who railed against the use of any militaristic force.

Einstein served as a consultant to the U.S. Navy for three years on a contract that began May 31, 1943 and ended on June 30, 1946. He had come to believe that a militaristic stance was the only way to keep the Nazi regime in Germany in check. Einstein was a brilliant theoretician, but he never lost his joy in creating new and different gadgets and inventions—a service the U.S. military effort could use. Almost weekly, fellow scientist George Gamow would arrive at Einstein's office with a briefcase full of confidential documents. Einstein clearly loved his work with the Navy and joked that he had a Navy paycheck, but wasn't required to get a Navy haircut. For $25 a day, he worked on theories of explosion and tried to determine why certain detonations would clearly go in one direction or another.

But Einstein's military experience never stopped him from championing what he saw as important political causes. He openly encouraged his fellow Americans to pressure the U.S. government to join the United Nations and stated that the only way to world peace was to have some overarching international government. Add in his vocal attacks on racism in the United States and one can see how, in a time of patriotism that appeared during the Cold War, Einstein's behavior could inflame the sentiments of those around him.

Einstein also spoke out against the powerful senator Joseph McCarthy during his anti-Communist crusades in the 1950s. Einstein was among the many who were famous enough to avoid a direct attack, but he nevertheless loudly advised others to stand up to the senator's Internal Security subcommittee.

As Einstein got older, he seemed to waver between optimism and pessimism about the fate of the world and was quick to interpret any government heavy-handedness as being too close to the fascism he hoped would die with Nazi-ruled Germany. He even gave voice to occasional extreme statements that the United States was now ruled by fascists or that he regretted having moved to the country. Most of his comments, however, were not so dramatic, though he was obviously still vocal about the United States avoiding war at almost all costs. As a person who had been given sanctuary in America, this could incite others against him. An editorial in the *Brooklyn Tablet* in 1938 said: "Professor Einstein at a time of personal peril was given sanctuary in this land. Now he is engaged in telling our government how to run its business. . . . Someone might say: 'Wouldn't you think as long as this country took Einstein in out of the storm he would at least wait a few years before dictating to the government?'" A lifelong editorializer himself, however, Einstein clearly believed in trying to improve even those things he valued.

And we know for sure that Einstein did value the United States. In a broadcast entitled "I am an American" on June 22, 1940, the day he was sworn in as a citizen, Einstein said: "I do feel that, in America, the development of the individual and his creative powers is possible, and that, to me, is the most valuable asset in life. In some countries men have neither political rights nor the opportunity for free intellectual development. But for most Americans such a situation would be intolerable. . . . I believe that America will prove that democracy is not merely a form of government based on a sound Constitution but is, in fact, a way of life tied to a great tradition, the tradition of moral strength."

Violin

In a life punctuated by strained personal relations and intense scientific thought on the highest reaches of physics, one of Einstein's greatest escapes was music. He played the violin all his life, he loved it as much as he loved anything and called it his "inner necessity." It was his constant companion.

Einstein began violin lessons at the age of six. At first, the lessons were forced upon him by his mother as part of her drive to create a perfect son. But Einstein soon fell in love with the instrument. As a young man, he would refer to his violin as his child, joking once that when he left it unplayed that "it probably thinks it has got a stepfather." Later, he called the instrument "my old friend, through whom I say and

> *Einstein's playing is excellent, but he does not deserve his world fame; there are many others just as good.*
>
> —A Berlin music critic in the 1920s

I sing to myself all that which I often do not admit to myself at all, but which at best makes me laugh when I see it in others." As he aged, the violin became part of the famous physicist's public persona, along with his messy hair and sloppy dressing. Cartoonists regularly portrayed Einstein clutching his violin, sheet music sprouting out of a pocket.

As much as he loved to play, no one would have called Einstein a brilliant musician; his playing was fairly average. Nonetheless, he relied on his violin to do the speaking for him at various events, performing as a representative of the League of Nations and at peace vigils. Until the end of his days, he gathered scientists and musicians alike to his home in Princeton to sit and play Mozart, Bach, and Schubert—his favorite composers. When he died, he left the violin to his grandson, Bernard Caesar Einstein.

Wave-Particle Duality

Over the millennia, scientists and philosophers alike have hypothesized about the nature of light, often alternating between believing that light is made up of individual particles or that it is a wave of some continuous substance. Modern physicists now believe it is both—or, more specifically, it can be either, depending on the way one examines it. The acceptance of this wave-particle duality of light follows directly from quantum mechanics, and its first inklings can be seen in some of Einstein's earliest writings and lectures.

While the question of what light was made of—waves or "corpuscles" as Newton called them—had been long in contention, scientists of the 1800s thoroughly convinced themselves that light was made up of waves, like waves in water. They based this idea on the fact that when two light beams interfered, they created patterns that one associates with waves like the precise alternating up-and-down ripples of two water waves combining. But there were one or two places where the wave theory of light didn't match up with reality. In a variety of famous experiments, scientists found that there didn't seem to be an ether through which light traveled and that the energy in light didn't transfer to electrons in the way one would expect. In 1905, Einstein stepped out on a limb and published a paper suggesting that if light came in discrete packets of energy (essentially particles, though he didn't yet call them that) all these remaining problems would be solved. This idea was fairly revolutionary at the time, flying in the face of all accepted science. It would be several decades before the theory was fully accepted.

Indeed, even Einstein took awhile to completely accept that his "packets" were particles just like atoms and electrons. During the same year in which he hypothesized particles of light, now known as photons, he published his theory of special relativity, and in that paper he continued to think of light as a wave. From the beginning, Einstein was comfortable thinking of light in the context of both theories.

In 1909, he gave a talk in which he said that light would ultimately be found to be both a wave and a particle. He was some fifteen years ahead of everyone else to make this prediction. In 1924, Einstein wrote: "There are therefore now two theories of light, both indispensable, and—as one must admit today in spite of twenty years of tremendous effort on the part of theoretical physicists—without any logical connections."

By the 1920s, all the famous physicists of the day seemed to agree that light truly behaved as both a particle and a wave. The particle theory seemed to accurately describe the basics of light, like reflection and refraction, and it took care of embarrassing issues like the missing ether. Wave theory, on the other hand, was the only way to explain that two beams of light quite clearly interfered in a wave-like way when they crossed paths. The various physicists of the time had varying hypotheses. Erwin Schroedinger thought that perhaps particles themselves were tiny "wave packets." Max Born believed that particles existed but that they moved in a wave-like pattern. Just what was going on was so unclear that one scientist once jokingly suggested that everyone should agree to use the particle theory on Monday, Wednesday, and Friday and use wave theory on the other days.

Ultimately, Niels Bohr (1885–1962) suggested that light and electrons quite simply should be analyzed as waves when it was useful for the experiment at hand and as beams of particles when that was better. It was an idea made possible by Bohr's acceptance of many such counterintuitive ideas of the new quantum mechanics, a science that based all its definitions and theories on what one could measure. Bohr made the definitive announcement that there was no need to figure out whether wave or particle was the correct description; just use the version that worked for you. The concept that both the wave theory and the particle theory were equally valid was named the "complementarity principle."

By the time Bohr made this declaration, Einstein had begun to have issues with the direction quantum mechanics had taken. While he believed that light could indeed be both wave and particle, he thought that the founders of quantum mechanics were too quick to embrace such vagaries. After Einstein's death, physicist Richard Feynman developed a theory in the 1950s known as quantum electrodynamics, which serves to explain why light is both a wave and a particle in a way that might well have satisfied Einstein more thoroughly than Bohr's simple pronouncement.

See **Photoelectric Effect; Quantum Mechanics.**

Women, Einstein and

Einstein clearly enjoyed the company of women—being flirtatious at best and unfaithful at worst—yet he also saw them as frustrations and obstacles. He described both of his marriages as "failures." Much later in his life, a student observed that Einstein obsessively cleaned and filled his pipe, and asked him if he enjoyed that more than smoking. Einstein replied that pipes were like women: much suffering was needed for a little bit of pleasure.

Without a doubt, Einstein had somewhat odd relationships with women. He seems to have put them into three categories: those who were younger to whom he was attracted, those who acted as a mother figure, and those whom he valued as scientific colleagues and thus didn't think of as women.

One manner in which Einstein was always comfortable interacting with women was when they treated him like a wayward child. It's a behavior that might be traced to his mother. While Einstein's father was congenial, he failed time and again in business. Consequently, Einstein's mother, who came from a wealthy family, seemed determined that her son would not follow in his father's footsteps. Pauline Einstein was constantly trying to "form" her son, hiring private tutors even before Einstein started grade school and forcing him to take violin lessons. So while Einstein claimed to resent overbearing female attention, he also seems to have sought it out. He met his first wife, Mileva, when he was eighteen and she twenty-two, and in the beginning, he played the role of a little boy in the relationship. In his letters, he refers to Mileva's scolding with anticipation and glee. But in the end, he found the maternal feelings to be suffocating and just as he had previously escaped his mother's control by taking his wife, he escaped his wife by taking up an affair with the woman who would become his second wife, Elsa Lowenthal Einstein.

Elsa, who was also a few years older than Einstein, remained his partner for the rest of her life. But the union was by no means blissful, due in part to that second category of women with whom Einstein interacted: the young and attractive. Just before he married Elsa, Einstein announced his attraction to her older daughter, Ilse, and he starkly suggested that perhaps he could marry the mother or the daughter—whoever wanted him. Not surprisingly, the suggestion was upsetting to Ilse and she decided to "step aside." While there's no record of Elsa's feelings about the incident, there are a few personal accounts of Einstein's life that mention "agreements" and sometimes "arguments" between Einstein and Elsa over his extramarital relationships.

Einstein was by no means a suave ladies' man, but he was world famous and he used it to his advantage. He seems to have encouraged attention from women who wrote him fawning letters, even inviting them over to his house only to subject them to boring lectures on physics—a joke that Elsa was in on. However, many of his relationships were not so chaste. There were many extramarital affairs; some noteworthy ones include some of his secretaries at the Kaiser Wilhelm Institute for Physics and various famous actresses. Although his wife clearly knew about some of these "indiscretions" and did not interfere, she would become highly upset if she believed the goings-on reflected badly on her or her husband's reputation. Interestingly, the fights between Einstein and Elsa seemed to be more about keeping up appearances than personal betrayal.

As for the last category of women, those whose intellect Einstein appreciated, they described him as respectful and considerate. For example, Einstein had a reserved, lifelong friendship with fellow physicist Marie Curie. Of course, Einstein stated he didn't think Curie was physically attractive. For Einstein, it was easy to respect a woman for her mind if she was neither a giggling starstruck admirer, nor an overbearing mother figure.

After Elsa's death, Einstein lived on in the house at 112 Mercer Street in Princeton and never remarried. However, mothering women continued to surround him: he lived with his younger stepdaughter Margot, his sister, Maja, and his secretary, Helen Dukas. He also continued to have affairs. According to letters that were put up for auction at Sotheby's in 1998, he maintained at least one relationship for several years while in his 60s in Princeton.

Wormholes

A wormhole is essentially a shortcut between two remote parts of space and, possibly, time. Previously known as an Einstein-Rosen bridge, wormholes were long thought of as nothing more than a mathematical curiosity; a possible outcome of general relativity, but one so inaccessible to us in practice that it was largely irrelevant. However, work in the last few decades shows that these wormholes might not be so abstract after all and, with very advanced technology, could potentially be used as bridges to travel through space and time.

Quite soon after the general theory of relativity was formed, there were those who realized distortions in space might lead to shortcut tunnels that could join otherwise vastly remote areas—something like a tunnel that creates a shortcut from Washington, D.C., to Sidney, Australia, by going right through the earth. In 1916, the same year Einstein published the theory of relativity, two separate physicists, Ludwig Flamm (1885–1964) and Karl Schwarzschild (1873–1916), independently found that tunnels in space were valid solutions to Einstein's relativity equations, which were tools to describe the shape of space. The equations show that gravity distorted the very nature of space, and in areas of immense gravity, a distortion, or tunnel, could appear. Schwarzschild had already postulated the existence of what would eventually become known as black holes—dead stars so dense and with such strong gravity that anything that came too close would be sucked in forever. The intense gravity associated with these black holes, postulated Schwarzschild, could well lead to huge spatial distortions.

In the 1930s, Einstein himself expanded on the idea of twisting space to create some sort of tunnel. In collaboration with his colleague Nathan Rosen (1909–1995), Einstein devised additional solutions to the relativity equations that show that a black hole's gravity might actually make a rip in space and, if joined to another black hole from another rip in an entirely different part of the universe, a short passageway connecting them would be created. This came to be known as an Einstein-Rosen bridge . . . and it was promptly forgotten.

After all, just because it was mathematically possible did not imply that such a thing actually existed. For one thing, Einstein still rejected the idea of black holes—back then referred to as Schwarzschild singularities—and so he believed that any such huge distortion of space would be next to impossible. But even those who could accept the possibility of a black hole knew that a bridge between two of them would be unfit for travelers. No object entering a black hole could go through it unchanged; humans and the strongest space ships alike would surely be stretched and ripped apart to their deaths. In addition, little things like the fact that the Einstein-Rosen bridge would be extremely unstable and could easily collapse or that time passes so slowly in such strong gravity that it would take an infinite time to pass through, made the Einstein-Rosen bridge a useless shortcut.

Several things, however, have led to a resurgence of the original Einstein-Rosen theory. In 1963, a physicist named Roy Kerr (1934–) devised new equations to explain how black holes formed, showing that some may form while spinning. A black hole created while spinning would end up in the shape of a ring, leaving a space right down the middle where, while the force of gravity would still be profound, it wouldn't be infinite. A strong enough object could make it through unharmed, shooting through the tunnel like a shortcut to a far away corner of space. These tunnels came to be known as "wormholes," a term coined by American theoretical physicist John Wheeler (1911–), since they're like the paths a worm carves through an apple.

Even these new-and-improved wormholes, however, are not particularly conducive to traveling, because they are so unstable that something like an entering space ship could cause the whole system to collapse. Cosmologist Kip Thorne (1940–) at the California Institute of Technology tackled this problem when author Carl Sagan asked Thorne to examine the book he'd just written, *Contact*. The characters in *Contact* traveled through a wormhole. Freed to think creatively—this was science fiction, after all—Thorne realized that an infinitely advanced technological society might well be able to hold a wormhole open using very exotic stuff (matter not made out of the protons, neutrons, and electrons we have detected in the universe thus far) that resisted the pull of gravity. Such exotic matter is not so far-fetched. Although a wormhole has not yet been detected, there are many physics theorists who believe it may well exist. (Of course, many theorists don't believe it.) And if such a wormhole could be created, then it would also be possible to manipulate it as a tunnel through time as well as space.

The bottom line is that Einstein-Rosen bridges are mathematically possible. Wormholes, in of themselves, do not violate the laws of physics as we know them. Whether they actually exist is unclear; some scientists believe that if they do, they do so only at microscopic levels, and are constantly fluctuating in and out of existence. (An interesting side point to this idea is that these many tiny wormholes may be what ensure that the laws of nature are the same on opposite sides of the universe, which would otherwise have no way of communicating with each other.) Lastly, it's possible that if exotic matter exists and *if* one had very advanced technology—two big "ifs"—that one might be able to hold a large wormhole open indefinitely and allow travelers to take a shortcut through space and time.

Zionism

Throughout his life, Einstein threw his considerable popular and political clout behind the Zionist movement. Although he was not particularly religious, Einstein was fiercely proud of his Jewish heritage. And although he was against nationalism, he also strongly believed that the Jewish people deserved their own identity and safe haven in which to live.

The nascent Zionist movement to create a homeland for the Jewish people had its headquarters in Germany. Kurt Blumenfeld (1884–1963), who recruited Einstein to the Zionists' side, served as the secretary-general of the Executive of World Zionist Organizations in Berlin around 1915 and was president of the Union of German Zionists from 1924 to 1933. Blumenfeld and Einstein were close and Einstein often added his name to Blumenfeld's statements on Zionist causes. Before his death in 1955, Einstein wrote an appreciation of his friend, thanking him "for having helped me become aware of my Jewish soul."

In addition to Blumenfeld, Einstein's support of Zionism stemmed from his conversations with what is often called "The Prague Circle." The Circle included the writer Franz Kafka, the man who would become Kafka's editor, Max Brod, philosopher Hugo Bergmann, and Bertha Fanta, Hugo Bergmann's mother-in-law. Einstein met them during his short stay in Prague as a lecturer at the Karl Ferdinand University from 1911 to 1912, and the ideas and discussions they shared with everyone in the klatch: Kafka was influenced by Einstein's views on nationalism; Brod based a literary character on Einstein; Einstein became swayed to the Zionist cause; and Bergmann went on to establish the Jewish National and University Library in Palestine.

In the 1920s, thanks to the popularity of his theory of relativity, Einstein was the toast of the intellectual world. Having a man so commonly referred to as "brilliant" supporting the cause of Zionism was a substantial boost to the movement. Einstein's first trip to the United States was from April 2 to May 30, 1921, when he traveled with Chaim Weizmann (1874–1952) on a mission to raise funds for the planned Hebrew University in Palestine.

> *Einstein explained his theory to me every day, and soon I was fully convinced that he understood it.*
>
> —Chaim Weizmann, after touring with Einstein to promote Zionism.

The timing of the trip meant that Einstein would miss the first Solvay Conference on physics to be held since the end of World War I. Einstein would have arrived at that Conference a conquering hero, for his fame and the movement to grant him a Nobel Prize in physics were at their peaks. But, as he would for the rest of life, Einstein juggled his two passions—physics and world politics—and chose to go to the United States instead. While Einstein didn't relish being in the public eye, he was well aware of how he could use his public persona as an influence. Originally, the trip was to be a quiet affair, but when it became known that the great Einstein was coming to the United States, universities and groups scrambled to offer him honorary degrees and invitations to lecture. Afterward, Einstein wrote about the trip to his friend Michele Besso: "Two frightfully exhausting months now lie behind me, but I have the great satisfaction of having been very useful to the cause of Zionism and of having assured the foundation of the University . . . I had to let myself be exhibited like a prize ox, and to give innumerable scientific lectures. It is a wonder I was able to hold out. But now it is over, and there remains the beautiful feeling of having done something truly good, and of having intervened courageously on behalf of the Jewish cause, ignoring the protests of Jews and non-Jews alike."

As much as Einstein strongly supported the Hebrew University, he was not blind to the political strife surrounding the formation of a Jewish homeland. In the wake of Arab attacks on Jewish settlements in 1929, Einstein told Weizmann not to make the same mistakes as Germany and warning him of "nationalism à la prussienne"—nationalism relying on force. Einstein wrote, "If we do not find the path to honest cooperation and honest negotiations with the Arabs, then we have learned nothing from our 2000 years of suffering, and we deserve the fate that will befall us."

The leaders of the Zionist movement found in Einstein both a champion and a gadfly. Einstein was openly critical of many Zionist policies and leaders, even pulling his support and name from the Hebrew University on occasion. Because he was bound to have just as many issues with a nationalistic stance from his own people as he was critical of it in anyone else, Einstein supported the creation of a strong Jewish identity and pride that could live safely and happily in any country in the world, not just locked to a single Jewish nation. He wrote: "I am a national Jew in the sense that I demand the preservation of the Jewish nationality as of every other. I look upon Jewish nationality as a fact, and I think that every Jew ought to come to definite conclusions on Jewish questions on the basis of this fact. . . . For me, Zionism is not merely a question of colonization. The Jewish nation is a living thing, and the sentiment of Jewish nationalism must be developed both in Palestine and everywhere else."

As the State of Israel was established in May 1948, Einstein was a supporter. It is not possible to understate Einstein's despair at the treatment of his fellow Jews at the hand of the Nazis, and this clearly led to his willingness to back the new country so fervently. At the formation of Israel, Einstein released a statement in which he called it the "fulfillment of an ancient dream to provide conditions in which the spiritual and cultural life of a Hebrew society could find free expression."

See **Anti-Semitism; Israel; Judaism; Nazism.**

Acknowledgments

The bulk of this manuscript was written in our apartments, while we sat on opposite couches, books piled high around us, cups of coffee leaving rings on the table, each of us typing diligently away on a laptop. This vignette was possible due to the support of so many people that it's hard to know whom to thank first—the friends and family (and dogs and cats) who put up with being ignored, the neighborhood coffee shops, the editors and agents who helped get the project started, or the scholars on whom we relied for research.

We'll start with the last. This book has brought together a huge collection of information, and we depended on the work of experts who have put in far more time poring over Einstein's archives than we. Abraham Pais, with his books *Subtle is the Lord . . .* and *Einstein Lived Here*, is known, deservedly, for writing some of the most thoughtful and comprehensive biographies on Einstein. "Hand me the Pais," was our official mantra while writing. Gerald Holton's essays on the thought that went into Einstein's science helped codify much of our understanding of Einstein's philosophies and theories. We were also supplied with endless details from the meticulously researched and yet dueling styles of the Einstein biographies written by Denis Brian and Albrecht Folsing. Professor Kannan Jaganathan and David Hall at Amherst College both read short excerpts of the first draft and gave comments. Any mistakes that made it into the book are entirely the fault of the authors, not the scholars mentioned here.

This project was conceived by Jeff Golick who was then at John Wiley & Sons. Mary Ann Naples at The Creative Culture is quite simply the best agent ever—it's like having an extra parent who looks out for you. We always know things will go smoothly with her in charge. We are indebted to our editor at Wiley, Eric Nelson, for bringing the book to fruition.

Thank you to the staff at the coffee shops of Café International and Tryst in Washington, D.C., Old City Coffee in Philadelphia, and the best rooftop bar anywhere, The Reef in Adams Morgan. How would a writer ever get anything done without you?

And friends and family:

Karen would like to thank, as always, her four spectacularly supportive parents who unquestioningly accept the fact that she goes underground for a month at a time whenever a deadline approaches. Noah gave invaluable editing comments, and just generally rocks. There are more good friends than can possibly be named here who helped provide the mental distraction (and bought the drinks) needed to get me successfully back to work the next day . . . or not. And, of course, thanks must go to Aries as well: co-authoring can be a tricky business, but working together was fun, rewarding, stress-free, and—most importantly—filled with an amazing amount of really good food.

Aries thanks everyone at WHYY who provided the time off, the emotional support, and the encouragement necessary to get the book done. Without the excitement and understanding from Rachel, Megan, Dave, Brenda, Brad, Joel, and especially Elisabeth, I simply would have gone mad. My family continues to show how to be daring and curious about the world. The atomicfriends must get a mention for endless amusement and insight. Amy, as always, manages to put up with a friend who may live a life more interesting than necessary; you've had an amazing year, and I'm honored to call you my friend. This book, and everything else I am and will be, is dedicated to Mykl. And of course, thank you to Karen, without whom this book would never have been started, or finished. I can only hope that our readers experience the same joy you showed me, when you had to explain to me, over and over and again, the difference between special and general relativity.

Selected Bibliography

Balibar, Françoise. *Einstein: Decoding the Universe*. Discoveries. New York: Harry N. Abrams, 1993.

Bodanis, David. $E = mc^2$: *A Biography of the World's Most Famous Equation*. Berkeley: Berkeley Publishing Group, 2001.

Brian, Denis. *Einstein: A Life*. New York: John Wiley & Sons, 1996.

Bucky, Peter A. *The Private Albert Einstein*. Kansas City, Mo.: Andrews McMeel Universal, 1993.

Calaprice, Alice, ed. *Dear Professor Einstein: Albert Einstein's Letters to and from Children*. Amherst, N.Y.: Prometheus Books, 2002.

———. *The Quotable Einstein*. Princeton: Princeton University Press, 1996.

Einstein, Albert. *Autobiographical Notes*. Paul Arthur Schilpp, trans. La Salle, Il: Open Court, 1996.

———. *Ideas and Opinions*. New York: Wings Books, 1954.

———. *Relativity: The Special and the General Theory*. Robert W. Lawson, trans. New York: Three Rivers Press, 1961.

Fölsing, Albrecht. *Albert Einstein: A Biography*. Ewald Osers, trans. New York: Viking, 1997.

Fox, Karen. *The Big Bang Theory: What It Is, Where It Came From, and Why It Works*. New York: John Wiley & Sons, 2002.

French, A.P., ed. *Einstein: A Centenary Volume*. Cambridge, Mass.: Harvard University Press, 1979.

Golden, Frederic. "Person of the Century: Albert Einstein." *Time*, December 31, 1999.

Goldman, Robert N. *Einstein's God: Albert Einstein's Quest as a Scientist and as a Jew to Replace a Forsaken God*. Northvale, N.J.: Jason Aronson, 1997.

Hey, Tony, and Patrick Walters. *Einstein's Mirror*. Cambridge: Cambridge University Press, 1997.

Holton, Gerald. *Thematic Origins of Scientific Thought: Kepler to Einstein* (rev. ed.). Cambridge, Mass.: Harvard University Press, 1998.

Highfield, Roger, and Paul Carter. *The Private Lives of Albert Einstein*. New York: St. Martin's Press, 1994.

Jammer, Max. *Einstein and Religion*. Princeton, N.J.: Princeton University Press, 1999.

Kantha, Sachi Sri. *An Einstein Dictionary*. Westport, Conn.: Greenwood Press, 1996.

Levenson, Thomas. *Einstein in Berlin*. New York: Bantam Books, 2003.

Overbye, Dennis. *Einstein in Love: A Scientific Romance*. New York: Penguin, 2001.

Pais, Abraham. *Einstein Lived Here*. Oxford: Oxford University Press, 1994.

———. *Subtle is the Lord . . . : The Science and the Life of Albert Einstein*. Oxford: Oxford University Press, 1982.

Parker, Barry. *Einstein: The Passions of a Scientist*. Amherst, N.Y.: Prometheus Books, 2003.

Paterniti, Michael. *Driving Mr. Albert: A Trip across America with Einstein's Brain*. New York: Random House, 2000.

Rosenkranz, Ze'ev. *The Einstein Scrapbook*. Baltimore, Md.: Johns Hopkins University Press, 1998.

Schilpp, Paul Arthur, ed. *Albert Einstein: Philosopher-Scientist*. The Library of Living Philosophers. London: Cambridge University Press, 1969.

Stachel, John, ed. *Einstein's Miraculous Year: Five Papers That Changed the Face of Physics*. Princeton, N.J.: Princeton University Press, 1998.

Zackheim, Michele. *Einstein's Daughter: The Search for Lieserl*. New York: Penguin Putnam, 1999.

Index